Employment Relations in Financial Services

Gregor Gall

Employment Relations in Financial Services

An Exploration of the Employee Experience After the Financial Crash

Gregor Gall
University of Bradford
Bradford, UK

ISBN 978-1-137-39537-5   ISBN 978-1-137-39539-9   (eBook)
DOI 10.1057/978-1-137-39539-9

Library of Congress Control Number: 2017937290

Printed on acid-free paper

This Palgrave Macmillan imprint is published by Springer Nature
The registered company is Macmillan Publishers Ltd.
The registered company address is: The Campus, 4 Crinan Street, London, N1 9XW, United Kingdom

*To my mother, Alisan, for all her love,
affection and dedication down the years*

Contents

1   Introduction   1

2   Players   39

3   Processes   109

4   Outcomes   177

5   Conclusion   239

Index   251

Abbreviations, Acronyms and Organisational Names

Accord	Successor to the IUHS
AfF	Alliance for Finance
ALGUS	Alliance and Leicester Group Union for Staff
AEGIS	AEGIS—The Aegon UK Staff Association
ANSA	Abbey National Staff Association
ANGU	Abbey National Group Union
BFSA	Brittannic Field Staff Association
BIFU	Banking, Insurance and Finance Union
BSU	Britannia Staff Union
CBG	Co-operative Banking Group
CBSSA	Cheshire Building Society Staff Association
CFS	Co-operative Financial Services (later CBG)
CGSU	Cheshire Group Staff Union
CWU	Communication Workers' Unions
DBSSA	Dunfermline Building Society Staff Association
DGSU	Derbyshire Group Staff Union
EWC	European Works Council
EUO	Employed Union Officer
FSA	Financial Services Authority
GMB	GMB general union
HBoS	Halifax Bank of Scotland
HBSSA	Halifax Building Society Staff Association
HSBC	Hong Kong and Shanghai Banking Corporation

ICT	Information and Communication Technology
IUHS	Independent Union of Halifax Staff
JSA	Job Security Agreement
LBSSA	Leeds Building Society Staff Association
LUBSSA	Leeks United Building Society Staff Association
LBG	Lloyds Banking Group
LFS	Labour Force Survey
LTU	Lloyds Trade Union (also known as Affinity)
MSF	Manufacturing, Science and Finance union
NAG	National Australia Group (owners of Clydesdale and Yorkshire banks)
NGSU	Nationwide Group Staff Union
PGSA	Portman Group Staff Association
PIP	Performance Improvement plans
PRP	Performance-Related Pay
RBS	Royal Bank of Scotland
RSA	Royal Sun Alliance
SEA	Security of Employment Agreement
SIPTU	Services, Industrial, Professional and Technical Union
SSA	Skipton Staff Association
SUWBS	Staff Union West Bromwich Building Society
TUC	Trades Union Congress
TUPE	Transfer of Undertakings (Protection of Employment) regulations
UBAC	Union for Bradford and Bingley Staff and Associated Companies
UFS	Union of Finance Staff
Unite	Union formed from Amicus and TGWU merger
USDAW	Union of Shop, Distributive and Allied Workers
WISA	Woolwich Independent Staff Association
YISA	Yorkshire Independent Staff Association

List of Figures

Fig. 2.1   Employment levels ('000s) in the financial services sector
           in Britain, 1978–2015   75

List of Tables

Table 2.1   NGSU membership leavers and joiners,
February 2016–June 2016   54

Table 2.2   Membership levels of unions organising within the
financial services sector, 1995–2015   71

Table 2.3   Union densities and presence (%) in the financial
services sector in Britain, 1996–2015   74

Table 2.4   Union presence within the financial services sector
in Britain, 1995–2014   77

Table 3.1   Strike activity in the financial services sector, 1999–2015   164

Table 4.1   Performance pay matrix determination   193

List of Insets

Inset 3.1   Partnership in HBoS   114
Inset 3.2   The War of Words—LTU Attacks Accord and Unite,
            Part 1   132
Inset 3.3   The War of Words—LTU Attacks Accord and Unite,
            Part 2   136
Inset 3.4   Selection of Headlines to Unite Press Releases   141
Inset 4.1   Letters of Discontent, Despair, Dismay and Dissatisfaction 205
Inset 4.2   Pleas of Pension Poverty   209
Inset 4.3   Market Pay Misery   211
Inset 4.4   Truth and Lies About Financial Services Sector Workers'
            Wages and Conditions   212

1

Introduction

Introduction

This study examines and analyses the employment experiences of workers in the financial services sector in Britain since the financial crash of 2007–2008. This is then to look at the human toll and tragedy of what has happened in terms of the erosion of workers' terms and conditions of employment in banking, insurance and financial inter- mediation. Widespread redundancies, reduced worth of pensions and oppressive performance management systems have been some of the most obvious and widespread outcomes by which rapacious employ- ers have responded to the deleterious impact of the financial crash upon their businesses and profitability. The purpose of these actions has been to protect and advance their material interests. The context of doing so has been that under an unchallenged regime of neo-liberal capitalism, the 'credit crunch' gave way to the financial crash and an unprecedented recession, with the financial services sector at its root and core, shortly leading the way to what has become known as an 'age of austerity'. Yet for a very short period of time in Britain, the financial and economic crisis also became a political and ideological

© The Author(s) 2017
G. Gall, *Employment Relations in Financial Services*,
DOI 10.1057/978-1-137-39539-9_1

crisis for capitalism, as capitalism itself wobbled and witnessed wide-spread government intervention in a failing, deregulated 'free market'. The weakness of the left and labour unions generally in Britain and, more specifically, in the financial services sector, meant that this crisis of capitalism was, utimately, resolved on capital's terms and in its favour—and at the expense of labour. This was true of economy and society in general but particularly so in the financial services sector. Escudero (2009: 2) ventured that along with the United States, Britain was the 'at the epicentre of the crisis and where its impact ... on the financial sector ha[s] been felt most strongly' with Soriano (2011: 1, 21) recording that: 'In the EU27 as a whole, 250,000 jobs were lost in the banking sector between 2008 and 2010 ... Importantly, 187,000 jobs were lost in the UK alone, the main European financial centre. ... The British sector was particularly exposed because its investment banking sector had a low level of regulation, and stocks and securities trading had gone further than elsewhere'. Meantime, on the third anniversary of the financial crash, Unite (press release, 13 September 2010) calculated that 'one hundred thousand finance sector jobs have been lost since the banking crisis began', with a year later, 'in excess of 150,000 jobs lost ... between 2008 and 2011' (Unite 2012: 6). By mid-2015, *Business Insider UK* (20 June 2015) calculated the number of jobs cut had risen to 186,111 in banking. Despite differences of opinion over the extent of labour shedding, it is clear that it has been the numbers of workers affected have been very substantial.

Originally, the subtitle of this book was envisaged to be *Fight, flight and falling-in-line* but, as the data gathering process progressed, it became clear that a revised subtitle of something like *Fright, flight and falling in line* would have been more appropriate as the absence of 'fight' became ever more palpable. Suffice it to say, for the moment, that the extremely limited presence of any strikes over the last decade indicated that where any 'fight' did take place, it was of a less forceful and collective nature than might have been otherwise expected. While this did not signal the triumph of partnership between capital and labour nor the complete hegemony of capital, the extant evidence of 'fight' in terms of resistance will be recorded and analysed as will its absence and inter-relation to the other components of 'flight' (leaving the sector) and 'falling in line' (acquiescence to the new managerial regimes). Upon further reflection, the four f's of fright, flight falling-in-line and fight were believed to be captured more eloquently and succinctly in the subtitle of 'An Exploration of the Employee Experience after the Financial Crash'. To date no other study has sought to provide an over-arching analysis of the fate of labour in this sector since the financial crash. In this sense, and even though some of the aspects have been well covered at a journalistic level, this study constitutes an act of exploring an unfamiliar area in order to discover new information and then present an analysis of it.

The significance of the study can be located in five particular aspects. The first is that the more general and wider crisis emanated firstly in the financial services sector and its effects have been more keenly felt in this sector than elsewhere. The second is that partnership, as the dominant means of organising the relationship between the representatives of capital and labour, has endured despite the crash (although, on occasion, capital has been prepared to step out with partnership when deemed necessary). The third is that the dominant historical form of labour unionism in the sector prior to the crash ill-prepared workers for resisting the terms of capital for responding to, and resolving, the crisis. The fourth is that despite the central concern of this book being the employee experience in terms of their jobs, working conditions and remuneration, the workforces of the major employers in the financial service sector are unionised, with their representative organs being recognised for collective bargaining on terms and conditions of employment. This necessitates an ample consideration of the industrial or labour relations of the sector as well as an examination of the activity of the labour unions themselves. The fifth is that many recent studies of the financial services sector have not considered what are the salient matters of the employee experience of employment and the processes and outcomes of employment relations within the sector (see, for example, Casu and Gall 2016 and Ertürk and Gabor 2017).

So the 'story' to be told in this study is one of increasing domination by employers and their managers as the basis of collective employee representation and resistance, namely, labour unionism, has become further eroded despite valiant efforts to arrest this decline. In other words, employees in the financial services sector in the post-financial crash period have faced a particularly sharp situation of considerable downward pressure upon their terms and conditions of employment and a marked inability to collectively defend themselves, making this a 'tale' of the reified hegemony of neo-liberalism in terms of the economy and the governance of employing organisations.

Intellectual Perspective

Following on from the radical political economy perspective deployed in Gall (2008), this section seeks to lay out a more developed and fleshed out one. Thus, compared to its predecessor (feudalism) and possible successors (socialism, communism, barbarism), capitalism is first and foremost an economic system whose *raison d'etre* is the accumulation of surplus value, namely, profit. Quintessentially, surplus value is produced by the exploitation of labour by capital for capital's benefit and interest (assuming it is realised into a usable form). The social structuration this gives rise to is a system of social classes, based primarily upon capital and labour. Capital gives rise to the superordinate (minority) class and labour the subordinate (majority) class. Within this radical political economy perspective, the role and place of the financial services sector is two-fold. First, financial services are but one part of the strategic means of exchange as per the means of production, distribution and exchange upon which capitalism is reliant to function and which embodies and facilitates the production of surplus value. Second, and at the same time, financial services are also a capitalist field of enterprise in themselves where surplus value is extracted as a result of the capitalist labour process and the consequent services provided being bought and sold (and in which labour exploitation of the workers which carry out these tasks is conducted). The state, as the other main actor in capitalist society in addition to labour and capital, is a capitalist one wherein its role and functions are primarily determined by the more powerful class, namely, capital. Its fundamental, historic role has been to support capital in any struggles with and against labour over the terms of exploitation and over exploitation itself. Notwithstanding this and the struggle by contending classes to exert control over the state, there have been different epochs of the capitalist state, with its previous social democratic form giving way to its neo-liberal form. Here, the state has been used to propagate the ideas and forms of neo-liberalism through deregulation of the labour and product markets and, on occasion, intervene in the economy to assist capitalist enterprises either for their own good or that of capitalism per se. Regulation of activities, involvement in money supply and state ownership are the main forms of intervention. The fourth actor in the employment relations of the financial services sector is the customer. However, its influence is weak, not because it sides with capital or labour but because it is atomised and unorganised. Unlike some employment relationships and employment relations, trifurcation has not occurred primarily but not exclusively because of this weakness. The issue of whether labour can form an alliance with customers to further their joint interests is addressed later on.

This brief outline provides the basis upon which to stipulate that the employment relations of the financial services sector, as with any other economic sector, can best be analysed and understood as the outcome of a symbiotic, two-way inter-change between the external (to unit of capital) environment and the internal (within the unit of capital) environment. In order to help do this whilst at the same time not becoming mesmerised by the process of interaction itself so that the intentions lying this become somewhat hidden, the aid of three derived conceptual categories from the above outline, namely, power, ideology and material interest, is helpful. These categories have particular pertinence for the financial services sector for, as previously alluded to in terms of the relative absence of open conflict between capital and labour in the form of collective industrial action as well as the prevalence of partnership, such conceptual categories enable a deeper and more insightful interrogation of the intentions, processes and outcomes of both parties in employment relations. In other words, it can be contemplated that partnership has not abolished the innate conflict of interests between capital and labour and that the absence of widespread, open signs of collective action may only indicate the inability of labour to mobolise to collectively prosecute its interests. Indeed, this does not suggest that the exploitation of labour has ended or been resolved for, as sometimes expressed, it may merely indicate a one-sided class war is taking place—in this case, waged by capital against labour. Power is normally conceived as 'power to' and 'power over', with the former facilitating the latter. Meanwhile ideology provides a worldview of how economic, social and political relations should be configured and for what purposes. Meantime, material interest is the category which—so to speak— binds the other two together in a mutually supportive way. Given that material interests give rise to power and ideology, they can also be protected and advanced by power and ideology. Applied to the financial services sector, the power of capital is a manifest one in terms of hiring and firing and setting terms and conditions of employment as well as determining the organisation of work and the labour process. This 'power to' do so involves a 'power over' labour, indicating little salient state regulation and that labour—through unions—is not a particularly strong force.

Yet it is possible, if not probable in the short-term, to conceive of a situation where labour develops its ability to exercise 'power to' and 'power over' because of the exploitation experienced by labour at the hands of capital. The dominant ideology of neo-liberalism has taken a specific form in the financial service sector, namely, a partnership variant of human resource management whereby a certain form or nature of labour unionism is recognised and legitimated. The roots of this are strongly historical in as much as the dominant employer means for dealing with independent unionism was to engage in a strategy of 'peaceful competition' (Bain 1970: 131) under which moderate and dependent staff associations were developed and/or supported. As these staff associations began to become more independent and 'unionate' (Blackburn 1967), best exemplified by merging with independent forms of labour unionism, the strategy of 'peaceful competition' gave way one of partnership by which the now dominant and more independent forms of labour unionism were, by and large, ideologically incorporated into the interests and agenda of the employers in the sector. The degrees to which positive and willing endorsement or reluctant and begrudging acquiescence existed on the part of labour unions varied (see Gall 2008). But it is clear that a significant factor for some unions in the sector was their lack of 'power to' and 'power over'. Again it is possible, if not probable in the short-term, to conceive of a situation where labour develops its own independent ideology in the sector and which takes account of its material interests from a radical standpoint leading to at least militant objectives (if not militant action itself). Material interests denote economic interest, and for capital this concerns the shareholders (individual, institutional) and senior management (in terms of their salaries, benefits, bonuses and share options). For labour, workers' concerns here are bound up with their remuneration (pay, pensions, etc.) as well as job security and conditions of work.

In the following chapters, readers should bear in mind that even if the attendant (radical political economy derived) links between the capitalist system as a omnipotent regime of accumulation, the agency of capitalists in the financial services sector and the process of the exploitation of wage labour are not always fully drawn out (because to repeatedly do so may look clumsy and over-bearing), there are very much implied and present. Thus, when the text examines the responses of employers to the financial crash, it is on occasion implied that they seek to respond in ways which re-inforce and deepen their means of control of workers (their power) and their terms and conditions of employment in order to enhance their ability to maintain or increase rates of profitability (namely, their material interests).

Conceptual Terms

Although exorcised from the subtitle of this study, the series of 'f' words provide a useful set of lower level concepts by which to form a framework for analysis. In other words, they help in the organisation of the analysis of data by providing categories in which to locate actions, behaviours and phenomena. Thus, 'fight or flight' is a traditional and commonly known binary conceptualisation of human reaction to adverse situations. It is derived from the American psychologist, Walter Bradford Cannon, who in 1915 coined the phrase to describe the responses of animals to danger. In psychological terms, the schema was later developed into a four-fold one of 'fight', 'flight', 'freeze', and 'fawn'. 'Freeze' refers to seeking isolation and reclusivity while 'fawn' comprises acquiescence and acted out acceptance. In employment relation terms, 'freeze' is not a particularly easily operationalised concept for it implies that workers could be at work but not part of a work group.

This would be difficult to achieve despite some tendencies towards atomisation. However, an unrelated sense of freeze is compatible with 'fright' whereby workers feel compelled and coerced into 'falling-in-line'. Meantime, 'fawn' approximates to 'falling-in-line' in a rather more willing—but far from positive—sense. Thus, to lay out the categories:

- *Fight* comprises acts of collective and semi-collective resistance against the actions and interests of the employer, most obviously taking the form of industrial action (striking and industrial action short of striking such as overtime bans and work-to-rules) as well as using ballots for those actions as bargaining chips. Less obviously, means of expressing employee voice (through surveys and consultative ballots) can be used as means of leverage and mobilisation. This depends upon strategic or tactical choice and circumstance (see later). As acts of individual resistance such as sabotage, sickness absence and appealing against performance management assessments are difficult to identify and measure because of their hidden and secretive nature (as well as sometimes being conflated with other behaviours), they do not form a primary concern of this category.
- *Flight* comprises those of working age leaving the sector through of their own accord as a result of some form or measure of dissatisfaction, those taking early retirement for similar reasons of dissatisfaction, those taking voluntary redundancy for similar reasons and those subject to compulsory redundancy or transferal to other organisations through outsourcing. Some indication of the extent of flight is given by the example of the LBG which cut 57,000 jobs between 2008 and 2016 through redundancies, retirement, sell offs, offshoring and outsourcing (*Guardian*, 25 August 2016).
- *Fright* and *falling-in-line* are related in terms of outcome although they differ in the process by which the outcome is arrived at. Under fright, workers are coerced by economic compulsion as a result of the prospect of the loss of their job (through either redundancy or dismissal for performance issues). This leads them to buckle under and buckle down in order to try to avoid such outcomes by working harder and longer. For example, Accord's president in 2011 reported: 'Our members' biggest worry is simply that they'll lose their jobs.

We're seeing a lot of people who are just keeping their heads down, working those extra hours and not being treated with the respect they deserve. They are just taking it and not speaking up because they are worried about their future' (*My Accord*, Spring 2011). By contrast, under falling-in-line workers seek to reproduce the attitudes and behaviours desired and demanded by their employers in order to secure pay increases and promotion under the regimes of performance management. This conveys the sense of game playing without genuine, positive commitment to the ideology and cultural norms of the company. Fright is, therefore, more grudging than falling-in-line.

A similar common conceptualisation to 'fight and flight' is that of worker mobilisation in the form of 'anger > hope > action' chain of reaction. Anger gives rise to the hope that action, which requires both to be created and taken, can resolve the issue which led to the anger in the first place. Mobilisation theory, following Kelly (1998), is a more much specified sequence by which workers develop grievances and then act to resolve these.

In journalese, what has happened in the financial services sector is often described in terms of 'shake out' and 'shake up', meaning the 'shake out' of jobs and the 'shake up' of employment practices and ways of working—both to the detriment of the workforce. But for the purposes of analysis here, and with a focus upon labour unionism, a better way of understanding the processes and outcomes is to return to a previous analysis of the industrial relations of the financial services sector (Gall 2008) which identified that union organisation had experienced disorganisation, dissolution and dislocation. In a revised and updated schema, to this can now be added the category of demoralisation in order to provide a more holistic means by which to assess union decline. Overall, the outcome has been atrophy of union influence and presence although suggesting that labour unionism is now 'hollowed out' or has become a 'hollow shell' would be inappropriate and inaccurate. This is because, on the one hand, the implied starting point—of being strong and influential—is wrong for labour unionism in the financial services sector has developed on a different trajectory from labour unionism in manufacturing, while, on the other hand, the extent of decline is not so advanced in either relative or absolute terms as the 'hollowed out' thesis suggests. Fleshed out, the four aforementioned categories are:

- *Disorganisation* has resulted from the consequences of the quasi-constant state of organisational flux as the structures of units of capital are reconfigured through mergers and amalgamations, disposals, demergers, outsourcing and offshoring. As the organisational structures of labour unionism are heavily influenced by those of capital for reasons of meeting and engaging with the representatives of capital, labour unionism has often experienced the need to mirror such changes in order to (re-)create more effective organisational forms. In this sense, more work and resources have been required to be put into getting labour unionism to a point where it can meet capital, rather than concentrating upon how to mobilise resources to exert leverage upon capital. Furthermore, the relationship between union personnel and management personnel are also in a state of flux with a constant churn of old relationships ended and new ones begun. This sense of disorganisation is for union organisation to become progressively less organised, rather than to never be organised in the first place. The latter sense is encompassed within the category of dislocation.
- *Dissolution* concerns the contraction of labour unionism's presence, most obviously in terms of overall membership but also in organisational presence in terms of members, structures and activities based in the workplace in the form of the some presence of workplace unionism. Increasingly, relations between members and their union are direct and individualised so that workplace and local unionisms have become denuded.
- *Dislocation* concerns established employment moving out of the realms of that which labour unionism has traditionally organised within. Both existing and new companies have developed their presence in new product markets and with new means of delivering these products as information and communication technologies (ICTs) have developed. For labour unionism, seeking to move its presence into these new areas through organising and recruitment activities has been difficult as a result of the attempts by capital to keep these

operations 'union free' by a variety of means while there has been a steep and arduous 'learning curve' for labour unionism to acquaint its own operations with in these new settings.

- *Demoralisation* revolves around the demotivation and disillusionment of members and activists as a result of the ascendancy of the power of capital and the prevalence of its ideology of partnership as a cloak for this power. The feelings of (relative) hopelessness and pointlessness then mount in a frustrating manner for members feel aggrieved but at the same time believe that there is little to no chance of ameliorative redress and change. Membership may be lapsed but for those that remain members there is little compulsion to be active in order to create the opportunity for such change. Collective confidence and oppositional consciousness are then denuded. The consequential triumvirate of anger > hope > action does not then come into play.

Of course, these four processes and outcomes are not the preserve of the post-crash period for they far pre-dated it but they have been deepened and extended by developments in the period since the crash as the subsequent chapters indicate. Notwithstanding the caveat entered into above concerning the extent of union decline, disorganisation, dissolution, dislocation and demoralisation do raise the potential (as opposed to prospect or probability) of de-unionisation of the sector in the longer term in both absolute and relative levels of union membership.

What makes this schema rather more idiosyncratic than might otherwise be the case is that the setting of employment relations in the financial services sector is largely comprised of partnership working (between representatives of capital and organised labour) amongst the largest organisations. This means that that movement towards union decline, with its sub-components of disorganisation, dissolution, dislocation and demoralisation, cannot be directly and automatically 'read off' employer strategy in a simple 'cause and effect' manner. This is because, as will become clear, the extent of employer support (financial, ideological, organisational) for labour unionism is substantial (albeit this is for a certain type and form of labour unionism). From capital, the conventional argument is its monopoly of knowledge warrants its power of unilateral initiative in order to be able to respond effectively and efficiently to changing market conditions in order to maintain market share and control costs. The components of power, profit (material interests) and ideology are not specifically spelt out in this perspective. However, so the partnership perspective goes, in an increasingly fraught and volatile marketplace, the input of employees is required so that employing organisations can be as competitive as possible in this environment. Herein lies the foundation of the mutual gains agenda of partnership (see later) whereby the interests of capital and labour can, it is argued, be aligned in a reciprocal—but not equal—manner.

Finance Capitalism, Capitalism and Neo-liberalism

As is now commonly understood, the general crisis of capitalism in the late 2000s and into the 2010s was triggered by a crisis within finance capitalism in the first instance. The increasing separation of finance capital from industrial capital, to become much more a circuit of capital in its own right, alongside the decreasing regulation of finance capital leading it to become less risk averse meant that, on the one hand, finance capital had become a more weighty fraction within wider capitalism, and on the other, a less stable part of capitalism. The two together became a dangerous mix. In Britain, this is best highlighted by the payment protection insurance (PPI) mis-selling scandal which saw around 30 million policies wrongly sold and financial institutions setting aside up to £30 bn in compensation schemes as well as mortgages being offered to those that could ill afford them (as well as mortgages over the value of the property). Within the financial services sector, the crisis triggered a massive process of restructuring (principally labour shedding, and reorganisation of work) which far outstripped that which happened elsewhere in other sectors of the economy. As explained elsewhere, this did not lead to the re-regulation of finance capital on a par with the regime that existed before the 'Big Bang' deregulation of 1986 onwards. Forms of 'light touch' regulation ensued as neo-liberalism continued its ideological and political dominance. However, this process of the continued sectional dominance by a fraction of capital within capitalism overall can be traced back to prior to the rise of neo-liberalism. Finance capital is best epitomised by—but not made entirely synonymous with—the City of London, indicating that its dominance has been bound up with the process of capitalist industrialisation, expansion and imperialism. The implications of this for employment relations are two-fold. First, state regulation of employment within the financial services sector has historically been weak, occasioning no particular forms of intervention like some other sectors of economic activity (for example, mining, ports, steel, sweated trades). It may be thought that the strategic importance of finance capital for capitalism per se would have occasioned particular forms of state control. Rather, the considerable relative strength of finance capital vis-à-vis other fractions of capitalism and the capitalist state has precluded this in Britain. The absence of any particular state oversight or intervention has meant that the second derivative feature has been that capital has dominated the employment relationship far more than in many other economic sectors. Consequently, the unitarist ideology, the material interests, and the power of finance capital have heavily coloured the complexion of employment relations leading to the prevalence of staff associations and now company-level social partnership.

Labour Unionism: Historical Trajectories and Contemporary Phenomena

Labour unionism in Britain has been subject to five main salient tendencies since the 1970s. The first has been the dismantling of job controls established by unions, representing a progressive surrendering by labour to capital of the controls labour had built up over the organisation of work. These were used to control the pace and nature of work, in order to lessen the exploitation labour was subject to in the wage-effort bargain. The second has been the restriction of collective bargaining to a smaller number of shallower issues. The main component of this tendency has been to remove traditional forms of collective

bargaining over pay rises and their replacement with individual assessment so that the sums of money available for pay rises are still bargained
over but not the manner in which the sums are then distributed. Allied
to this has been the emergence of performance measurement of individuals. The third has been the end of the 'something-for-nothing' bargaining agenda and its replacement with the 'something-for-something'
agenda. Thus, for many years and influenced by years of relatively high
inflation, unions sought annual pay increases to keep up with or better the level of inflation in order to protect and advance their members'
standards of living. Negotiations with employers concerned arguments
about how much should be paid and whether the employer could afford
this. The rise of productivity bargaining from the early 1960s began
to change this culture, with employers starting to insist upon concessions in effort bargaining and work practices in return for pay rises. By
the end of the 1970s and beginning of the 1980s, employer routinely
began insisting upon gaining different forms of flexibility (task, tem-
poral) from their workers in return for pay rises. The fourth has been
the emergence of vertical forms of labour unionism. Previously, different grades of workers in both public and private service sectors were
represented by different unions. This was especially so with regard to
workers and their managers and supervisors. Over time and as a result
of employer reorganisations and union mergers, workers, managers and
supervisors have become members of the same unions (even if they had
different internal union sections to represent them). Lastly, workers end
or lapse their union membership when made redundant—and prior to
gaining any subsequent employment—as unions no longer, to the limited extent that they once did, provide access to jobs by organising job
pools. Moreover, as the cost of membership becomes an issue too in the
context of unemployment, this also leads to lapsing. Compared to a
number of continental European countries, state unemployment benefits are not operated through unions in Britain, and unions now do not
provide extensive unemployment benefits to members themselves.

With regard to the financial services sector, such job controls did not
exist in any palpable way. Professional banking or insurance qualifica-
tions which exerted a mild form of job control were not determined
by unions or staff associations. Although seniority existed in terms of

general and specific banking activities, again this was not determined in any way by staff associations or unions. However, the financial services sector has been a prime example of employers introducing individual performance systems to determine workers' pay rises, beginning with performance-related pay (PRP) and transmogrifying into systems of performance management. Not only has this development removed a significant area of influence from the unions in the sector but the effect has been to further fragment and stratify a workforce and membership (see below and subsequent chapters) so that collective mobilisation is much more difficult to achieve. Similarly, negotiations over the size of the available pay pot—even when distributed by means of individual performance measurement—have been bound up with gaining other changes in employment conditions and practices in the financial services sector. Pen-ultimately, membership of staff associations and unions in the financial services sector has often catered for workers and their managers and supervisors (albeit with different internal union sections to represent them) up to the level of directors. This de facto right to union membership for senior staff was fought for by the emerging financial service sector unions and its take up became relatively common. This tendency was underscored by the moderate nature of many of the organisations and subsequent union recruitment strategies to maximise membership. Thus, the lowest paid bank tellers through to highly paid senior managers (but not directors) held union membership. Lastly, and like most contemporary unions, unions and staff associations did not provide access to employment opportunities and so membership lapsing upon redundancy was extremely common. And, the same is true of retired members for there is little in the way of activity for retired members to undertake.

In the financial services sector, the effect of continued widespread usage of performance-related pay has been to put workers and union members into different, though not entirely atomised or individualised, stratified positions so that a sense of overall or majority collectivism is harder to re-create and sustain. Stratification takes place whereby workers are put into different bandings as a result of individual performance assessments. Normally, there are no more than four or five bandings but these are then transposed onto a matrix based on market levels of pay so that the number of final groups of outcomes by category can be up to 20. When members are unhappy or aggrieved with the outcomes of their performance appraisals (with regard to the impact on pay and development needs), they can appeal on an *individual* basis with union help and representation, and in turn, this strengthens the directness of the link between the concerned member and union but also atomises the member from other members given this representation will in all likelihood the most extensive and deep form of interaction with their union. This fragmentation is added to, as with outside the financial services sector, by workers and members being in different pension schemes such as remaining final salary schemes, other defined benefits schemes, and other defined contribution schemes. So there are considerable pressures towards fragmentation of macro-collective identities, raising the prospect of de-collectivisation and atomisation, with union resources increasingly expended on individual case work. This presents a challenge to unions to reconfigure and reconstruct collectivism (in terms of organisation, identity and consciousness).

Before moving on, it is important to recount that, along with the relative underdevelopment of workplace unionism, historically and contemporarily the 'servicing', rather than 'organising', approach has dominated in the financial services sector (Gall 2008).[1] Thus, the tendency is for 'the' union to be viewed as an external third party essentially hired to provide services, often in the vein of an insurance policy when needed, and to members where members do not perceive themselves as an active agency, much less the most important resource of a union.

Partnership

Formal partnership agreements and partnership working, referred to hereafter as simply 'partnership' and embodying the frameworks, processes and outcomes of a mutual gains ideology, continue to comprise the dominant modus operandi for organising the relationship between capital and labour in the financial services sector. The extent of partnership in the financial services sector is such that it may no longer provide competitive advantage although by the same token not having it would in all likelihood incur competitive disadvantage. In the private sector in Britain, the financial services sector continues to be the single sector most affected by partnership in terms of the number of employees covered. Only in the public sector is there more extensive coverage of employees, with the NHS being the most obvious example. In both cases, the extensive of coverage is facilitated by employer structure whereby a relatively small number of very large employers exist. However, the significant difference between the two examples concerns government policy. Whilst there has been encouragement, if not instruction, from government policy for the NHS employers to institute and practice partnership with employees and unions (along with the attendant leverage of funding), no such higher compulsion has existed in the financial services sector. Here partnership has been at the behest of the employers acting in an independent manner, and with only limited government support (and often this has been quite late in the day). And, the continued prevalence-cum-hegemony of partnership in the financial service sector is despite the deleterious consequences of the financial crash of 2007–2008 upon the terms and conditions of financial service sector workers.

One might have expected that the unions themselves, or under pressure from their memberships, may have withdrawn from partnership and brought about its crisis or even dissolution. This would be to say that they were no longer prepared to continue as normal in abnormal times (as a number of unions in Ireland did over their social partnership agreement after the financial crash). But instead, unions have, by and large, clung to partnership as the 'best way' to manage the fallout from the financial crash. Their memberships have, by and large, accepted and endorsed this stance. Employers have continued to be willing to preach and practice partnership because, in such troubled times, it has been to their benefit and their shareholders to do so. The no little matter of the extent of new public ownership following the government bailouts of a number of financial services sector companies has had no bearing upon this, for the governments did not seek to play an active role in managing their new acquisitions. The bailed out financial services sector companies were left to continue to act in regard of employment relations as they had before the crash (with the partial exceptions of bonuses and sales cultures). This reflected the bizarre notion inherent in neo-liberalism that, despite the crash, (private sector) management continues to 'know best'. No amount of pressure upon the last Labour government (2005–2010) by the likes of the largest union and largest Labour union affiliate, Unite, made a difference here. The arrival of the Conservative-Liberal Democrat coalition (2010–2015) and Conservative (2015 onwards) governments merely deepened this trajectory. All in all, this brief sketch suggests that there are quite deep ideological, political and economic as well as institutional-cum-organisational roots to partnership in the financial services sector. This is in spite of this particular form of social dialogue having little or no statutory underpinning or state resourcing (as alluded to above and for Britain more widely) compared to similar economies in Western Europe.

At this stage, and recalling the analysis put forward previously (Gall 2008), it can be proffered that the prevalence of partnership as a meaningful and accurate representation of the mode of capital-labour relations hides not just the power dimension of managerial dominance and union weakness but also the existence of an influential ideological construct to reify and deepen dominant power relations in pursuit of continued material gain for capital and its representatives. Whether labour merely and contingently acquiesces to the nature of this relationship because of weakness will be explored later.

The Financial Crash

The financial crash in Britain began in September 2007 with Northern Rock being unable to pay off the large sums it borrowed to fund mortgages for customers, necessitating its 'nationalisation' in February 2008 after two private takeover bids did not materialise. The run on Northern Rock in mid-September 2007 was the first on a bank in Britain for 150 years. Meanwhile in 2008, weakening investment bank, Bear Stearns, was bought out by JP Morgan, the US government bailed out Fannie Mae and Freddie Mac, being two companies that had guaranteed thousands of 'sub-prime' mortgages, and Lehman Brothers filed for bankruptcy, prompting worldwide financial panic. In September 2008,

HBoS, was rescued by Lloyds TSB after a huge drop in its share price. Back in the US, investment banks were pummelled on the stock markets, with Goldman Sachs and JP Morgan Chase changing their status to banking holding companies to end their investment banking model, the Washington Mutual and Wachovia banks collapsed, and Congress passed a $700 bn financial bailout bill. In Ireland, the government promised to underwrite the entire Irish banking system while Iceland's three biggest commercial banks—Glitnir, Kaupthing, and Landsbanki—collapsed. In October 2008, to avert the collapse of the UK banking sector, the government bailed out several banks, including the Royal Bank of Scotland, Lloyds TSB, and HBoS.

State Attitude and Intervention

The bailing out of four financial services sector companies (Bradford and Bingley, LBG, Northern Rock, RBS), along with vast tranches of 'qualitative easing' (through the Special Liquidity, Credit Guarantee Scheme and Asset Protection schemes) for other financial services companies, were commonly but wrongly perceived to be cases of nationalisation and 'socialism for the rich'. In early 2008, Northern Rock was completely 'nationalised' while 6 months later so was Bradford and Bingley, costing together £57 bn in total to do so. Partial 'nationalisation' took place in Royal Bank of Scotland (RBS, 84%) and Lloyds Banking Group (LBG, 43%) over a number of tranches of capital injections amounting to £65.8 bn from late 2008 to late 2009. On 13 October 2008, the Labour government, through its Chancellor of the Exchequer in the House of Commons, announced that the injection of public capital would be managed 'on a fully commercial basis by an arm's length body with a precisely defined remit to act in the interests of taxpayers'. This new body was the UK Financial Investments Ltd. (UKFI). UKFI (2009: 7) then stated that its role was 'to manage the Government's investments, not to manage the banks'. So the purpose of UKFI was made plain—in other words, this would not be any nationalisation of old where civil servants within a government department and led by a minister would run and control economic activities with broader economic and social objectives in mind. Suffice it to say, there was no social democratic intention behind the 'nationalisation' where the goals of stabilising capitalism and ameliorating market outcomes for workers are foremost. Instead, the 'nationalisation' was forced upon a government of a social liberalism, a variant of neo-liberalism, persuasion, and as its successors, in the form of the Conservative-Liberal Democrat coalition (2010–2015) and Conservative (2015–), were able to implement the commitment that government holdings would be only temporary measures so that the financial services companies could get back to 'business as normal' as quickly as possible. Thus, by mid–2017, the government stake in LBG was reduced to zero and 73% in RBS.

The consequence of the nature of this state intervention and ownership was that it closed down the political space, and strangled the political opportunity, for the finance sector unions to exert leverage over the financial services companies via the government. Indeed, as Unite national officer, Dominic Hook (interview, 6 September 2016), commented: 'UK Financial Investments, the Treasury, the regulators were all arms' length from unions but not alas from the banks … We asked for a meeting with UKFI but didn't even get one … State oversight has been a clever camouflage to get on with rationalisation'. Leverage could be envisaged to have been operationalised in three ways. First, the government as the ultimate employer would instruct senior management to act in a more favourable way towards union demands within the collective bargaining process. Second, the government would introduce institutional means of co-determination like worker directors. Third, the sector would experience re-regulation of its activities which would indirectly provide unions with an additional means of leverage over management. Historically, more politically amenable governments have been susceptible to pressures for such forms from strong unions where public ownership or regulation existed. However, the encroachment and then hegemony of neo-liberalism resulted in governments becoming forcibly insensitive, if not hostile, to the demands of weakened unions. What was most telling in this situation was that the Labour Party in government and then in opposition could not be relied upon to act in the manner that would be expected of a social democratic party, whereby it would act in a different way and with different purposes and then contest the actions of the government from a different ideological standpoint. Indeed, Labour's minister for the City stated in 2009: 'We believe in commercially led, private sector banks ... We have not become shareholders in banks as a political objective, it's as a consequence of taking necessary action' (*Daily Telegraph*, 18 December 2008). No amount of lobbying by Unite, the largest union, largest union affiliate to Labour and its largest financial donor, made any difference here.[2] For example, Unite hoped that while Labour was in office (until 2010) it would make a condition of the continued state financial support that employers would desist from offshoring jobs at a time of widespread redundancies.

But it was not just a neo-liberal ideology and the weakened state industrial and political state of labour unionism that explains this outcome. As alluded to before, there was also the no small matter of the crucial and central positon of finance capitalism within British capitalism-cum-capitalism in Britain. Finance capital within capitalism in Britain exerts a disproportionate amount of influence compared to finance capital in other advanced economies for historical (the City of London as one of the world centres of finance) and more contemporary (deregulation of the finance sector, entry into European capital markets) reasons. Coupled with the relative weakness of industrial capital, this suggests that in power terms the government/state was rather more dependent upon the financial services sector (banks especially) than the financial services sector was upon the government/state even within the period of the crisis. So while the financial services sector did require state intervention and government bailout, the terms upon which these were given were more favourable to the companies than might have otherwise been expected. In summary, neo-liberalism, weakened labour unions and the power of finance capital explain the trajectory taken over 'business as normal'.

The unwillingness of the state to regulate finance capital and finance capital's unwillingness to be regulated by the state were further indicated by four events. Firstly, by the Financial Conduct Authority (FCA) shelving its plan for an inquiry into the culture, pay and behaviour of staff with regarding to mis-selling and risk taking in late 2015 where the

FCA stated: 'We have decided that the best way to support these efforts is to engage individually with firms to encourage their delivery of cultural change as well as supporting the other initiatives outside the FCA' (*Guardian*, 1 January 2016). Secondly, by the limited measures taken to increase the prowess of whistle-blowing regulations in the financial services sector (*People Management*, 8 October 2015, 26 February 2016). Thirdly, after sustained lobbying by banks in 2015, the bank levy—which was introduced after the financial crash—was reduced by over half and only applied to operations within Britain (*Guardian*, 9 July 2015, 16 January 2016). And, fourth, no action has been taken against senior banking executive for their responsibility in creating the financial crash. Thus, despite a report by the FCA and PRA finding senior HBoS management were responsible for its massive failings and similar findings made concern senior RBS executives for its near collapse after producing in 2009 the biggest annual loss in corporate history in Britain of £24.1 bn, no prosecutions were forthcoming until early 2017 (*Guardian*, 20 November 2015, 13 May 2016; *Morning Star*, 31 January 2017). Such a situation was not a foregone conclusion for in some countries much stronger action has been taken against employers in the financial services sector. One example is Israel where a law was passed to cap bankers' salaries (*Guardian*, 30 March 2016). It is a matter of political will and a reflection of the configurations of power, material interests and ideology.

Again, as alluded to before, the root of the explanation for the actions of the state in rescuing the banking and financial system was not just neo-liberalism—the ideology—but also power and material interests, indicating a rather greater level of dependence and reliance of the state and economy upon the financial services sector than vice versa. The percentage of GDP accounted for by the financial services sector (using The City UK's definition of financial and related professional services) had risen from 6% in 1995 to 10% by 2009 (while manufacturing fell from 22 to 11% in the same period) and between 1999 and 2009, the share of GDP accounted for by financial services in Britain far exceed that of the United States, Japan, France and Germany (The City UK 2011). By 2016, the proportion of GDP contributed by financial services had risen to 12% (The City UK 2016), while manufacturing fell further. Consequently, the state as the ringmaster for capital was compelled to act for the wider good of finance capital and general capital for the prospect of an economic crash following a financial crash was perceived to be highly probable.

Research Methods

The means of data gathering for this study comprised four primary methods. Firstly, information obtained directly from the financial service sector unions (correspondence, documentation) and their publications, press releases, conference agendas and membership communications (bulletins, magazines, newsletters). The unions were Accord, Advance, Aegis, Affinity/Lloyds Trade Union, Communication Workers' Union (CWU), IBOA/Financial Services Union (FSU), NGSU, UFS, Unite,[3] and USDAW.[4] This material dated back to the beginning of the financial crash in 2007–2008. Secondly, interviews and correspondence with officers and activists from the main financial services sector unions. Thus, I wish to record my warm thanks to a number of union officers: Accord (Ged Nichols), CWU (John East), NGSU (Tim Rose), UFS (Alan Wood, Nick Caton), and Unite (Liz Cairns, Dominic Hook, Rob MacGregor). They gave either generously of their time for interviews or extended email correspondence and/or also arranged for the provision of union materials. A number of Unite seconded representatives and senior lay representatives (activists) in Capita and LBG were also interviewed or corresponded with on multiple occasions but, given that all but one of them at the time of writing were still employed within the sector, they are not named. Thirdly, to this were basis were added publications and information from the Certification Office, Department for Business, Enterprise and Regulatory Reform (BERR)/Department for Business, Innovation and Skills (BIS), Incomes Data Services (IDS), Office of National Statistics (ONS), and pro-partnership organisations like the Involvement and Participation Association (IPA) and Engage for Success. As the financial services sector comprises a high proportion of partnership agreements within Britain, these were more than amply covered in the publications of a number of these aforementioned organisations. Lastly, reports and interviews in the quality or broadsheet media (like the *Guardian*) were used to provide an element of independent verification of the materials gained from the financial services sector unions.[5]

As before (see Gall 2008), no attempt to was made to speak to employers or their senior managers because this was not believed to be necessary as neither the focus of the study was capital per se nor was it reasoned that the route to identifying capital's actions and associated outcomes could not be achieved by means other than interviewing or surveying management. Had attempts been made to carry out interviews or surveys, the potential worth of the material derived from them was brought into doubt by the tight-lipped and un-effusive nature of those interviews that were carried out (by journalists) of senior managers. For example, an interview with Neil Roden, former RBS human resources director, was not revealing as the journalist himself noted (*HR Magazine*, 24 September 2010). Roden was no more forthcoming after leaving RBS than when he was interviewed while still in post (*People Management*, 3 December 2009). Whether the result of an added public sensitivity surrounding the ramifications of the financial crash or just the routine lack of frankness displayed by senior management, such interviews were not productive and further attempts to carry them out with a more specific purpose in mind were not believed to be worth entertaining.[6] Data on company employment levels was not gained directly from individual employers because their annual company accounts (or other publications) did not provide data for *annual* employment levels for their operations *within* Britain. Even this data— as aggregate data—would not have provided for inflows and outflows of employment. Consequently, other sources, most obviously from unions, were required to be used.

That said with regard to employer access, it is a little more controversial to take the same stance regarding workers and union members (though not labour unions themselves). In other words, to decide not to interview or survey workers or union members when their experiences are the central subject matter of this book requires explanation. Thus, the purpose of the study is not to give workers a voice for, although of limited extent, the expression of worker voice can be found elsewhere, facilitated via their unions, and social media. (However, worker voice is given substantial coverage in Chap. 4.) Rather, the purpose is to examine at a generalised level of focus what has happened with regard to fight, flight, fright, and falling-in-line. Open examples of fight were identified through union and media sources as were numbers in flight. This was a relatively simple task because unions produced ample numbers of press releases on such matters and mainstream media displayed a greater than normal level of interest in the financial service sector in the post-crash period because of the heightened political significance of the sector.

With regard to fright and falling-in-line, this was achieved by a combination of the aforementioned use of secondary materials, particularly where a close reading of the publications of unions' member magazines was deployed. This allowed the use of summary reporting of unions' own now numerous membership surveys, and their letters, advice and problem pages in magazines. Letter pages comprised members writing into express their views, advice pages comprised the subject matter of common issues members were raising with their unions, and problem pages comprised the question and answers from members and unions. Setting aside the issues of gaining the necessary financial resources and then the appropriate access to conduct regular and large scale surveys of unions' members (as opposed to smaller, single 'snapshots') from 2007 to 2008 onwards, it was not believed that conducting such surveys would have added anything particularly more beneficial than could be gained from the aforementioned sources. This was because this study did not seek to measure specific levels of instances of employer actions (such as performance appraisal outcomes, disciplinaries) nor worker reactions (such as discontent or grievances) by company, union or year. Nor did it seek to identify the extent of such phenomenon across the sector. Consequently, the sources of data were deemed to be more than adequate because this study is an exploration and an overview.

Of course, there are limitations to using this approach (especially in regard of fright and falling-in-line). The first issues revolve around using union sources where union members were the focus of attention. By doing so, non-union members in unionised companies and non-union companies and who are sizeable in number (see later) are excluded from consideration. The most obvious implication is that the focus upon union members suggests that the more oppositionally-minded employees were studied. However, such an inference is problematic for several reasons. Thus, the close association of unions with employers—through partnership working—does not necessarily mean that holding membership makes members more oppositionally-minded. It may in cases concerning LTU and Unite (with the exception of LBG) but not for the raft of other unions. This point is emphasised given that the counter could hold, namely, non-membership reflects that unions are believed to lack independence from employers. Moreover, union weakness and a predominant 'servicing' (and not 'organising') culture within unions could easily disincline employees from joining unions where they wished to join more oppositionally-minded unions. One means of gaining the views of non-union members would have been to access the surveys on employee engagement carried out by individual employers. However, gaining access was not attempted because the veracity of the surveys was brought into doubt by reports—via unions—from employees whereby they felt a mixture of compulsion to undertake the surveys, and scepticism towards the management of the surveys vis-à-vis their results. Hence, unions made widespread use of their own surveys, showing that surveys of employees are a means of prosecuting contention.

There are also a range of other consequent issues revolving around using union surveys and materials. First, the questions in, and timings of, membership surveys were matters for the unions themselves, reflecting their concerns and interests with regard to generating data to be used for bargaining, agitation, propaganda, organising and an array of self-promotional purposes. In other words, the questions were not formulated by researcher and those that were used meet the more immediate needs of the union (without necessarily allowing for consistent longitudinal questioning). That said, response rates may have been higher than for surveys carried out by unknown third parties and surveys seeking retrospective, rather than contemporaneous prospective, views are problematic. Second, some of the documentation deployed has an inherent tendency to emphasise the aggrieved and discontented—because these workers are more likely to write into express their views, seek advice and representation, respond to a questionnaire, and take individual action such as a grievance or appeal—so that a measure of the relative balance of views ranging between contentment and discontentment (and including fright and falling-in-line) cannot be ascertained. Similarly, it is also not possible to ascertain the impact of flight upon the balances of contented and discontented, and upon fright and falling-in-line, within the existing workforces at any one point in time. It can be speculated that flight might remove many of the aggrieved workers from the workforce. Yet it can also be speculated that the experience of those workers that remain after widespread bouts of flight may produce new or increasingly aggrieved workers. Such omissions are not irrelevant but they are not crucial to the task of this study because its purpose was to provide a *generalised* overview of developments and, with the documentation and evidence considered, there is sufficient, consistent material to highlight broad phenomena and patterns of attitudes and behaviours. Third, there is more material concerning LBG than other employers for two reasons. One is that there are three unions operating within LBG (Accord, LTU, Unite) so that there are three sets of publications. The other is that the competition between the three (with Accord and Unite, on one side, and LTU, on the other) has provided a further reason to publish a greater than normal level of membership communications. Fortunately, as LBG is one of the major four banks and along with RBS the biggest of the four major banks, this is not an untoward situation.

Separate from these concerns is that explaining the absence of collective actions as per fight is a fraught business at the best of times because it involves asking the counter-factual questions of the kind: 'why did 'x' happen and not 'y'?' or just 'why did 'x' not happen?' This pertains to issues of why did not more members vote for industrial action when a majority was not gained (as well as why did as many as they did vote for action), why did more not vote in the ballot and so on and so forth. By using interviews and surveys of members, much more may not have been revealed or illuminated because of limited recall of the detail of sequences and processes or simple lack of knowledge of what did and did not motivate others to act as they did. But to the extent that interviews with specific subjects can help here, interviews and correspondence with a number of union officers were conducted on these matters.

As such, the methods deployed here are more than suitable and appropriate to provide a broad exploration and overview of the main trends occurring within the financial services sector. The depth of inquiry into the employee experience in particular companies has been heavily influenced by the presence and extent of union organisation and activity. It also follows from this that the concentration upon union-based data does mean that the reach of this study into the newer, non-traditional—and unorganised or weakly organised—parts of the sector is limited.

Previous Research

In examining the studies of employment relations in the financial services sector in Britain since the publication of Gall (2008), nearly all the fieldwork of these studies were carried out before the financial crash (namely, Arrowsmith and Marginson 2011; Arrowsmith et al. 2010; Butler 2009a, b; Cebulla 2016; Hoque et al. 2017; Johnstone 2010, 2011; Johnstone and Wilkinson 2015; Johnstone et al. 2009, 2010a, b, 2011; Malhotra et al. 2007; Marginson et al. 2008; McCann 2013, 2014; Samuel 2014; Stuart and Martinez Lucio 2008; Traxler et al. 2008; Waddington 2013).[7] However, this does not mean that they are necessarily 'out-of-date' or of no relevance to understanding the post-crash period. For example, Johnstone et al. (2009: 273–274) argued, inter alia, there was a need to have more longitudinal research on partnership; to have 'firm-in-sector' case studies; studies which looked at stakeholders other than unions; and studies of partnership as a process. Moreover, and given that Johnstone (2011) and Samuel (2014) both demonstrated that partnership enjoyed a high degree of institutional support from employers, this has a salience for the survival of partnership in spite of—or because of—the ramifications of the financial crash upon employment relations. But care is required in coming to such judgements. The study by Hoque et al. (2017) is a case in point. Their conclusion from a survey of some 3000 Unite members on the influence of workplace representatives upon job quality was that (i) there was a strong positive relationship between the presence of an onsite representative and respondents' perceptions of the extent to which their local union provided them with effective collective voice; (ii) respondents' perceptions of three of the four aspects of job quality under observation (job content, work—life balance and job stress, but not job security) were more favourable where an onsite representative was present; and (iii) the association between onsite union representation and respondents' perceptions of job content and work—life balance was mediated by their perceptions of the extent to which their local union provides effective collective voice. As Hoque et al. (2017: 46) acknowledged, the survey on which the analysis was based was conducted in spring 2008 so that 'the worst effects of the 'credit crunch' and subsequent crisis in the finance sector' had yet to take hold so it was 'open to question, therefore, whether union representatives will have continued to be able to mobilise collective voice to improve job quality outcomes during this period'. But they (Hoque et al. 2017: 46) were on weak ground to have suggested: 'it is possible that in the period following the credit crunch, onsite unions may have had an important role to play in preventing redundancies' as Chaps. 3 and 4 indicate. Moreover, the nature of Unite as a union compared to other unions like LTU or NGSU also needs consideration if their conclusions were to be applied more widely.

Chapter Structure

The following substantive chapters cover the players, processes and outcomes of the period in the financial service sector since the financial crash of 2007–2008. Thus, Chap. 2 examines the primary institutions of employee representation (without regard to their processes or outcomes in terms of the relationship between capital and labour). Union organisations have continued to weaken in their presence and influence within the sector, and now no longer have a significant presence (let alone influence) outside of a few companies. This is despite the occurrence of various union mergers being premised upon 'unity is strength' and 'economies of scale'—indeed, the concentration of their organisational form has not led to any concentration or maintenance of influence. The atrophy in staffing levels has led to older workers leaving the sector through redundancy (overwhelmingly voluntary) and these are predominantly the more unionised workers and the more active members. Furthermore, new entrants to the sector bring with them less propensity to be union members and union activists and this trajectory is reinforced by the organisational cultures which they encounter for the first time. This disorganisation has taken place despite a number of unions investing heavily in the employment of union organisers to recruit, retain and organise members. Put another way, the situation would be much worse without these efforts. Within the major union, Unite, which was established in 2007, its finance sector has experienced a loss of identity and coherence within what amounts to a much larger and more general union (than Amicus was). Unite no longer has the benefit of a wide cadre of leaders for the sector which were grounded and experienced in that sector as was the case prior to one of its main constituent unions, Unifi, joining Amicus. This phenomenon has been compounded by the dissolution of an occupational identity within the sector and not constrained by the weak set of institutional rights existing under various partnership agreements between unions and employers. Indeed, the proliferation of partnership agreements has undermined the ability of the unions to respond robustly to the employers' initiatives to retrench and restructure organisations. Staff forums and work councils amongst a small handful of non-unionised organisations have fared no better, and in some cases, much worse than their union counterparts in influencing the actions and attitudes of management.

Chapter 3 assesses the *processes* of employment relations whereby a number of aspects of fight, flight, fright and falling-in-line are examined. As alluded to before, the first notable phenomenon is the absence of fight, most obviously denoted by strikes and industrial action, suggesting that a number of factors have resulted in the unwillingness and inability of unionised financial services workers to undertake collective action. The unsettling presence of continual tranches of widespread redundancies has been only one of the factors at play. Other factors include organisational churn which has had a dislocating effect on union organisation. The few cases of industrial action—actual or threatened—have predominantly taken place in small and highly idiosyncratic areas where strategic leverage is greater than elsewhere. More common are collective protests outside company buildings by activists from other employers and where the tactic is to damage the brand or reputation of the targeted employer (and not halt or disrupt its operations). The process by which large-scale flight has taken place is one largely of employer unilateralism. Elsewhere in terms of pay structures and structural reorganisation, the same pattern of employer behaviour is manifestly discernible. Previously, negotiation had increasingly been superseded by consultation (especially under the guise of partnership agreements). Now consultation has increasingly been superseded by merely being informed of changes in advance of the changes taking place. In the context of the absence of fighting to preserve jobs and conditions of employment, the relative attractiveness of flight has increased even if the terms for leaving are not quite now as 'generous' as they once were. Similarly, for those left in employment, the demands from employers in the wage-effort bargain have become greater by virtue of (a) the reduction in staffing levels through redundancy and natural wastage, and (b) increased usage of a more virulent form of performance management. Yet for fear of the consequences of non-conformity and the inability to move jobs elsewhere, a process of falling-in-line has taken place.

Chapter 4 concerns the substantive *outcomes* of employment relations associated with fight, flight, fright and falling-in-line. Unions have had no obvious or widespread success in preventing tens of thousands of redundancies in the sector. Where they have been able to exert some influence has been on the terms of severance and not on the numbers leaving. Even here, the influence has been rather marginal. Pay continues to be regulated under employer regimes of performance management so that union influence is again marginal—it has been restricted far more to establishing the size of the overall 'pay pot' and ensuring the procedural means by which pay awards are distributed are either adhered to or seen to be fair rather than on what principles are used for individual distribution. In comparison to the past of collective bargaining establishing across-the-board rises for all staff, this emphasises not only the lack of co-determination but that employees are treated as a set of increasingly atomised individuals. Low pay is now becoming a feature of employment as is precariousness. No longer is there a psychological contract of stable, long-term employment with increasing remuneration through either seniority or promotion. For those that are left in employment, the main outcome of flight has been the emergence of a more pronounced and sullen resignation to, acceptance of and acquiescence with their fate under a regime of increased management power. 'Performance management' has now come to involve far greater scrutiny of work performance, meeting targets and monitoring of sickness and absence. Critically, it is now also linked to what are termed 'market rates' for the geographic region in which employees undertake their roles. Chapter 5 comprises the conclusion, whereby the significance of the preceding substantive chapters is assessed and a number of important issues are drawn out for the study of employees' experience of work, employment relations and labour unionism in the sector.

Conclusion

This present study seeks to builds upon the previous study of labour unionism in the financial services sector (see Gall 2008). It takes as its point of departure the juncture at which that study finished, being the beginning of the 'credit crunch' precipitating the financial crash that occasioned a recession and the age of austerity. However, this present study also has a wider concern, focussing directly upon the experience of employees at the hands of employers since the financial crash as well as continuing to chart the trajectory of the organs of employees' collective representation in this environment. Given the latter, some of the main questions posed in this study are: has partnership triumphed at the expense of, and as, independent labour unionism declined?; why has partnership managed to survive the trauma of the financial crash?; what has happened to the trajectory towards 'unionateness' identified in the previous study (see Gall 2008)?; what has been the fate of the model of 'internalism' in the form of single institution staff associations as company mergers continued apace?; what is the relationship between 'internalism' and partnership?; and where does the strategic leverage of finance workers lie?

Notes

1. This thesis was well received—see, for example, Ellis (2011) and Martinez Lucio (2011).
2. Initially, opinion was divided amongst Unite's finance sector members over whether banking should be nationalised. This resulted from concern over the terms (given many Unite members held shares in their employers) and over the scale. But later Unite called for RBS, given its higher state ownership, to be turned into a state-owned bank which could act as an investment bank in order to increase lending for small businesses, local authorities and agencies to create a 'green infrastructure' (Unite press release, 17 June 2013, *uniteWORKS*, July/August 2013). This was an extension of its call made in late 2012 for the total nationalisation of RBS to be part of a 'root-and-branch reform of the UK's banking system' (Unite press release, 10 September 2012). Unite called for both RBS and LBG to be fully brought into public ownership as a national investment bank (Unite press release, 29 September 2012). Earlier, it also called for 'A Social Contract for Financial Services' in late 2008. This comprised demands for (i) recognition of Unite as a key stakeholder in the future of the financial services industry; (ii) ensuring the employment security of employees in the finance sector; (iii) protecting and improving the terms and conditions of employees, including pension arrangements; (iv) ending the remuneration packages of senior executives which reward short-termism and irresponsible risk taking; and (v) overhauling of the regulatory structures of the financial services sector to include union involvement in order to enhance the accountability of finance institutions. This was followed up in 2012 with 'A finance sector for the real economy' which argued for (i) stronger regulation; (ii) introduction of a Financial Transactions Tax on speculative trading to help repair the damage caused by the financial crisis and curb the most risky transactions; (iii) fair and transparent pay systems for all workers, including employee representation on remuneration committees; (iv) employment security and an end to the jobs cull in the sector and the rush to outsource and offshore, and; (v) reassessment of performance management systems with greater emphasis given to service rather than sales and delivering fairness for both customers and employees.
3. A number of Unite's memberships in different insurance companies had their own websites (AXA, Capita and Prudential for example) as well so these were used.

4. Only Advance did not respond to requests for information so, in its case, the only materials used were those publicly available on its website, namely, its members' magazine. Additionally, Unite was unable to provide access to more than a sample of its membership newsletters by each company it organised within. However, collation of on-line materials meant that did not prove to be a significant problem.

5. In regard of the *Guardian*, Joris Luyendijk, a Dutch journalist, provided for it a banking blog called 'Voices of finance' consisting of interview-based articles or opinion pieces by staff working in banking and finance. Luyendijk deployed what he described as an anthropological approach to understanding the financial services sector by 'going native' by means of getting participants in the sector to write self-portraits of what they do and what their work involved. Begun in September 2011, by 2 years later it had recorded well over 100 such portraits. These were then put together to produce a book (Luyendijk 2015). Unfortunately for the purposes of this book, very few concerned the experiences of those other than senior management personnel who worked in trading and investing. The most useful account in this banking blog on the experiences of an employee relations manager at a major bank based in Canary Wharf in London and which concerned managing the disciplinary, grievance and redundancy processes of such traders and investors. This paucity of material on the self-reported experience and views of the majority of finance workers is reflected in the dearth of blogs by financial services sector workers. Unlike *Maid in London* (about the experience of worker organising by maids in hotels in London), *Angry Workers of the World* (about working in west London) or *Roy Mayall* (concerning the experience of postal workers working for Royal Mail), blogs were not unearthed after internet searches so that ethnographical type accounts of workers' own work experience, unfortunately, remained closed to this study.

6. The limited access which Martin and Gollan (2012) secured to interview eight current and former RBS executives is not believed to contradict this assessment, especially as their research focussed upon management practices in a way which limited critical inquiry. They also heavily relied upon the aforementioned interviews with Roden. Moreover, also see McCann (2014: 245) on such access difficulties to management in the financial services sector in Britain. Participative research as with Brannan (2017) was not an option for this study while Liu et al. (2017) relied upon media reportage to generate their data.

7. Despite repeated requests, a copy of Taylor and Moore (2014) could not be obtained. Although Fraser (2015) briefly examined recent employment matters in RBS, he did so using secondary sources. One exception is Johnstone and Wilkinson (2017) which examines 'BuSoc', a building society, from 1990 to 2014. However, the anonymising of the organisation militates against much use being made of the study with regard to the post-crash period.

References

Arrowsmith, J., & Marginson, P. (2011). Variable pay and collective bargaining in British retail banking. *British Journal of Industrial Relations, 49*(1), 54–79.

Arrowsmith, J., Nicholaisen, H., Bechter, B., & Nonell, R. (2010). The management of variable pay in European banking. *International Journal of Human Resource Management, 21*(15), 2716–2740.

Bain, G. (1970). *The growth of white collar unionism.* Oxford: Clarendon Press.

Blackburn, R. (1967). *Union character and social class: A study of white-collar unionism.* London: Batsford.

Brannan, M. (2017). Power, corruption and lies: Mis-selling and the production of culture in financial services. *Human Relations, 70* (6): 641–667.

Butler, P. (2009a). 'Riding along on the crest of a wave': Tracking the shifting rationale for non-union consultation at FinanceCo. *Human Resource Management Journal, 19*(2), 176–193.

Butler, P. (2009b). Non-union employee representation: Exploring the riddle of managerial strategy. *Industrial Relations Journal, 40*(3), 198–214.

Casu, B., & Gall, A. (2016) *Building Societies in the Financial Services Industry,* London: Palgrave.

Cebulla, A. (2016) The social orientations and ideologies of UK finance employees at the onset of the Global Financial Crisis. *Capital & Class,* forthcoming.

Ellis, V. (2011). 'Greed is (not) good': The causes and consequences of the financial crisis. *Work, Employment & Society, 25*(1), 163–169.

Ertürk, I., & Gabor, D. (2017) (eds.) *The Routledge Companion to Banking Regulation and Reform,* London: Routledge.

Escudero, V. (2009). Effects of the crisis on the financial sector: Trends and policy issues. International Institute for Labour Studies. Discussion paper 197/2009, Geneva.

Fraser, I. (2015). *Shredded: The Rise and Fall of the Royal Bank of Scotland*, Edinburgh: Birlinn.

Gall, G. (2008). *Labour unionism in the financial services sector: Fighting for rights and representation*. Aldershot: Ashgate.

Hoque, K., Earls, J., Conway, N., & Bacon, N. (2017). Union representation, collective voice and job quality: An analysis of a survey of union members in the UK finance sector. *Economic and Industrial Democracy*, 38(1): 27–50.

Johnstone, S. (2010). *Labour and management cooperation: Workplace partnership in UK financial services*. Basingstoke: Gower.

Johnstone, S. (2011, March 25). *Partnership working in UK financial services*. London: IPA.

Johnstone, S., & Wilkinson, A. (2015). Employee voice in a dot com: The rise and demise of the employee forum at WebBank. In B. Kaufman, P. Gollan, D. Taras, & A. Wilkinson (Eds.), *Voice and involvement at work: Experience with non-union representation* (pp. 146–165). Basingstoke: Routledge.

Johnstone, S., Ackers, P., & Wilkinson, A. (2009). The British partnership phenomenon: A ten year review. *Human Resource Management Journal*, 19(3), 260–279.

Johnstone, S., Wilkinson, A., & Ackers, P. (2010a). Critical incidents of partnership: Five years' experience at NatBank. *Industrial Relations Journal*, 41(4), 382–398.

Johnstone, S., Ackers, P., & Wilkinson, A. (2010b). Better than nothing? Is non-union partnership a contradiction in terms? *Journal of Industrial Relations*, 52(2), 151–168.

Johnstone, S., Wilkinson, A., & Ackers, P. (2011). Applying Budd's model to partnership. *Economic and Industrial Democracy*, 32(2), 307–328.

Johnstone S., & Wilkinson A. (2017). Assessing the dynamics of labour management partnership: a longitudinal case analysis. *British Journal of Management*, forthcoming.

Kelly, J. (1998). *Rethinking industrial relations: Mobilisation, collectivism and long waves*. London: Routledge.

Liu, H., Cutcher, L., & Grant, D. (2017). Authentic leadership in context: An analysis of banking CEO narratives during the global financial crisis. *Human Relations*, 70(6), 694–724.

Luyendijk, J. (2015). *Swimming with sharks: My journey into the world of the bankers*. London: Guardian Faber Publishing.

Malhotra, N., Budhwar, P., & Prowse, P. (2007). Linking rewards to commitment: An empirical investigation of four UK call centres. *International Journal of Human Resource Management*, 18(12), 2095–2128.

Marginson, P., Arrowsmith, J., & Gray, M. (2008). Undermining or reframing collective bargaining? Variable pay in two sectors compared. *Human Resource Management Journal, 18*(4), 327–346.

Martin, G., & Gollan, P. (2012). Corporate governance and strategic human resources management in the UK financial services sector: The case of the RBS. *International Journal of Human Resource Management, 23*(16), 3295–3314.

Martinez Lucio, M. (2011). Labour unionism in the financial services sector— Fighting for rights and representation—By Gregor Gall. *British Journal of Industrial Relations, 49*(1), 200–201.

McCann, L. (2013). Managing from the echo chamber: Employee dismay and leadership detachment in the British banking and insurance crisis. *Critical Perspectives on International Business, 9*(4), 398–414.

McCann, L. (2014). Disconnected amid the networks and chains: Employee detachment from company and union after offshoring. *British Journal of Industrial Relations, 52*(2), 237–260.

Samuel, P. (2014). *Financial services partnerships: Labor-management dynamics.* Abingdon: Routledge.

Soriano, C. (2011). *Recession and social dialogue in the banking sector: A global perspective.* Dublin: Eurofound.

Stuart, M., & Martinez Lucio, M. (2008). Employment relations in the UK finance sector: Between globalisation and re-regulation. CERIC Working paper 1, University of Leeds.

Taylor, P., & Moore, S. (2014). *Employee representation in the finance sector.* London: Unite.

Traxler, F., Arrowsmith, J., Nergaard, K., & Molins Lopez Rodo, J. (2008). Variable pay and collective bargaining: A cross-national comparison of the banking sector. *Economic and Industrial Democracy, 29*(3), 406–431.

UKFI. (2009). *Annual report, 2008–2009.* London: UK Financial Investments.

Unite. (2012). *A finance sector for the real economy.* London: Unite.

Waddington, J. (2013). The views of members towards workplace union organization in banking between 1999 and 2008. *British Journal of Industrial Relations, 51*(2), 333–354.

2

Players

Introduction

Although labour unions, whether originally staff associations or independent unions, represented a minority of staff working throughout the financial services sector by 2015 (see Table 2.2) and in only a few employing organisations do they represent a majority of employees, labour unions, nonetheless, remain the sole representative and independent institutions for protecting and advancing the collective interests of employees in the sector. In this context, it is also worth noting that employer provision of (dependent) means of collective interest representation remains limited, the utility of European Works Councils continues to be somewhat restricted, and the extent of coverage of collective bargaining is considerably wider than the extent of union membership alone would imply (see Table 2.3). The structure of this chapter is to examine each labour union individually before identifying and assessing a number of common characteristics to these unions. When examining each union, the focus is upon their geneses, trajectories and developments, especially in terms of membership levels and participation as well as their overall industrial perspectives and relationships

© The Author(s) 2017
G. Gall, *Employment Relations in Financial Services*,
DOI 10.1057/978-1-137-39539-9_2

with employers. While some attention is paid to inter-union relations given that multi-unionism is a feature of labour unionism in a number of employing organisations in the sector, this subject matter is primarily dealt with in the following chapter as part of examining the *process* of relationships. However, for the moment, it is worth noting that the extent of multi-unionism has recently grown given the spate of mergers, takeovers and divestments since the financial crash of 2007–2008. This primarily, but not exclusively, concerns LBG.[1] Following the consideration of the institutions of labour unionism, there is also a brief consideration of employers in terms of new entrants to the financial services sector and employer programmes of employee engagement.

Accord

Accord traces its origins back to 1978 when its predecessor, the Halifax Building Society Staff Association (HBSSA), was founded and gained its certificate of independence the following year. In 1994, the association was renamed the Independent Union of Halifax Staff (IUHS). Following acquisition and merger activities by the Halifax Building Society, whereupon a number of staff associations transferred to IUHS, the union was renamed Accord in 2002. Its membership steadily increased from just under 20,000 members in 1995 to just under 33,000 by 2008. Most, but not all, of this growth was organic (see Gall 2008: 89). From 2008, membership fell from this peak to around 23,000 by 2015. Like other financial service sector unions, membership levels were hit by the shakeout in the sector after the financial crash, albeit some were more affected than others depending upon which companies they organised within and where they had most of their members. Nonetheless, Accord was able to report that it 'recruited more members in 2015 than in any year since the financial crisis and our net membership increased on a year by year basis for the first time since 2008' (*My Accord*, Winter 2016). And 'Already in 2016 more new members have joined us than in the whole of 2013 and the whole of 2014 and our membership in the Lloyds Community Bank is growing fastest of all' (Accord press release, 14 July 2016). The number of

Lloyds members was 'almost 2000' (*Accord Mail (TSB)*, September 2016). Similar to other unions, Accord found that 'one in two people who are not union members have never been asked to join' (*My Accord*, Summer 2012). The impact of falling membership upon union density was not straightforward given the widespread shedding of labour, company merger and the decision taken by its 2010 conference to recruit outside of HBoS. In late 2008, Accord's general secretary reported Accord had density of 50% in HBoS (*Tribune*, 8 December 2008). But by 2012, Accord stated: 'Even though thousands of jobs have gone since then—and, inevitably, membership has reduced—we now have more than 60% of all HBoS staff in Accord' (*My Accord*, Summer 2012) and 'in the Halifax branch network, [density is] around 85%' (*My Accord*, Autumn 2012) whilst in 2016, it commented: 'Accord now has more LBG employees in membership than any other union—but that is still less than 50% of the workforce' (*My Accord*, Spring 2016). Within, TSB density was around 10% in late 2016 (*My Accord TSB*, October 2016). Further details on union density could not be gained from Accord because: 'As you appreciate, we are in a competitive situation with Affinity (trading as LTU and TSBU) so I'm reluctant to provide sensitive information that may be useful to them …' (Ged Nichols, email correspondence, 28 October 2016). However, Accord did state: 'our density is lower in the heritage Lloyds parts of [LBG] because we only started to try to recruit members in those parts of the business in September 2015 [but] … I will say that we recruited more members in the year from September 2015 than we did in any comparable period since the financial crisis' (Ged Nichols, email correspondence, 28 October 2016). Overall, Accord aims to recruit around 400 new members per month to 'stand still' (Ged Nichols, email correspondence, 28 October 2016).

In terms of Accord organisation, the number of Accord workplace representatives reached 'almost 1000' (Accord press release, 23 June 2010, *My Accord*, Spring 2011) in mid-2010 before falling back to 850 by late 2015 (*My Accord*, Autumn 2015). Around 200 of these attend the union's biennial conference. Accord has eleven full-time seconded organisers with LBG. Most of the costs of their facility-time are met by Accord (Ged Nichols, email correspondence, 28 October 2016). Membership participation can be judged by reference to ballot turnouts on proposed agreements on terms and conditions of employment and election turnouts.[2] In the former, whilst majorities voting for deals were often very high, turnouts were low at a third or below (see later). In the latter, and without any contested elections for the position of general secretary, the regular election for union president is the main indicator. Turnouts were low at 8% in 2016, 9% in 2014 and 6% in 2012. However, these are turnouts are not substantially different from other unions within and without the financial services sector.

Through its general secretary, Ged Nichols, Accord outlined its philosophy:

[We believe in] … consultation not confrontation, negotiation not imposition. Intelligent, responsible adults should be able to reach agreement based on mutual respect and understanding. That's Accord's way – although we will not, of course, roll over if such agreement is not forthcoming. (*My Accord*, Summer 2010)

[Partnership is] when management and the unions agree to work together for the good of the company and the benefit of the staff, working out the best solutions to potential problems. … So what does it mean exactly? … Accord knows that a successful company means better rewards and job security for its members. (*My Accord*, Winter 2011)

Whatever our differences, it is important that the bank and unions work together in a positive way to try to change things for the better. (*My Accord*, Summer 2012)

I believe in mature and balanced trade unionism and working with decent employers to help their businesses to be successful. This in turn helps them provide secure jobs and fair rewards whilst treating their workforce with the dignity and respect that working people are entitled to expect from decent employers. Decent employers who treat their staff and customers fairly and make a positive contribution to our economy and our communities. (*My Accord*, Autumn 2013)

In the context of the decision to recruit in areas where LTU was dominant (see later), Accord described itself 'an open, transparent, responsible and accountable union' (*My Accord*, Autumn 2015) and 'a union run for, and overseen by, our members' (*Accord Mail (Lloyds)*, October 2016) with the following statement of aims and objectives:

> We are asking Lloyds heritage staff to join us and participate in building a better bank and a better future for all employees in the Lloyds Banking Group. The business brands that employees work in may be different and may have different histories, cultures and traditions but the people and our aspirations are the same. We all want secure jobs that are meaningful and satisfying, we want to be recognised for the good work we do, be fairly rewarded and treated with respect at work. We want our employers to recognise us as individuals and that we have lives outside of work. We care about our colleagues and our customers. We want to work for a successful business that does the right things so we can be proud of it and our contribution to it. But we live in tough times where nothing can be taken for granted – so we need a strong, inclusive union that helps us as individuals if things go wrong and works hard with our employer to make working life better for everybody. This is what Accord does. (*My Accord*, Autumn 2015)

Its general secretary then outlined the union's continued philosophy and modus operandi:

> Our style is collaborative but that is a source of influence and strength – it doesn't mean that we are soft or that we will always agree with what employers want. We will continue to remain an independent union. But we don't disagree for the sake of it. We try to resolve problems (such as with 'targets' and behaviours) where they occur rather than running to the press or regulators. The joint statement of principles that underpins our new working relationship with Lloyds Banking Group recognises organisational independence and is respectful of differences. (*My Accord*, Autumn 2015)

Consequently, it is not surprising to find Accord (and its predecessors [see Gall 2008: 89]) has never held a strike, although it has balloted for industrial action (see later) and that its arguments for its demands are couched in terms of mutual gains (whereby job losses are viewed as being detrimental to the interests of both members and the company as reducing staffing provides for lower levels of service provision to customers which in turn impacts deleteriously upon profitability and employee's experience of work).

Accord implicitly pursued an underlying three-fold operational strategy. One part concerns attempting to keep the employer to its word in regard of the implementation of the employer's own unilaterally determined policy and rules. This means monitoring the behaviour of junior, middle and senior management and assessing their behaviour against stated policy and rules, and where a divergence exists—and which does not favour its members—lobbying senior management to rectify this. Often the contention is that the implementation of one policy contradicts the implementation of another (higher order) policy, the process of implementation has skewed the intended outcome or that there has been a lack of transparency. The second part is, having accepted management policy, to help manage implementation to ensure procedural fairness. Thus, Accord made statements on various occasions like: 'We will work to ensure that employees are treated with the dignity and respect that they are entitled to expect at this worrying time' (*Accord press release*, 29 June 2016). The third part to the implicit operational strategy is to act as a resolver of questions and queries that members have about their terms and conditions of employment that arguably the employer's human resource department should be carrying out. However, the role for Accord here is engage as a player in the regime of information and consultation, namely, the framework of micro-social dialogue.[3]

Advance

Advance is the dominant union[4] in Santander and its subsidiaries.[5] Its forebearer was the Abbey National Staff Association (ANSA). ANSA was created in 1977, gained its certificate of independence in 1978 and affiliated to the TUC in 1998. Along the way, it changed its name to the ANGU in 2001 and to Advance in 2007 in recognition of Abbey's integration into the Santander Group with the Santander group also acquiring Alliance and Leicester and Bradford and Bingley. Following the acquisition of the Bradford and Bingley, the Union for Bradford and Bingley Staff and Associated Companies (UBAC) amalgamated with Advance in 2009.[6] Advance's membership grew from 4895 (1979) to 6575 (1985) to 8210 (1991) before peaking at some 9000 in 1996, and then falling back to 6945 by 2015 (despite the addition of just over 1000 UBAC members). In spite of membership decline, in the early 2000s its union density increased from around 30 to 35% (Hall 2004: 2) as a by-product of company restructuring, offshoring and downsizing. By 2015, according to its annual report for 2016, Santander UK had 19,992 employees.[7] With Advance having 6945 members in 2015, this represents a density of 35%, indicating no change from more than a decade earlier. However, Advance's union density throughout Santander is not uniform. In the Geoban division with 3700 employees, density was 81% in the early 2010s (*Your voice at work* magazine, Summer 2011).

Advances' current partnership working arrangement with Santander dates back to its initial recognition by Abbey in 1977. This was formalised into written agreements like that of 2003. Up to this point, Hall (2004: 2) noted 'the union has never undertaken a strike or other industrial action' and this has remained the case. Under Abbey, there was a high level of incorporation of Advance's senior officers into the company's operational structure in terms of meetings for information and consultation. It has four secondees who are, in effect, the equivalent of EUOs and around 60 lay reps (one for every 150 members). It has commonly talked in terms of shared values and mutual objectives with the employer. Annual pay awards are not put out to membership ballots and there was no failure to agree on issues between 1989 and 2004 (including on offshoring when ANGU believed that Abbey took part in open dialogue). De facto partnership has, therefore, been practiced—but only at the company not intra-company level for line management has been resistant to ANSA and workplace presence has been extremely 'underdeveloped' (see also Bain et al. 2004). As with Accord, ANGU/Advance displayed only organisational , thus, limited moves toward 'unionateness'.

Somewhat similar to Accord, Advance's role is very much constructed around representing to management its members' concern and relaying back to members management's responses in the manner of a sub-contracted agency by both labour and capital. At one level, there is nothing instinctively odd or unusual about this for this is one of the basic aspects of the work of any union. Yet, Advance exists rather more to act as a communicator between two parties than a bargainer for one (labour) not because it does not seek to bargain but because the emphasis given to the transferal of information and views upwards to management and downwards to members means that this fits into an exchange relationship between capital and labour where consultation takes precedence over bargaining (even though the two overlap). Moreover, because this takes place within the context of mutual gains and partnership, the manner in which this task is carried out and the intention lying behind the practice become more distinctive. Thus, the choice to work within the confines of such a cooperative ideology and institutional framework denudes workers of the ability to robustly challenge the terms of the wage-effort bargain and the organisation of work. Consequently, Advance places itself in the position of trying to make management better and more effective for Advance's own ideology stipulates that by working with the employer and by advising management of its best (supposed) interests, Advance can best progress its members' interests.

The Advance partnership ideology comprises the following components: an efficient and effective employer operation within the competitive marketplace is the best guarantor of workers' job security and terms and conditions; workers need to be well motivated to help attain this with improved remuneration as well as being treated as partners being the best way to achieve this; and so on. Therefore, Advance contests employer actions and advises other courses of action when it believes that the employer has departed from this desired trajectory. And, by the same token, when the employer pleads poverty or makes case for the need to take actions to safeguard the business and which result in deleterious consequences for workers, Advance makes its case against this but ultimately accepts the thrust of the employer rationale (and for reasons other than lack of power to stop the employer). In such cases, Advance argues that the process of redundancy or performance management should be carried out as humanely, professionally and properly as possible. Thus, voluntary redundancies rather than compulsory redundancies are sought, with attendant retraining and deployment also available. In the case of performance management, it warns against the outcome and consequences of demotivation of staff as a result correct and incorrect ratings.

The endpoint of the argument here is that Advance's ideology cannot situate workers' interests in anything other than contingent and dependent terms, where this contingency and dependency exist with regard to capital. In this sense, there is no construction of the independence of workers' interests. Concomitant, the basis to this partnership is more than an ideological super-structure for there has to have been—and has been—some indication of the maintenance and advance of material interests. Quite how much is difficult to precisely ascertain in relation to the other factors of what would have the employer done in the absence of Advance (see later on 'challenger' bank status) and what labour market forces would ordinarily suggest. Even in a situation of bargaining, employers' first offers are predicated on there being room for an improved final offer so that a semblance of bargaining can be said to have occurred.

Aegis

The origins of the Aegis union date back to the formation in 1971 of the Scottish Equitable Staff Association as an internal staff association. When Scottish Equitable was renamed Aegon UK[8] in 2010, the union changed its name to Aegis, and affiliated to the TUC in the same year. With the outsourcing of 'non-core' parts of Aegon from 2012, Aegis followed these workers to their new employers by recruiting them and gaining union recognition to represent them (at Origen Financial Services, AEGON Global Technologies Europe and Kames Capital). This brought about a number of wider changes. First, Aegis union officers terminated their employment with Aegon and became employees of Aegis, thus relinquishing the company resource of facility time and in the process gaining further independence from the company. Second, a decision was taken to pursue a strategy of membership growth into other parts of the financial services industry. Part of this saw the

SURGE[9] and YISA unions merge into Aegis in 2014 so that Aegis now represents members in the Skipton and Yorkshire building societies (even though Aegon did not take over the Skipton or Yorkshire societies). The logic to amalgamating with SURGE and YISA was to benefit from economies of scale, protect financial security, expand Unionlearn activities and increase external profile. All three unions had small and declining memberships, with relatively little in the way of financial reserves to sustain themselves in the longer term. Aegis's membership had declined from 2500 to 3000 in the 2000s and dipped below 2000 (when density was 70% [Carley 2012]) in the 2010s before SURGE and YISA transferred to it. It now stands at just under 5000 members (see Table 2.2).

Britannia Staff Union

The Britannia Staff Union (BSU) is a small, independent finance union with members employed by the Co-operative Banking Group (CBG, formerly Cooperative Financial Services). The Britannia building society, the second largest building society,[10] was bought by the Co-operative Banking Group in 2009. BSU membership has fallen from a highpoint of just under 3500 in 2009 to just under 1500 by 2015. This was heavily related to the financial crisis of CBG, whereby many Britannia branches were shut rather than rebranded after the takeover, with 240 of its 350 branches being closed. The forebearer of the BSU was the Leek and Westbourne Building Society Staff Association, which was founded in 1972 and certified as an independent union in 1976. In 1984, it was renamed the Britannia Building Society Staff Association, becoming the Britannia Staff Union in 1994. BSU signed a partnership agreement with the building society in 1998 and this has set the tone for its subsequent relationship with both CBG and Unite (which is the other main union recognised by CBG). In order to cut operating costs, the union heavily used electronic surveys of members in order to 'take the temperature' on issues, formulate pay bargaining objectives and ratify agreements. It surveys gain between a 30 and 50% response rate. Finally, the BSU is likely to seek merger or transfer in the short- to medium-term as its membership continues to fall while its cutting of costs remains insufficient to accommodate to this trajectory. Added to this, and reflecting its own financial crisis, CBG ended its subsidy to BSU. Thus, in mid-2016 BSU sought to sell its costly to maintain headquarters and move into rented accommodation whilst recognising that selling the property would be neither quick nor easy (*BSU Newsletter*, July 2016). It also sought to define itself at the 'Banking Staff Union' which allowed it to keep its acronym while seeking to broaden its membership basis within and without CBG.

Communication Workers' Union

The Communication Workers' Union (CWU), representing staff in retail, commercial, corporate, customer service and support roles in Santander UK, has enjoyed a relatively benign relationship with Santander. This has resulted primarily from a strategy pursued by the bank of being a challenger to the existing, established companies (see below). Currently, the CWU has some 3500 members in Santander and its associated companies and providers along with a small number in iPSL, the cheque clearing organisation. According to its annual conference documents, this number has remained relatively stable in the mid-2010s, with around two-thirds of these members paying into the union's political fund. So some 95% of these CWU members are employed in the Santander operations, and this constitutes 19% of the Santander workforce represented by unions and is based only upon the specific workplaces the CWU organises within. These are determined the historical legacy of organising in Girobank (which was originally part of the Post Office) either directly since its creation or through the Alliance and Leicester Group Staff Union (ALGUS)[11] amalgamating with the CWU (in 2007) when Alliance and Leicester was bought by Santander (and following on from the Alliance and Leicester acquiring most of Girobank operations in 1990). Swiss Post Solutions (SPS) acquired the mail and logistics contract for Santander whereby the CWU retained bargaining rights for the former Alliance and Leicester sites but also gained those rights for SPS staff which work at other Santander sites. Meanwhile, Advance retains negotiating rights for the former Abbey National and Bradford and Bingley sites, constituting 81% of the unionised workforce. John East, CWU assistant secretary with responsibility for financial services, reported that 'relations [with Advance] are cordial, many of the negotiations are undertaken jointly where they relate to overall conditions of service, whereas the two unions represent different sites within the group so some negotiations are discrete and only appropriate to one union' (Email correspondence, 3 September 2016). As mentioned before, the CWU also organises in IPSL, the cheque clearing organisation, but the size of IPSL operations has dwindled as electronic means have superseded paper means. Consequently, CWU membership has fallen from 1000 to 200 by the mid-2010s (even with PCS members transferred to it in 2011). As with other unions organising in the financial services sector, the CWU heavily uses membership ballots to affirm the results of negotiations with Santander (although it does not use membership ballots to guide or form bargaining demands). For example, in 2016 CWU membership accepted a 2.1% pay deal following an electronic ballot which recorded an 80% turnout. With a highly feminised membership, 33% of the (lay) Santander National Committee members were women in late 2013 (CWU 2014: 2).

Financial Services Union

The Irish Bank Officials' Association (IBOA), founded in 1918, was renamed IBOA—the finance union in 2007 before becoming the Financial Services Union (FSU) in 2016.[12] With the expansion of two major Irish banks, the Allied Irish Bank (AIB) and Bank of Ireland, into Great Britain in the 1960s, the IBOA consequently operated in three jurisdictions. The main one is the Republic of Ireland, but for the purposes of this study, the other two of Northern Ireland and Great Britain, are salient. From a high of 32% in 2003, the proportion of the union's membership located in Northern Ireland and Great Britain, that is, the

United Kingdom, fell to 28% by 2015 while the union's overall membership rose from 18,152 members in 2003 to a peak of 22,555 in 2009 before falling back to 14,313 in 2015 (see Table 2.2). In line with a number of other financial services sector unions elsewhere, the utilisation of new technologies saw the IBOA/FSU organise amongst not 'just bank tellers, but [also] software developers, derivative traders, financial advisers and sales teams … [so that i]n the past few years the make-up of the union's membership has already begun to change with around 1000 members now drawn from outside the traditional banking sector' (FSU press release, 6 May 2016). In 2016, following a 3-year strategic review of its internal operations and structures, this new course was formalised as the IBOA adopted new rules to encourage wider membership engagement and adopted the new name, FSU, to reflect more properly its broadening membership base within a much more diverse economic sector. In tandem with this, the FSU stated that while 'members will continue to benefit from the collective strength of the union … we'll also be reconfiguring our services to provide more personal and career development' (FSU press release, 6 May 2016).

The onset of the banking crisis from the summer of 2008 onwards plunged the IBOA into a period of unprecedented turmoil as it moved into defensive mode aimed at protecting members' jobs, terms and conditions against the backdrop of a severe contraction in the workforce of the financial services sector (see Chap. 4). The landscape of Irish banking also changed quite dramatically. Of the six domestic banking institutions in existence at the beginning of 2008, only three now remain: AIB and Permanent-TSB, which are essentially and fully state-owned, and the Bank of Ireland which is 15% state-owned. Of the other three, EBS was merged into AIB while Anglo Irish Bank and Irish Nationwide Building Society were nationalised and merged to form the Irish Bank Resolution Corporation (IBRC) on the basis that it would do no more new business and wind down by disposing of all assets. Of the foreign-owned institutions in existence in 2008, the National Irish Bank, owned by Danske Bank Group, ended its personal and business banking operations in 2014, now only providing corporate banking service. Nevertheless, Danske remains a significant presence in Northern Ireland (through Northern Bank).

Lloyds Trade Union

In terms of absolute membership, Lloyds Trade Union (LTU) continues to be the largest dedicated financial services sector union. Its membership grew from 1995 to the early 2000s, reaching a peak of around
45,000 and before falling over a decade later to well under 40,000 members. By 2015, it had 34,000 members (see Table 2.2). Within LBG, it
claims to be the dominant union by size, although whether its membership is greater than the combined membership of both Accord and
Unite is unclear. According to the contents of a series of letters to bodies like the United Nations, Financial Conduct Authority, Pensions
Regulator and Prudential Regulation Authority (see LTU *Newsletters*,
May and June 2016) over—and following—derecognition in May 2016
by LBG, LTU claimed between 25,000 and 30,000 members in LBG.
In terms of relative membership, it reported in 2009 it had a density of
87% in the branch network in England and Wales and 73% in Scotland
(LTU press release, 23 November 2009). A year later, it claimed an
average density of 86% in the branch network (LTU press release, 24
September 2010). In the branch network of TSB in 2013 it claimed
an 87% density (LTU press release, 22 February 2013). Reflecting the
changes in the creation of the merged bank, LBG, from late 2010,
Lloyds TSB Group Union changed its name to Lloyds Trade Union
(LTU). In 2013, LTU changed its name in LBG to Affinity, and operated as the TSB Union (TSBU) inside TSB as it attempted to move
outside its former base of Lloyds within the enlarged LloydsTSB/Lloyds
Banking Group. Although LTU is now the name the trading company
of Affinity, for the sake of simplicity, the union is referred to as LTU
throughout. Given that the period of 2008–2015 had such an important
influence on the philosophy and perspectives of LTU, these are covered
in Chaps. 3 and 4 as part of the processes and outcomes of the financial
crash and its aftermath with the sector. Suffice it to say for the moment
that LTU became a much more oppositional union to LBG compared to the other two unions within LBG, namely, Accord and Unite.
However, there is much more to this 'story' than first meets the eye so it
is not quite one of a former staff association transmogrifying into a militant labour union. Indeed, it remains very much a servicing-orientated

union (see also Gall 2008). In terms of the effect of derecognition and increased inter-union competition upon on LTU membership levels, it is now yet clear what impact these have had. It will take until the beginning of the next decade for a clear picture to emerge here.

National Association of Co-operative Officials

The National Association of Co-operative Officials (NACO) organises just under 1500 members in the various parts of the cooperative movement including insurance and financial services. It is both a labour union and a professional management association, representing over 90% of management and professionals in the co-operative movement, according to its website. Membership has fallen from around 2500 in the early 2000s to 2233 in 2008 to 1388 in 2015 with around a third of members being women.

Nationwide Group Staff Union

The Nationwide Group Staff Union (NGSU) is an independent union, representing workers within the Nationwide Building Society Group and its associated companies (Nationwide, Cheshire, Derbyshire and Dunfermline building societies). The NGSU is the sole recognised union by the Nationwide Building Society Group for collective bargaining but it also has recognition for bargaining groups within Computacenter, Carillion, Swiss Post and IBM following the outsourcing of these operations by Nationwide. With staffing levels fluctuating, for example, between 15,900 in 2010 and 15,500 in 2011, the NGSU's membership has remained around 12,000 over the last decade with a substantial portion of this outcome being due to inorganic additions. Stable absolute membership has resulted in a 70% union density for a number of years (*Rapport*, January 2011, Summer 2016) while Traxler et al. (2008: 42) put NGSU density at 'over 70 percent' for the period up to 2005–2006. Ebbs and flows in membership are, according to Tim Rose, NGSU Assistant General Secretary (Services), 'tied to the fortunes of Nationwide. During the financial crisis our membership fell to around 11,400 as a direct result of redundancy programmes at Nationwide. As things have improved and the Society has recruited again (huge growth in risk and compliance roles), our membership has gone up. We're currently at just under 12,500 and we think this is pretty healthy state—we can operate without too much pressure to increase subscriptions. Looking back over the past few months, new joiners have exceeded leavers, but generally we have to work pretty hard to stand still' (Email correspondence, 27 July 2016). Table 2.1 shows a net gain of 150 members with just under 1% of members leaving per month. Aggregated to a yearlong period, the NGSU loses about 10% of its membership but is able to recruit 13% additional members.

The NGSU was formed in 1990 by the merger of Anglia Building Society Staff Association and Nationwide Building Society Staff Association. Both associations date from the 1970s. In 1999, the union affiliated to the TUC. The Portman Group Staff Association (PGSA) transferred engagements to NGSU in 2008 as did the Staff Union Dunfermline Building Society and OURS (One Union of Regional Staff) in 2011. These transfer of engagements and amalgamations were influenced by change in capital ownership whereby the Nationwide acquired the Cheshire, Derbyshire and Dunfermline building societies in 2008 and 2009. The Derbyshire Group Staff Union was founded in 1972 as the Derbyshire Building Society Staff Association. In 1979, it applied for a Certificate of Independence but was refused. This was then gained in 1986. It affiliated to the TUC in 2003 and adopted the nomenclature of staff union in 2004. In 2010, it merged with the

Table 2.1 NGSU membership leavers and joiners, February 2016–June 2016

Month/ Membership	Leavers	Joiners
Feb-16	114	163
Mar-16	117	141
Apr-16	102	139
May-16	93	111
Jun-16	112	134
Totals	538	688

Source NGSU, email correspondence, 27 July 2016

Cheshire Group Staff Union (CGSU) to form One Union of Regional Staff (OURS) which affiliated to the TUC. The CGSU organised workers in the Cheshire Building Society. Members of OURS voted to merge with the NGSU in 2011. The Staff Union Dunfermline Building Society was previously entitled the Dunfermline Building Society Staff Association while the Cheshire Building Society Staff Association became the Cheshire Group Staff Union in 2008 and affiliated to the TUC in the same year. The NGSU is also affiliated to Unions 21, War on Want, Amnesty International and Justice for Colombia.

With regard to the labour–capital relationship, NGSU 'seeks to work in partnership with Nationwide Building Society to secure the best possible working conditions for our members' (NGSU, n.d.) where both parties 'are committed to achieving the common aim of an efficient and successful business in the best interests of employees and customers ... by working together to develop high levels of employee commitment ... based on mutual respect and ... conducted in a spirit of openness, trust and integrity that acknowledges the legitimate differences and interests of each party' (NGSU 2016). Regularly, the NGSU said of itself through iterations of the following: 'NGSU is very proud to be a staff union ... we share many of the same aims as the society—a successful business means better terms and conditions for employees' (*Rapport*, January 2011). A dense network of institutional mechanisms exists for conducting this relationship, comprising a Joint Consultation and Negotiation Committee,[13] an Employee Involvement Committee, an Organisational Change Committee and Business Committees. The processes of negotiation, consultation and exchange of information sometimes result in joint communiques to members and employees. Collective representation exists for non-senior executive staff with individual representation for employees of senior executives. Outside of this framework, the NGSU engages in a dialogue with the company's human resources function or local management. NBSG provides paid time off to NGSU lay representatives to carry out their union duties and encourages union membership so that it has a representative partner to deal with. There is, in effect, a 'no-strike' agreement for 'both parties agree that, provided the procedures outlined in this Agreement are followed, they will not take action that may be prejudicial to the effective operation of Nationwide or the Union, or the interests of employees … Both parties are committed to ensuring that there shall be no impediment to normal operations and therefore there will not be any form of industrial action taken and normal working will continue to apply at all times' (NGSU 2016). The dispute resolution procedure states that if no agreement can be reached then there is to be the use of internal and external conciliation and mediation culminating in binding arbitration facilitated by ACAS. Indeed, the long serving general secretary, Tim Poil, commented: 'We have never called a ballot for industrial action and our relationship with Nationwide is such that I can't imagine the circumstances when we would' (*Rapport*, Winter 2015). Nonetheless, tensions have been evident over the way the NBSG has sought to control wage costs since the financial crisis. Thus, 'Nationwide lost sight of the importance of maintaining good employee relations in the drive to survive the recession' (*Rapport*, January 2011). Membership participation within the NGSU can be judged to some extent from turnouts for elections to the national executive committee, being 10% in 2013 and 2015, and by the existence of 140 workplace representatives in 2013 and 180 in 2016.

Portman Group Staff Association

The Portman Group Staff Association was a non-TUC affiliated union. Prior to dissolution, membership had increased steadily from around 700 members to 1400 as a result of a merger with the Staffordshire Building Staff Association after the merger of the two building societies in 2003, and a Union Modernisation Fund (UMF) project helping to revitalise the association. However, membership fell again to just over 900 by 2007. With the merger of the Portman Building Society and the Nationwide in 2008, the PGSA amalgamated with the NGSU. The consequence of the merger of employer operations saw 800 posts 'lost' from the Portman side (Stuart et al. 2009: 155). Before and after the merger of employers, the process of consultation had been shallow and rudimentary (Stuart et al. 2009: 15), so a partnership agreement was developed under the auspices of the UMF. This involved developing union capacity to act as a partner which included independent communications with members and a greater distance from the employer, both of which the employer supported so that it could have an effective partner with which to deal with (Stuart et al. 2009).

UFS

UFS, originally standing for Union of Finance Staff and accompanied by the strapline of 'the union for the future', was a registered, independent union, originally established in 1988 and with its headquarters and most of its membership in south-west England. It was not affiliated to the TUC or any political party. Although not constitutionally a union exclusively for financial services staff for its last few years of existence, the majority of its members continued to be employed in a small number of financial service companies (and those that were contracted to provide services to these companies through outsourcing). The main companies were those of the Zurich financial group and then Swiss Post, Capita, IBM and CSC. In the new millennium membership fell from a high of just over 4300 in 2004 to just under 2000 by 2014 and 2015. The origins of UFS lie in BIFU being derecognised by Eagle Star in 1988 and a staff association being set up to take over its function as the sole recognised body. This was the Eagle Star Staff Association which became the Eagle Star Staff Union. In 1998, this body became the Union of Finance Staff after the company's takeover by the Zurich Financial Services group. It operated on the basis of seeking partnership with employers, both in de jure and de facto terms. It also had a section for managers, the Finance Managers' Association.

Like many other unions in the financial services sector, UFS presented itself as a collective organisation providing individual representational services.[14] This accorded with the 'servicing' model of the 'rainy day' insurance variety, with a good articulation of this being:

> It may be only once in your career, it may be over a series of events driven by personal circumstances. Whatever the reason it is clear to us that, when difficult things happen to you at work, it is vital to have somewhere to turn. UFS provides that service, whether it is some general friendly

advice or a formal legal opinion and representation. The ability, at a time of severe stress, to turn to somebody that understands how you are feeling and knows what advice to give is a life saver. (*In Touch*, Winter 2015)

Compared to Unite, the perspective adopted by UFS was not so much as to condemn a change and seek to fight it but rather to accept the nature of the change and as best tailor the union's help and advice to resolving the problematic nature of the change rather than trying to reversing it.

As a result of the knock-on effect on its membership of the reduction in the size of the workforce of the main employer it organised within whilst wishing to maintain the level of its membership services, UFS considered increasing membership subscriptions substantially, asking employers to provide more facilities and support, join with other like-minded independent unions to form a confederation (like OURS) or merge with a substantive union. Before considering these, there is another side to falling membership through redundancies and that is recruitment. The annual level of membership recruitment for UFS to stand still was around 10%, with the 'churn in our part of the financial sector rang[ing] from 3% in older established departments, (but now gradually being dismantled) to potentially 35% in call centres. Anecdotally, we have recruited new starters in the morning and they have left the employer by the afternoon!' (Alan Wood, UFS general secretary, email correspondence, 19 August 2016). Raising subscriptions was not considered to be a viable long term solution and neither was reducing the level of services as '[this] would eventually take away what we are trying to preserve' (*In Touch*, Winter 2015). Meantime, as UFS already received substantial support from many of its key employers,[15] no more support could be anticipated and the problem with a confederation was believed to be that it would have insufficient resources. After internal discussions, a transfer of engagements to Community was the recommended course of action as it was a well-resourced union that allowed smaller unions joining it to retain considerable autonomy. In order to assuage any member concerns, UFS pointed out that its membership would be continue to be serviced by its EUOs, partnership with employers was sacrosanct and members did not have to contribute to Community's political fund and, thus, its affiliation to the Labour Party (UFS *Report*, Summer 2016). The membership ballot resulted in a 92% vote for the merger on a 26% turnout of the 1688 members. Consequently, on 1 January 2017, UFS merged into Community, a general union having its roots in the ISTC steel union. The reduction in absolute union membership reflected another weakness which was low union density. Thus, density 'ranges between operations, so in the general business of Zurich we may have 48% density but in the whole UK company it might be as low as 20%. The range of density in actual bargaining units is still around 40%, dropping slowly annually' (Alan Wood, UFS general secretary, email correspondence, 19 August 2016). Despite, the declining union base, the UFS characterised its relationship with the main employers it organised within as 'excellent' with the rider that 'the trend of shifting key decision makers regularly … constantly introduces risk to the relationship at that level' (Alan Wood, UFS general secretary, email correspondence, 19 August 2016).

Unite

Unite organises in some 30 companies in the financial services sector. The main ones in banking are the Bank of England, Barclays, CBG, HSBC, LBG, NAG, RBS, and Virgin Money while, in insurance, the main companies are Allianz,[16] Aviva, AXA, Cooperative Financial Services, Friends Provident, Legal and General, Prudential and RSA. In only in a few cases of the smaller companies in the sector does Unite have more than 50% membership density levels. For example, in late 2008 an internal Organising Support Unit report found Unite density was between 30 and 40% in Barclays, HSBC, NAG and RBS and between 10 and 20% in HBoS and LBG (Unite 2008: 4–5) while in insurance of ten of the major companies, it varied between 15 and 55% with only two companies having density in excess of 50% (Unite 2008: 7–8). Traditionally, such a situation of low union density for independent labour unionism resulted from the multi-union form of 'peaceful competition' whereby employers favoured internal staff associations. However, by the turn of the new century, with the creation of Unifi and its merger with Amicus (which drew upon its insurance sector membership from pre-merger constituent, MSF [see Gall 2008]) as well as the increasing tendency for those staff associations to become independent unions and merge with larger independent unions (often as a result of changes in company ownership and structures), multi-unionism is a much less extensive phenomenon. The remaining examples of multi-unionism are Aegon (Aegis, Unite), CBG (BSU, Unite), Ulster Bank (FSU, Unite) and Zurich (UFS, Unite).[17] Yet the single biggest remnant of this phenomenon is to be found within LBG and concerns LTU, where it co-exists with Accord and Unite after the mergers of the Halifax (Accord organised) with the Bank of Scotland (Unite organised) to form HBoS in 2001 and Lloyds' acquisition of TSB (Unite organised) to form LloydsTSB in 1995 and then the takeover of HBoS by Lloyds in 2009 to form LBG.[18] But even where Unite is the sole and major union (Barclays, HSBC, RBS), it does not hold majority membership so that Unite also does not have membership density above 50% in any of the major banks. Its overall density in the banking sector was put at 31% in 2008 (Unite 2008: 5) and 26% in 2009 (Prosser 2011). Its overall density in insurance was put at 22% in 2008 (Unite 2008: 8) and by 2012 at between 16 and 20% (Carley 2012). Total membership in insurance was put at 33,000 in 2008 and 2009 and then 25,000 in late 2013 (Unite 2008: 8; Carley 2012; Liz Cairns, email correspondence, 16 October 2013). But in a number of individual insurance companies, Unite does have just above 50% union density (see above). But, for example, in Aviva after its acquisition of Friends Life in 2015, in the new merged organisation Unite had a 20% density, with 4000 members out of 19,700 employees (Unite press release, 26 March 2015).

Publicly, Unite's membership in its finance and legal section (where members in legal services amount to just a couple of thousand) has fallen from 180,000 in 2009 to 150,000 in 2010 and then 130,000 in 2012 and to 100,000 by 2016 (Unite 2009, 2012; Dominic Hook interview, 6 September 2016). However, elsewhere it was still claiming 'over 170,000 members' and 'over 150,000 [members]' in late 2011 and 'over 130,000 members' by mid-2015 (*uniteWORKS* November/December 2011; Unite 2011; Unite *The Spark*, Autumn 2015) as well as '150,000 members in financial services' (Unite press release, 19 December 2013) in late 2013 and representing '120,000 staff in financial services' (Unite press release, 17 June 2013) 6 months earlier. Indeed, as late as early 2017, Unite's website still proclaimed 'Unite's finance and legal sector is comprised of over 130,000 members throughout all major employers in banking and insurance'. Of this approximate period, industrial reporter, Barrie Clement, observed: 'Most unions have felt the heat. For instance, the massive and largely private sector union Unite lost half its paying membership in the finance sector over the last five years or so' (*The Journalist*, June/July 2013). This clearly contradicted the view of Dave Fleming, Unite national officer for finance, in 2011 that: 'Now could be our time [for membership growth]. When people think things are unfair the union becomes increasingly relevant' (*uniteWORKS*, November/December 2011) and this was despite Unite membership being 'up 5000 in the last year' (*uniteWORKS*, July/August 2012).

Despite tidying up of membership records in Unite shortly after it was formed, its membership data appears to have continued to contain a number of significant ambiguities.[19] First, the combined membership of the two merged constituent unions was claimed by the new union to be 2 million in 2007 but this was then revised down to 1.5 million and then to 'over 1.4 million members' in its media releases between 2013 and mid-2017.[20] In 2014, total paying membership was 1,140,551 (United Left report of Unite Executive Council, March 2014). Second, for the finance and legal section of Unite, internal figures recorded a membership of 167,674 members in early 2008 (Gall 2008: 128). This represented the number of members balloted for the Executive Council elections (see also below). However, in late 2008, an internal Organising Support Unit report (Unite 2008: 5, 8) put membership in banking and insurance at 118,811. Third, figures for the number of ballot papers dispatched in Executive Council elections in 2011 and 2014 for the union's finance and legal section were much lower than the aforementioned membership figures. In 2011, the 'number of eligible voters' was 110,711 while in 2014 the number of 'ballot papers distributed' was 89,912 (United Left Executive Council reports, June 2011, June 2014). These two categories are roughly synonymous. Thus, matching the c. 111,000 (2011) figure against the 130,000 (2012) figure and the c. 90,000 (2014) figure against the 100,000 (2016) as well as a figure of 101,730 for 2014 (United Left Executive Council report, March 2014) suggests that the number of members in arrears or for which current and correct postal addresses were not held is highly unlikely to be able to completely account for the disparity. This is because, drawing upon the union's annual returns to the Certification Officer for the four years between 2012 and 2015, the average proportion of members which Unite did not have a current and correct postal address (for which ballot papers in internal unions elections and industrial action ballots are needed) was between 5 and 7%. Taking this as rule of thumb for the union's finance and legal sector membership, where the figures for the early 2010s and mid 2010s were 15 and 10% respectively, highlights a substantial (and unexplained) disparity. This is especially so when it was reported to the September 2013 Executive Council of Unite that there were 89,630 members in the finance and legal sector (Unite Now! Executive Council report, September 2013) and that by late 2016, there were just 77,884 members.[21]

According to the Electoral Reform Services scrutineer's report for the 2017 Unite Executive Council elections, only 66,965 members were balloted in the finance and legal section, suggesting another substantial fall in actual membership. (with 1.062m members balloted overall). Nonetheless and setting this aside for the moment, Unite faced a situation of having to 'run quite fast just to stand still' - if that is still an appropriate analogy to use - in membership levels. Thus, in November 2013 finance and legal section membership was reported to stand at 101,318 (United Left Executive Council report, December 2013) but just a few months later, in March 2014, was reported to be 101,730 (United Left Executive Council report, March 2014). In 2015, 9000 new members were recruited but 8000 were lost and in 2014 with similar levels of joiners and leavers there was a net loss of 2000 (Dominic Hook interview, 6 September 2016). Prior this 3039 new members were recruited in 2010 (United Left Executive Council report, September 2010) with 1800 new union members recruited at Barclays in 2013 (United Left Executive Council report, March 2014) and 3484 new members in LBG in 2010 (United Left Executive Council report, December 2010).

The composition of membership is predominantly female. In 2013, 60% of finance and legal section members were women (with 10% black and minority ethic) (Unite Now! Executive Council report, September 2013). In late 2016, the figure the proportion of all members being women remained at 60%.[22] In December 2014, the Unite

Executive Council was informed that the union had 'Unite has 133,383 young members spread across all regions and industrial sectors, largely concentrated in five [regions and five sectors]' (Unite Now! Executive Council report, December 2014). One of these was Finance and Legal with 11,669 young members. Young members are those aged thirty and under.

The scale and nature of the recruitment and organising challenge facing Unite was highlighted by an internal Organising Support Unit report in late 2008. It showed that where Unite had union recognition and members (and excluding members of other unions), there were 311,000 non-union members (Unite 2008: 5, 8). It also showed that in banking (56%) and insurance (75%), the majority of workers were employed in workplaces of 50 or more workers while 30% of workers in banking and 25% in insurance worked in workplaces with over 500 workers (Unite 2008: 11–15). The majority of non-union workers in companies with Unite recognition were found in banking (where a smaller number of employers employ most workers compared to a large number of smaller companies in insurance employer most workers). Consequently, Unite's recruitment, retention and organising activities in the financial services sector primarily concentrated upon workplaces with existing union recognition and membership, that is, 'brownfield' sites, rather than 'greenfield' ones. And within this, a number of companies and workplaces have been targeted with organising resources as part of the union's '100%' and Organising Unit campaigns to increase the quantity and quality of membership and workplace representatives. The purpose behind the '100%' campaign has been to create active and sustainable groups of memberships which are capable of campaigning on local issues affecting members within their workplaces. Thus, LBG and RBS were the main targets for the work of the Organising Unit within the financial services sector for a sustained period of time after the financial crash.[23] In both, the larger workplaces—such as call and contact centres or mortgage centres—were targeted in particular. However, other companies with similarly large workplaces such as Barclays and Prudential have also been focused upon. The choice of a smaller number of larger workplaces, rather than say a greater number of smaller workplaces like branch offices, reflects a belief that the most effective

deployment of resources and the most conducive conditions for collectivism exist in the larger workplaces. Typically, these workplaces
have over 1000 workers. So although recruitment and organising can
be carried out by virtual means, Unite has found that a regular physi-
cal presence (in the form of its EUOs and workplace representatives) is
essential to making and maintaining contact with members which leads
to participation and activity. With collective bargaining taking place
at the national company level, the issues and grievances addressed by
Unite's organising strategy have been localised ones. For example, Unite
activists at an LBG Merseyside contact centre identified through use of
a survey that what workers wanted most there were fridges. Unite campaigned on this issue, successfully gaining the installation of fridges and
in so doing helped raise membership density from 2% in 2010 to 80%
amongst the 350 workers in 2015 (*uniteWORKS*, September/October
2013, *Huffington Post*, 19 January 2014, *UniteLive*, 18 November
2015). Meanwhile, Unite activists at RBS's Thanet Grange workplace
identified through using a survey that a key issue of concern was the
annual leave booking system. Unite was able to engage with management so that it put in place a better system, and in doing so recruited
new members and raised its profile (*Unite Finance e-bulletin*, November
2014).

The winding down of the operations of the Organising Unite within
LBG was not due to pressure from other members in other companies
within financial services seeking the application of the Organising Unit's
resources to their workplaces. Rather, it was as a result of the clash
between activists and officers within LBG and the Organising Unit over
aims and style in developing leverage within a partnership environment.
This was indicative of the continuing autonomy of the national company committees as the de facto leadership of Unite within these companies (see Gall 2008: 125; Undy 2008: 69, 70, 72, 100). Under this
tendency, there has been a disintegration of Unite's attempt to prosecute
coordinated pay bargaining across the sector.[24]

In spite of the dedication of organising resources to specific companies and targets, increasing membership participation and activity has
been extremely difficult on the major issues of redundancies, pay and
performance management. In no small measure this has been the result

of the willingness of workers to leave the employ of the companies in the sector (as per flight), rather than stay and resist (as per fight) the erosion of their jobs and conditions. The successive waves of redundancies across the sector with a combination of relatively good severance terms and an age structure that has allowed many to effectively take early retirement has meant that the point at which there are no longer sufficient reservoirs of workers willing to take voluntary redundancy has not yet been reached—and nor did the officers of Unite believe it was likely to be reached any time soon (Dominic Hook interview, 6 September 2016; Rob MacGregor interview, 7 September 2016). This is because the experience of working in the sector had led many to be willing to leave and, to the extent that calls for voluntary severance were routinely over-subscribed, some members took out grievances against their employers for not being granted severance. Severance terms have been relatively good because of an historical factor, namely, that the other side of a 'gentleman's agreement' over the non-poaching of staff was that banks would seldom then employ those who had worked at their competitors. Consequently, severance terms were to allow for an extended period of unemployment. But more recently such severance terms have been viewed as a payoff for having had to work for an employer in the sector for so long with the experience being onerous and dissatisfying. The effect of this for union influence and power has been that it has been 'near impossible' (Rob MacGregor interview, 7 September 2016) to mobilise members to fight when so many want to leave with the rider that the wish of most members is for the union's role to be to protect existing severance terms and oversee the implementation of rationalisation in as fair and transparent way as possible. In other words, the union's role had been to 'negotiate the terms of exit' (Rob MacGregor interview, 7 September 2016). The latter has meant opportunities for severance being made open to all, with the criteria clearly laid out.

The degree of participation by Unite members in the structures and processes of their union can be gauged by examining the following. As with other unions and parts of Unite, membership participation in national executive council (or committee) elections was low. However, it was lower for the finance and legal section than for other sections of

Unite and other unions. For the 2014–2017 Executive Council elections, the turnout was 3.2% while the average for other Unite trade sections was between 5 and 6%. For the 2011–2014 Executive Council, the turnout for the finance and legal section was 4.7 and 5.5% for the 2008–2011 Executive Council (with this being the lowest of any industrial sector within the union). For the 2017–2020 Executive Council elections, the turnout rose to 5.9% of finance and legal members but this was still the lowest for any trade section within the union in this round of elections. Meantime, the PCS union saw the turnout for its National Executive Committee elections from 2012 to 2014 fall from 10.7 to 9.5% and then 8.0% (although there was an increase thereafter, being 8.3% in 2017). In consultative ballots on pay, namely, those asking members to accept or reject an offer, some sections of Unite in the financial services sector also experienced relatively low turnouts. For example, in the Prudential, turnouts were seldom over 50% and often considerably less. Meanwhile, in AXA and although falling over the period, Unite membership provided high levels of participation on ballots on pay issues, being between c. 85 and c. 65%. While the two current (and longstanding) national officers for Unite's finance and legal section are male, women officers have existed in some numbers (see below) and the Executive Council allocation for the union's finance section has been dominated by women and is now comprised of only women.[25]

Although Unite is an 'organising' union, this did not mean that throughout the financial services sector there was not strong evidence of the continuation of a 'servicing' approach. For example, in a Unite newsletter of January 2015 within Barclays, and which was entitled 'Protect yourself at work—Join Unite the Union today', Unite stated:

> When you start a new job you don't expect to have a bad experience at work. However, as with other things in life, the unexpected can and often does happen. As car or home owners, we prepare for the worst by taking out insurance cover. Why should your attitude to your job be any different? Be prepared and insure yourself, join Unite the union today. On a daily basis Unite makes a huge difference for our members in all forms of individual representation. With a Unite workplace representative at your side you are never alone and will be professionally supported through

difficult times. This assistance can range from phone advice on general queries, help with Performance Improvement Plans (PIP) or Performance Development (PD) issues, all the way through to personal representation at formal meetings for Disciplinary, Capability and Grievance (DC&G) or Long Term Sickness (LTS) cases and other more complex legal issues. Unite will be there to give you support when you need it the most.

Even in the case of a successful organising drive at an LBG contact centre, members took up membership as "'back up' just in case something happened" (*uniteWORKS*, September/October 2013). This attested to a considerable degree of variation in Unite's stated and actual practice in time and space across the financial services sector. This included variation *within* the individual companies of the sector. That said, the distinction between servicing and organising is not set in stone, and this is reflected in the use by Unite in a number of large workplaces in the sector of union learning as both a recruitment and organising tool.

USDAW

The Union of Shop, Distributive and Allied Workers (USDAW) has around 3000 members in the financial services sector, originally by way of organising the Cooperative Insurance Society (CIS) which arose out of the cooperative movement. As a result of the financial crisis of the parent company, CBG, CIS was sold to the Royal London Mutual Insurance Society in 2013. Prior to this, CIS had outsourced its life insurance operations to Capita in 2007. Consequently, USDAW members are now employed by both these companies where it has union recognition for them. USDAW also has members in the Provident Personal Credit and Provident Financial Management Services companies. As a result of the establishment of Tesco Bank by the Tesco supermarket chain in 1997 (as a joint venture with RBS) and then operated as a sole venture since 2008, USDAW has added to its financial services sector membership. USDAW is the major union recognised by Tesco for its retail workforce so that it had a good claim on seeking to organise within Tesco Bank (especially after 170 RBS staff were transferred over to Tesco through TUPE).[26] Some 3500 staffs work for Tesco Bank in Edinburgh, Dundee, Glasgow and Newcastle. USDAW secured a partnership agreement with Tesco for the Tesco Bank and, by 2013, USDAW had recruited some 400 members since 2010 for the Glasgow and Edinburgh workplaces (equating to a 26% density) (USDAW *Network* magazine, September/October 2013).

VIVO

VIVO, the staff association for Standard Life employees, is not an independent, registered trade union (with the consequence that its membership numbers are not publicly available). It originated from a staff consultation committee which existed within the company since 1970 and was relaunched as the LINK in 1998 as a result of the widespread perception of the former's ineffectiveness and lack of profile (Gall 2008: 135). LINK was the peak organisation for the five Standard Life staff associations which corresponded to its five divisions. A formal partnership, instituted in 2000, is based upon consultation and not negotiation. Amicus and Unite have both sought to organise within Standard Life but with little success (Gall 2008: 135–136). Their organising attempts, in the context of widespread redundancies, demtualisation and the crash, provided the stimulus to the reorganisation of LINK into VIVO in 2008, the revamping of information and consultation arrangements, and the signing of a new partnership agreement. VIVO is funded and resourced by Standard Life (Koukiadaki 2010) so that a certificate of independence from the Certification Officer will not be forthcoming. VIVO will face a major challenge to protect members' jobs and terms and conditions as a result of the merger of Standard Life with Aberdeen Asset Management in 2017, with 800 redundancies anticipated out of a combined workers of just over 9000.

Other Unions

The GMB general union held membership amongst a small section of LBG for which it had bargaining rights. These were in two Asset Finance workplaces. After the new recognition agreement of 2015 (see Chap. 3), the GMB was derecognised with these members being encouraged to join either Accord or Unite. The GMB also has some members in AA insurance. The Transport and Salaried Staff Association (TSSA) also has a small number of members in the foreign exchange businesses of travel agents such as Thomas Cook's and other money exchange companies like Travelex.

Inter-union Relations

The relations between various unions within the financial services sector, focussing largely upon those organising within LBG, are dealt with in the following chapter on processes. This is because while the substantial nature and dynamics of inter-union relations pre-date the financial crash, the influence of employer reaction to the consequences of the financial crash in the financial services sector has greatly coloured and developed these relations. Where unions have amalgamated through transfers of engagements, these cases have been detailed above. Given that most labour unions other than Unite still remain narrowly focussed upon particular employers, the extent of interaction between unions is limited other than where they organise in the same companies. For example, the advice given to Advance by Accord on modernising the former's partnership agreement with Santander in 2010–2011 (*My Accord*, Spring 2011) was high unusual as an instance of a high level of productive inter-union cooperation across companies. The routine inter-action between unions in the sector has been that of a lower and less productive level through the Alliance for Finance (AfF). The AfF was established in 1996 with 27 affiliates with this quickly rising to 36 affiliates. Its purpose has been to constitute the lobbying organisation for labour unionism in the sector by seeking to influence decision-makers in government, the sector's regulatory bodies and the financial services industry in general to try to ensure that the interests of staff are properly taken into account when these organisations and agencies make decisions. These areas included training, mergers and acquisitions, and stakeholding where a collective industry approach was deemed desirable. As a result of mergers and transfers of engagements, AfF's number of affiliates fell from just over twenty in the late 2000s to ten by 2016.[27] It superseded the Financial Services Staff Federation (FSSF) whose purpose was similar and increasingly provided a forum for the exchange of information about developments in collective bargaining in each company. Although it almost goes without saying, whether over job losses, erosion of pensions or performance management systems, there has been no generalised and coordinated fightback by the unions within the financial services sector. Other than on the issue of pensions in the public sector, and epitomised by the one-day strike on 30 November 2011, this has also been true of the union movement more widely in Britain in the post-crash period.

Total Union Membership

Only Advance, CWU and LBSSA recorded marginal increases in membership from 2007 to 2015. Consequently, it comes as no great surprise to find that when putting together the total membership data contained in Table 2.2 together with that of Unite, CWU and a handful of other unions which do not exclusively represent workers in the financial services sector (like GMB, NACO, SIPTU, TSSA and USDAW)—and for which annual data is harder to then come by—that overall union membership in the sector in Britain fell from 293,926 in 2006 (Gall 2008: 128) to either 191,531 members or 171,531 members in 2015. The higher figure is based upon Unite having 100,000 members in 2015 and the lower figure is based upon Unite having 80,000 members (see above). Neither figure include Unite's membership in the Republic of Ireland which comprised between 5000 and 10,000 members (see *uniteWORKS for Ireland*, January/February 2012, March/April 2013). This means union density has then fallen from 25.1% in 2006 when the total employment compliment was 1.171 million to 16.7 or 14.9% (depending upon which Unite figure is used) in 2015 when the total employment compliment was 1.148 million.[28] The resulting figures from the calculation of either absolute or relative membership sizes bears an uncanny resemblance to those from the LFS. Table 2.3, using,

Table 2.2 Membership levels of unions organising within the financial services sector, 1995–2015

Year/Union	Accord	Advance	AEGIS	Affinity	BSU	CWU	DBSSA	DGSU	IBOA	LBSSA
1995	19,652									
1996	25,124	9000			1800			554		
1997	26,217	7612		28,340	2184			549		
1998	25,652	7468		30,472	2172					
1999	25,263	8306		36,039	2243					
2000	23,995	8322		c.36,000	2353					
2001	24,170	8514		c.45,000	2358					
2002	23,772	8924		c.45,000	2352			464		
2003	24,941 (70%)	8874 (74%)		43,778 (64%)	2358		232	476	5815 (66%)	
2004	25,759 (70%)	8952 (74%)	2518 (60%)	43,848 (64%)	2337		236	477	5804 (66%)	122
2005	25,936 (70%)	8063 (75%)	2693 (67%)	44,411 (64%)	2971		250	498	6247 (66%)	126
2006	27,477 (68%)	7216 (76%)	2484 (59%)	41,998 (63%)	3193		286	504	6250 (67%)	119
2007	30,415 (69%)	6763 (76%)	2500 (45%)	40,516 (62%)	3397		315 (78%)	506 (77%)	6095 (73%)	409 (71%)
2008	32,745 (70%)	6822 (73%)	2769 (50%)	40,264 (62%)	3240		298 (79%)	445 (75%)	6315 (72%)	500 (69%)
2009	30,803 (67%)	7645 (73%)	2456 (43%)	40,227 (62%)	3492		211 (78%)	405 (75%)	6276 (67%)	474 (66%)
2010	28,902 (68%)	6998 (75%)	2317 (54%)	40,273 (62%)	3328	2899	CE	391 (71%)	6094 (72%)	471 (68%)
2011	27,995 (67%)	7482 (73%)	2120 (54%)	40,268 (62%)	3149	2799		CE	5775 (72%)	442 (68%)
2012	26,028 (68%)	7452 (73%)	1692 (52%)	38,649 (62%)	2802	2968			5305 (71%)	415 (70%)
2013	24,338 (67%)	6784 (74%)	1653 (52%)	38,601 (62%)	2373	2898			4655 (70%)	424 (67%)
2014	22,616 (67%)	6996 (72%)	2651 (59%)	37,089 (62%)	1777	3435			4276 (70%)	415 (70%)
2015	22,639 (68%)	6945 (72%)	4933 (62%)	34,020 (62%)	1449	3591			4016 (70%)	515 (66%)

Year/Union	LUBSSA	NGSU	OURS	PGSA	SABB (UKR)	SBSSA	SURGE
1995							
1996		9300	347				637
1997		9409	351				748
1998		9706					
1999		10,254					1276
2000		11,108					1337
2001		11,291					1397

(continued)

Table 2.2 (continued)

Year/Union	LUBSSA	NGSU	OURS	PGSA	SABB (UKR)	SBSSA	SURGE
2002		11,633					1366
2003		11,940 (75%)					1089
2004	122	12,078 (74%)	449	704 (63%)	96 (35%)		1337
2005	126	12,402 (73%)	411	741 (68%)	90 (36%)	173 (59%)	1310
2006	119	12,832 (73%)	422	1090 (68%)	88 (35%)	183 (62%)	1434
2007		12,919 (73%)	407	1425 (70%)	87 (36%)	134 (63%)	1338 (64%)
2008	106	13,952 (73%)	402 (84%)	913(65%)	86 (35%)	220 (63%)	1259 (64%)
2009	97	12,786 (72%)	351 (79%)	CE	83 (33%)	161 (61%)	1605 (62%)
2010	96	11,802 (72%)	306 (82%)		84 (33%)	CE	1448 (63%)
2011	98 (79%)	12,005 (72%)	564 (79%)		84 (33%)		1314 (64%)
2012	91 (80%)	11,628 (71%)	407 (76%)		82 (33%)		1307 (58%)
2013	90 (79%)	11,852 (70%)	CE		91 (38%)		CE
2014	83 (78%)	11,951 (70%)					
2015	84 (78%)	12,197 (70%)					

Year/Union	SUWBBS	UBAC	UFS	YISA
1995		2800		
1996				
1997		2662	4225	
1998		2648	4910	
1999		2584		
2000		2803		
2001		2796		
2002		2720		
2003	484	2690	3846	
2004	493	1813	4343	
2005	547	1568	4040	
2006	615	1593	3739	
2007	624 (62%)	1557 (66%)	3266 (55%)	1214 (68%)
2008	665 (62%)	1079 (69%)	3101 (54%)	2314 (67%)

(continued)

Table 2.2 (continued)

Year/Union	SUWBBS	UBAC	UFS	YISA
2009	579 (63%)	1065 (70%)	2647 (53%)	1325 (70%)
2010	496 (62%)	CE	2535 (47%)	1342 (68%)
2011	522 (63%)		2238 (54%)	1586 (68%)
2012	502 (63%)		2182 (55%)	1727 (69%)
2013	523 (66%)		2035 (54%)	2131 (69%)
2014	500 (67%)		1935 (55%)	2220 (68%)
2015	482 (66%)		1860 (57%)	CE

Source Annual returns of unions filed with the Certification Officer (with the exception of the CWU for which its annual conference agendas were used). Figures for 2016 were not available at the time of writing.

Note 'CE'—ceased existence after transfer of engagements, i.e., amalgamation or merger. Figures in brackets indicate the percentage of women members where available.

Table 2.3 Union densities and presence (%) in the financial services sector in Britain, 1996–2015

Year	Sectoral density	National density	Density for men	Density for women	Density of full-timers	Density for part-timers	Absolute numbers ('000)	Extent of bargaining on pay	Workplaces with union presence
2015	14	25	10	19	13	20	165	23	37
2014	17	25	13	21	15	27	180	23	38
2013	17	26	13	21	16	25	181	24	39
2012	16	26	11	21	14	26	171	24	38
2011	17	26	12	22	14	26	188	25	40
2010	17	27	13	22	15	27	186	28	42
2009	20	27	15	26	18	n/a	226	28	43
2008	21	27	16	26	27	36	237	28	45
2007	22	28	18	27	18	33	297	31	45
2006	24	28	21	27	19	30	n/a	31	46
2005	24	29	20	28	33	n/a	n/a	35	50
2004	27	29	22	31	23	33	n/a	36	49
2003	26	29	22	30	24	40	n/a	37	51
2002	27	29	22	31	29	37	n/a	n/a	n/a
2001	27	29	23	30	n/a	n/a	n/a	38	n/a
2000	30	30	25	34	n/a	n/a	n/a	41	n/a
1999	29	n/a	24	35	n/a	n/a	n/a	41	n/a
1998	31	n/a	26	36	n/a	n/a	n/a	44	n/a
1997	33	n/a	29	37	n/a	n/a	n/a	n/a	n/a
1996	36	n/a	32	39	n/a	n/a	n/a	n/a	n/a

Source Labour Force Survey (BIS 2016c)

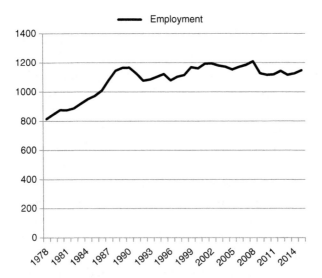

Fig. 2.1 Employment levels ('000s) in the financial services sector in Britain, 1978–2015. *Source*: Labour Force Survey

LFS data, records that absolute membership fell from 297,000 in 2007 to 165,000 in 2015 and 24% density in 2006 to 14% in 2015.

LFS data also shows that between 1986 and 2015, total employment in the financial services sector has remained around just over 1 million (see Fig. 2.1). The peak of 1.209 million was reached in 2008, with a decline of less than 100,000 in the 8 years thereafter, with no year having less than 1 million employed in the sector. Meantime, employment in banking rose from 680,000 in 2000 to 772,000 in 2007 before falling to 562,000 in 2010 according to Soriano (2011: 20) while the European Banking Federation (2005–2015) reported employment levels in banking had fallen from 534,437 in 2005 to 505,661 in 2007 to then 454,087 in 2011 and 402,561 in 2015. Although variance in figures reflects difference in sub-sectoral definitions of composition, the direction of travel is clear. And, while the composition of employment (such as full-time/part-time, permanent/temporary which have a bearing on union density) is unknown throughout, and bearing in mind the level of redundancies, it is reasonable to conclude that thousands of new posts and jobs have also been created in order to explain the less sharp anticipated fall in overall employment levels in the financial services sector. Moreover, the traditional sub-parts of the overall sector continue to decline by size of employment (although they remain substantial). So, according, for example, to TheCityUK (2014, 2016), a membership-based advocacy group for the financial services sector established in 2010, employment in banking and insurance declined from 436,000 and 315,000, respectively in 2014 to 416,000 and 309,000, respectively in 2016. This means that some 30% of employment in the sector is now in non-traditional activities. Related but not synonymous to this is that, and although definitions vary, data for late 2008 (Metcalf and Rolfe 2009: 7) and early 2012 (Tarren 2013: 44) indicated that around 30% of employment in the financial services sector in Britain was in the sub-sector of 'auxiliary' (with the remainder being financial and insurance activities). Auxiliary covers the administration of financial markets (for example, the Stock Exchange), fund management and security broking, together with activities such as mortgage broking and *bureaux de change*. The consequences of these employment shifts for labour unionism are significant. With a falling overall absolute membership, it can be suggested that not only has membership declined in established or traditional areas of organising but that the newer areas of employment growth are not being successfully organised either. This tendency was identified prior to the financial crash in terms of dissolution, disorganisation and dislocation (Gall 2008: Chap. 5). The salience of this for the post-crash period is that given the only slight overall fall in employment levels, the process of organisational restructuring is likely to have increased in pace in terms of the stripping out and shedding of existing, 'older' posts and jobs in the 'older' parts and creating 'newer' posts and jobs in the 'newer' parts (whether by new or existing units of capital).

As Table 2.3 indicates, union density in the financial services sector has fallen by nearly two-thirds in the last 20 years. It has also moved from being the equivalent of the national union density in 2000 to just over half of this by 2015. Density for men has continued to be considerably less than that for women. Table 2.4 shows that financial services excluding pensions and insurance have historically experienced a higher level of unionisation than the insurance sub-sector, with the

Table 2.4   Union presence within the financial services sector in Britain, 1995–2014

Year	Financial services excluding insurance and pensions			Insurance, reinsurance and pensions		
	National sub-sector density (%)	Men (%)	Women (%)	National sub-sector density (%)	Men	Women
2014	25	17	33	11	12	n/a
2013	24	19	29	11	10	12
2012	22	15	30	11	12	n/a
2011	25	18	32	10	n/a	11
2010	23	14	33	12	15	n/a
2009	29	20	37	15	12	17
2008	28	19	35	22	n/a	26
2007	28	21	35	27	n/a	28
2006	29	24	35	22	n/a	n/a
2005	31	23	37	18	n/a	n/a
2004	32	25	37	21	n/a	n/a
2003	33	26	39	25	n/a	n/a
2002	35	26	43	27	n/a	27
2001	33	27	39	21	n/a	n/a
2000	37	28	44	31	39	n/a
1999	36	25	44	29	34	26
1998	38	30	45	31	n/a	28
1997	43	37	48	29	n/a	27
1996	43	35	49	26	31	n/a
1995	47	41	51	26	37	n/a

Source BIS (2016a) using Labour Force Survey data
The availability of this data for classifications within the Standard Industrial Classification resulted from the publication of the response to a parliamentary question. As such this was an unusual turn of events for previous requests to ONS for access to breakdowns of data within the 'Financial and insurance activities' category were turned down due to difficulties in disaggregating the data (and the cost implications of this).

gap between the two widening while both have declined in absolute terms. Throughout both sub-sectors women continue to have a higher union density than men. The dimensions of the contraction of union presence have constituted a fall from a majority of workplaces in 2003 to a little above a third by 2015 whilst those of collective bargaining on pay have witnessed a steeper fall from two-fifths in the late 1990s to less than a quarter by 2015. The existence of performance management (see later) is believed to account for this decline whereby a limited amount of collective bargaining on the size of the pay pot to be distributed individually still exists. These indications of decline are notable given two particular aspects. The first suggests union density should have been higher because the financial services sector has a far higher percentage of big workplaces (500 employees or more) than do other industries and the economy as a whole, this being 35% compared to 18% between 2003 and 2008 (see Metcalf and Rolfe 2009: 10). Yet, the second aspect points in the opposite direction, for it also the case that 28% of all financial services sector employment was to be found in London compared to an average of 12% for all industries between 2003 and 2008 (see Metcalf and Rolfe 2009: 10), and it is known that union density levels in London are far lower there than those found elsewhere. For example, density in London fell from 24% in 2008 to 18% in 2015 while, over the same period, the national average fell from 28 to 25% and 32 to 28% in north west England, 33–32% in Scotland and 37–35% in Wales (BIS 2016c: 46).

In 2014, the percentage of full-time workers unionised in financial services excluding insurance and pensions was 22.5% while the percentage for those part-time workers was 39.0% (BIS 2016b). Union density amongst permanent workers in financial services excluding insurance and pensions was 26%. For insurance, reinsurance and pensions, only 10% of full-time workers were unionised in 2014, with 12% of permanent employees being unionised (BIS 2016b).

The sense, notwithstanding some significant declines in membership amongst some unions, that labour unionism has been 'running very fast just to *try to* stand still' in terms of recruiting new members to offset the loss of membership since the financial crash is quite acute (cf. Gall 2008: 108, 128). So many unions saw an increase in the number of new recruits in response to the numerous tranches of redundancy exercises. However, those affected by redundancy relinquished their membership so that were no net gains. Even where there were some net gains as a result of the response to changes in terms and conditions of employment, whereby in this period of change more joined than left, over the whole period there were still net losses. Any absolute gains in membership have been inorganic ones. Consequently, there has been considerable churn in union memberships. The implications for resources in this context are that considerable energy is expended upon recruitment and retention rather than representation and bargaining, and the quickly 'revolving doors' of membership militates against establishing and maintaining coherence of members.

Common Characteristics

This section brings together the main common characteristics of unions which have been studied so far, or alluded to, in this chapter. The purpose is to convey a sense of what is common to the different unions in spite of their different geneses, trajectories and outlooks in order to develop an overview of their nature and characteristics, especially with regard to attitudes that influence behaviours and resource availability. The first of these concerns membership characteristics, having significant implications for the provision of resources for representation and mobilisation and the deployment of these. Following this, issues of the form of labour unionism, democracy and membership participation, and relations with customers are amongst the other issues examined.

Atomisation, Churn and Fragmentation

An increased tendency towards atomisation of memberships has taken place as a result of performance management and redundancies. Existing upon the foundation of a servicing orientation which tends to atomise (rather than individualise[29]) member-union relations, and aided by the way in which democracy and participation have been operationalised (best epitomised by consultative ballots and memberships newsletters as the main form of members-union contact (see below) and the absence of workplace unionism with workplace meetings), the tendency towards atomisation has been extended and reinforced by the rise of individual member casework which has significantly increased as a result of the processes of performance management and redundancies. The processes and outcomes of atomisation concern the rise in the number of cases where unions provide advice and representation to individual members over their appeals against performance ratings, size of bonuses and selection for redundancy (see Chap. 3). Ratings for pay rises and bonuses are appealed against as being below lower than was expected or warranted while in the latter refusal to gain an offer of voluntary severance has been the main source of grievance (as opposed to being selected for redundancy when the desire has been to stay in existing employment).[30]

While precedents can be set and used subsequently so there is a collective aspect to individual cases and while the provision of the resources to allow such advice and representation stem from the existence of collective organisation, the primary union relationship here is predicated on being directly between the individual member and the union. Sometimes, this is with a (lay) union official (with facility time). Sometimes, this is with an EUO. Often members are specifically encouraged to directly contact their own union's national headquarters in order to obtain such support and advice. The relationship between the member and the union is based upon the provision of specialist knowledge and not collective strength through mobilisation (as per fighting victimisation or unfair through industrial action). This provision of such a service is likely to be the highpoint of the union member's relationship with the union. In the process, relations with other union members are de-prioritised or non-existent.

Atomisation is distinctive from fragmentation for fragmentation stratifies members into broad collective bandings as a result of experiences on pay and pensions (see Gall 2008: 117) while atomisation does not differentiate members from each other—rather, it separates members from each other, notwithstanding the prevalence of any collective consciousness and identity. Fragmentation of the interests of union membership was previously identified within the financial services sector in regard of the ending of multi-employer bargaining (which also gave rise to the greater autonomy of national company committees in Unite and its predecessor, Amicus) and the spread of PRP (see Gall 2008). However, in the post-financial crash period, the extent of fragmentation has significantly increased, now posing a further and greater challenge to the ability of unions to collectively mobilise their memberships. The axes of differences between members now concern a more virulent type of PRP found within performance managements systems, reformed pension systems, and working hours. Instances of these will be detailed in Chap. 4 on outcomes but, for the time being, a couple of examples suffice to substantiate the point. In the case of the NGSU, it reported that the change in working hours contracts in 2012 in the Nationwide from 9 am–5 pm to 8 am–8 pm:

> prompted some to ask why the [it] didn't consult directly with members or hold a ballot to canvas views before reaching an agreement with Nationwide. To answer the question directly – we simply didn't believe that a ballot of the membership would be helpful in achieving a successful outcome to the negotiations … [because] the changes … directly affected members in the branch network who … now represent the minority of the total branch workforce. The majority are employed on the 8 to 8 contract and the actual contractual position for these employees was not adversely impacted – in fact the operational framework in which they could be asked to work has improved. Because of the different impacts, we felt it was unlikely that we could achieve a clear mandate from a ballot and that this would be unhelpful in the negotiation process – without convincing support from the membership our position would have been weakened. The situation also poses the question about who exactly we should ballot and what action we would seek. It is reasonable to assume that those directly impacted would not support the changes but if we were unable to persuade Nationwide to drop its proposals – what action would we then take? Some members have called for a ballot to take industrial action. A resolution of this significance would impact on all NGSU members and we would therefore have been required to ballot the whole membership. With many members in the admin centres working on 8 to 8 terms and for some in telephone channels, a requirement to work their hours between 6 am and 10 pm – we did not believe that support would exist for industrial action. (*Rapport magazine*, December 2012)

The development of different pension schemes (moving from defined benefits to defined contributions) and different pension terms (differential closure of schemes) for workers in the same company has also led to fragmentation in this form of deferred wages. In Santander, of its 24,000 staff in 2013, only 5000 were still members of its final salary scheme (defined benefits). For the CWU, this meant only 20% of its members were members of the final salary pension scheme. Meanwhile in Aviva, Unite faced a situation where only one third of staff were members of the final salary pension scheme.

Lastly, churn refers to both organisational and membership churn and the impact of the former upon the latter. Internal and external organisational restructuring (see introduction to next chapter and Chap. 4) has continually presented challenges for unions. Existing, settled relationships between unions and employers have been subject to change and rupture, requiring resources to be deployed to try to bring these back up to where they were or to try to re-establish them in their entirety. Meanwhile, membership churn, although far from exclusive to the financial services sector, has been as extensive as any given the degree of labour shedding and changes to the composition of the sector's workforce. Organisational and membership churn converge together when new capital-labour bargaining relationships occur and unions are compelled to establish new union structures to accommodate to the changes. This is most obvious in the case of acquisition, mergers and outsourcing.

Declining Institutional-Based Labour Unionism

The period since the financial crash has witnessed the further erosion of the once dominant form of institutional-based labour unionism. On the one hand, further mergers and transfers of engagements amongst unions have meant that there is now only one remaining major employing organisation which has a single financial services sector union dedicated to their operations. This is the Nationwide with the NGSU—although even here the two institutions are not their original selves in terms of takeovers (by the Nationwide) and consequent transfers of engagements (to the NGSU). In the case of LBG, there are now three unions while in Barclays, HSBC and RBS there is just one union, namely, Unite, but it is not a union specifically for any one of these three employing organisations. On the other hand, the process of outsourcing has meant that, in the context of falling memberships, some unions have felt compelled to follow their members to their new employer so that they have also ceased to organise within one employer-cum-institution. The declining sense of internalism has been underpinned by further affiliations to the TUC. In addition to afore-mentioned unions affiliating to the TUC since 2008 (Aegis, Cheshire Group Staff Union, OURS), the Staff Union Dunfermline Building Society affiliated in 2009 as did the Staff Union West Bromwich Building Society in 2013. This adds to an existing marked trajectory of the majority of the major financial services sector unions being affiliated (see Gall 2008: 95). As before (Gall 2008: 95), in affiliating an ideological impulse to join the wider labour movement was not the primary motivation. Rather, a strong collective voice over employment issues with access to research facilities was. A counter to this trajectory of declining institutional-based labour unionism has been the prevalence of partnership whereby close affinities between unions and employers are established and maintained. The result is a form of intra-sector competition between different units of capital and their employees. This has a particular salience for Unite for its national company committees were believed by a number of its senior lay activists not to uphold the policy established by the union's national finance sector committee, on the grounds that the policy of the latter is not appropriate or realistic for the organisation in which the national company committee exists within. Some of these activists believed that national company committees had become too 'cosy' with their employers, such that 'company exceptionalism' and 'company unionism' had been allowed to emerge. For example, one senior lay activist (interview, 19 September 2016) commented: 'Members elect reps—reps stand for regional sector committees—then National committees. In theory, it is bottom up democracy and represents the views of the sector as a whole. However in practice, how any committee (in any sector) acts is down to the people who take up the elected positions'. Despite the aforementioned decline of instutional-based labour unionism, it still remains a potent force in the sector in that most unions have neither the interest nor the resources to organise outside their main constituences, that is, more widely in the sector. Here, Unite can be contrasted to Accord, Advance, LTU and the NGSU. This tendency plays a significant part in accounting for the shrinking presence of union membership overall in the sector.

Union Mergers

The pace of mergers (transfers of engagements, amalgamations, creations of new unions from existing ones) had considerably slowed down by the 2010s (compared to the periods 1990–1999 and 2000–2007)—see Gall (2008: 94, 124–126) and Undy (2008). There have been just eight cases since 2008 (see above and Table 2.2). Given the scale of turbulence as a result of the financial crash, more may have been expected. That this did not happen is partly a factor of there being fewer unions which are potential merger suitors and fewer suitable merger partners. But there are other ways to look at the issue. These are to observe that (i) employer subsidy (largely, facility time) to unions under partnership agreements may have been sufficient to enable a number of unions to remain independent organisations for longer than would have been normally expected; and (ii) those unions which now exist are sufficiently robust in financial and membership terms in the short- to medium-term to not need to consider merger. This was not the case with BIFU, MSF finance members and UNIFI (see Undy 2008). Nonetheless, the eight mergers since the financial crash further indicate efforts to consolidate union presence in the sector while in a continuing defensive mode.

Forms of Democracy and Participation

Financial service sector unions have regularly used surveys and ballots to ascertain membership views on various issues such as responses to employer initiatives, developing bargaining agendas, and consenting to negotiated deals (Gall 2008).[31] This represents a certain type of union democracy where workplace unionism and its activists have less of a determining role than in many other unions. Thus, seldom do members, within the forums of the workplace or local union, come together to discuss matters. By the same token, this form of democracy strengthens the centre or top of the union, whether lay or employed officers, for it allows these agents to more easily frame the issues and interpret the results. Historically, this form is derived from a type of labour unionism where workplace unionism was relatively underdeveloped as a result primarily of a multitude of small workplaces, centralised employer practice and the existence of centralised company or industry level bargaining (see Gall 2008).[32] This form of labour unionism can be characterised as 'directed democracy', with the direction being set by the centre or national leadership.

The representative nature of union democracy within the vast majority of unions in the financial services sector is based, ultimately, upon annual policy making conferences, consisting of delegates, who are often also workplace union reps. Financial pressures due to falling membership have led a number of other unions to also have biennial conferences or short annual conferences (one day or half a day). However, at these conferences most financial services sector unions like Accord and Advance, unlike many other unions in the private or public sectors, permit senior managers as employer representatives to speak at their as part of an on-going process of social dialogue.[33] This is not a particularly new development but the practice has taken on a new dimension with the spread of formal partnership agreements covering what once were staff associations and independent unions as well as continuing to operate in the context of the post-financial crash period. Speaking to union activists gives employer representatives the opportunity to explain and legitimise employer actions with a view to reinforcing and extending a mutual gains agenda as well as receiving feedback. Consequently, this fits into the dominant practice of consultation and information based upon partnership, rather than bargaining between opponents with perceived conflicting interests. However, allowing senior managers to speak can also provide an opportunity for activists, where the personal wherewithal exists, to grill senior managers with a view to scrutinising employer behaviour and sending a sharp public message of discontent and dissatisfaction to the employer. It was for this latter reason that Unite permitted managers to address its seminars but this did not extend the invitation to its conferences.

Financial service sector unions also organise vertically so that managers up to the level of director are eligible for membership and a minority of directors often do hold membership. For example, Accord has a Managers' Advisory Committee and a Branch Managers' Forum. However, it was not evident that lower grade employees were less likely to join a union because of this or for members who were lower grade employees to be less inclined to participate in the affairs of their union (as has been the traditional fear in other unions which now often allow managers into their ranks).

Organising and Servicing

The task of recruiting and retaining members, as well as organising them for collective interest representation, in the financial services sector presents a number of longstanding and more recent challenges regardless of partnership agreements and working. In banking, branches have tended to be relatively small workplaces without union reps while workplaces in insurance tend to be long established large sites with core workforces with long service. The absence of union reps in workplaces is known to exacerbate problems of union visibility and contact. Within banking, the largest workplaces are now call or contact centres, employing workers who tend to be more transient and have less affinity to the sector (in terms of career trajectories and any occupational identity). In the other large workplaces within banking, namely, processing centres, the jobs tend to be low paid ones, with a high turnover of workers (and again producing little affinity to the sector in terms of career trajectories and occupational identity). However, where union organisation has been established in these larger workplaces, workplace union reps exist by which unions can make their presence felt and bargain over local issues.

It is within this overall context that the balance of servicing (representation and negotiation) officers to recruitment and organising officers in a number of unions is roughly equal,[34] indicating that recruitment and retention of members takes a high priority. However, this does not imply that an organising culture is present and forceful across and throughout the unions. As mentioned in Chap. 1, and as alluded to with regard to UFS and Unite before in this chapter, the servicing culture remains both pervasive and persuasive. Under this, recruitment (and retention) is based more upon the individual buying of services provided by the union and delivered by EUOs and lay officials than upon any other motivation. This may only be just for the 'rainy day' scenario of grievances, disciplinaries and redundancy. Consequently, the union is something of a 'third party' in the relationship between capital and labour. Waddington's (2013) data, albeit gathered between 1999 and 2008, revealed an increasing reliance upon EUOs rather than a shift in responsibility towards lay representation and no discernible evidence of renewal of workplace or branch unit of organisation. In particular 'workplace organization in banking regressed after 1999 on three counts: the coverage of lay representation, the improvement of local union activities and the continued reliance of members on FTOs' (Waddington 2013: 349). There is no evidence that this situation has been reversed or moderated since as this—and the following chapter suggests this has been the case in terms of the quality and quantity of members' activism and participation in the affairs of their union or the determination of their terms and conditions of employment vis-à-vis the capital-labour relationship.

Union Financial Resources

Some of the dedicated financial services sector unions (such as Advance) appear to be resource rich in absolute financial terms as a result of their accumulation of fixed and liquid assets but on a proportionate basis in relation to the size of their memberships they do not appear to be so. Meanwhile others (Advance, Aegis, Affinity, NGSU) are not and some are very poor (SUWBBS, UFS). Nonetheless, and judged from figures from the annual returns of unions to the Certification Officer, a surprisingly high percentage of unions from the financial services sector paid their general secretaries more than £100,000 in total remuneration. For example, they represented 10% in 2008–2009, 11% in 2011 and 13% in 2016. These comprised Accord, Affinity/LTU, IBOA/FSU, NGSU, and UFS while the number of all unions paying over £100,000 in remuneration fell from 38 to 36 to 30 in those years. No dedicated union in the financial services sector has a political fund. Those unions that do are the more general unions with financial services sector members, namely, CWU and Unite.

Lotteries

Different specialised unions have different esoteric characteristics compared to general unions. For example, some exist as quasi-professional bodies. In the case of the financial services sector, one important feature of unions work—but not in the case of Unite—is to organise sizable monthly lotteries. The top prizes can easily equate to a month's salary for average finance sector workers, with some of the money raised going toward combinations of running costs of the lottery and union organising and recruitment. For example, the NGSU retains 25% of what is raised to help meet the running costs of the NGSU. Common to all schemes is that eligibility to join the lottery is one of the advertised benefits of union membership. The existence of lotteries is a further indication of the prevalence of a servicing orientation.

Union Names

In the financial services sector, as with many other sectors in the economy, unions have adopted names for their organisations which are not obviously those of unions. Examples are Accord, Advance, AEGIS, Affinity (LTU), SURGE and VIVO for unions specific to the sector and Community and Amicus/Unite for general unions which organise within the sector. As with elsewhere, the removal of the nomenclature of 'union' from union names could be read as an indication of a move away from labour unionism and towards associations (as per staff associations) as the primary form of identity within the framework of partnership with employers.

Ageing Activism

All unions can point to one or two young activists who are potential future national leaders but this tends to mask the paucity of young members and young activists. Of those that are the leading young activists, many were politically active (in progressive political and campaigning groups) prior to working in the financial services sector, and in this respect, represent a somewhat unusual route into union activism. In other words, and notwithstanding any long-term 'Corbynista' effect, if labour unionism is reliant upon this route into activism, its activist base will further atrophy as it is unable to persuade some of the overwhelming existing 'non-political' active members to become activists. The other side to the coin to the paucity of young union activists is that most of the senior lay positions (especially those with facility time attached to them) are held by members in the 40+ age range. However, one senior shop steward (interview, 19 September 2016) recounted that there was a glimmer of hope in that '[f]or many of the workers of my generation there were no negative ideological beliefs in trade unionism, for most they simply did not know what a trade union was. I viewed this as an opportunity as it allowed the reps to shape the ideological and practical benefits of trade unionism. ... [By contrast some] people of an older generation ... had negative experiences in the past with trade unions ...'.

Gendered Relations

Historically, most of the unions and staff associations within the finance services sector have been led by men even though the vast majority of members of these unions and staff associations have been women, itself reflecting that the majority of the workforces are often women. For example, Metcalf and Rolfe (2009: 9, 13) found that women comprised just over half of workforce in the sector between 2003 and 2008 and women comprise the majority of staff in banks, building societies, insurance but not in other sub-sectors like auxiliary and investment banking. By 'led by men', it is meant that the positions of general secretary primarily, but also senior officer corps, are dominated by men and have been for long periods of time. Thus, former unions and staff associations BIFU, MSF, NUIW, SURGE, UBAC, Unifi and WISA fall into this category (so critically comprising the largest unions in the finance sector). In this regard, Kirton (2014: 501) noted that the 'male-dominated Unifi ... seemed to be doing little' in advancing women's influence. More contemporaneously, Accord, Affinity, BSU, IBOA/FSU, LBSSA, LUBSSA, NGSU and UFS have been led by men for long periods of time, sometimes being periods of over 20 years. The equivalent lead officials within the CWU and Unite unions have also been mostly male and for similarly long periods of time.[35] A small number of unions like Aegis are led by men at the level of general secretary but not dominated by men at the senior officer corps level. By contrast, current unions and staff associations like Advance and SUWBBS, and former unions and staff associations like ALGUS and YISA, have been led by women or not dominated by men at senior officer corps level. Meanwhile, a number of others like DBSSA/DGSU, OURS and SSA have been led by a mixture of men and women (although it should be noted that these are small unions and staff associations). The continued dominance of the officer corps and senior officer corps by men has existed within the context of the continued numerical supremacy of women amongst union memberships (see Table 2.2). The manner of the domination of these unions by men has seen incumbent general secretaries returned unopposed in subsequent elections. The only major exception is that of Advance where a woman has been the longstanding general secretary. The extension of long standing male domination downwards into the ranks of EUOs below the general secretary level has not existed to the same degree as for general secretaries. For example, of Accord's employed officers in 2016, six of the eleven were male. However, of the senior lay personnel such as members of national executives, the composition of women members approximates more closely to the level of female memberships. Advance is the best example here.

The salience of this consideration of gendered relations is the potential ramification for membership participation and the importance of this participation for the generation of union resources (rather than in the area of having sufficient 'women-friendly' and 'women-centred' formal policies—which most unions do). Thus, the dominance of men may constitute a further obstacle or barrier to the participation of the majority of union members. The counter-argument that women participate in their unions far less for reasons of lower work attachment because they are often part-time workers does not seem to hold much water given that the levels of union density amongst part-time workers have been consistently considerably higher than for full-time workers (see Table 2.3) and, for financial services excluding insurance and pensions, union density was higher for part-time workers than for full-time workers (39.0% contra 22.5%—see above). It is the issue, then, of participation which is foremost (as opposed to inferring any direct link between the far higher than usual gender pay gap in the financial services sector compared to that in the economy as a whole).[36]

Broader Influence of a Mutual Gain Agenda

One aspect of partnership and the mutual gains agenda was that a number of unions openly stated that becoming a union rep was a positive career move. For example, Accord stated: 'Oh, and being a Rep is seen as a good career move too, helping members to resolve difficulties, understanding business needs, recruitment etc.—whilst still doing their 'day' job' (*My Accord*, Winter 2011) while UFS reported: 'being a union member or a UFS rep should not cause any problems [with your employer] and, in many cases, the skills and experiences you gain lead to new career opportunities … Becoming a UFS rep can further your career by building positive relationships with management' (*Report*, Summer 2015). The BSU in an undated document called 'Why being a rep is good for your career' observed that: 'You can see from the list below [of acquired skills and aptitudes] that today's Union representatives can quite possibly develop into tomorrow's leaders'. Meanwhile, Unite merely stated: 'You'll learn a whole new skill set. From negotiating to organising, Unite reps develop valuable skills that you can't gain anywhere else … allowing you to properly represent your colleagues and grow the union' (*TSB Newsletter*, May 2016) without extolling any personal benefit. However, in AXA, it stated: 'The skills you learn as a union rep are extremely helpful from a career development point of view as they cover many that team leaders and managers need to be successful' (Unite press release, 30 September 2010).

Employer Subsidy

With the obvious exception of LTU in the 2010s (see Chap. 3), unions within the financial services sector receive from employers a relatively high level of subsidy for union organising and representation compared to other parts of the private sector. Indeed, the level of subsidy appears to be on a par with that received in the public sector until recently and within manufacturing several decades ago.[37] Provision of facility time, namely, the ability to carry out union work in work time, is considerable[38] and is supplemented by office facilities and the availing of use of communication mechanisms as well as access to new staff induction events and encouragement to join from the employer. In 2010, Unite alone—and across some 20 companies in banking and insurance—had some 650 workplace representatives with facility time with around 40 of these being on full-time release. In the case of Barclays in the mid-2010s, all 120 workplace reps had 2 weeks facility time for recruitment and there were 14 full-time secondees comprising six health and safety reps, six caseworkers and the chair and vice-chair of the union's national company committee. As alluded to by this example, often the facility time is concentrated in the hands of a few lay activists so that a small number of activists on full-time facility. The extent of partnership agreements not only protects union recognition but also safeguards such a level of facility time. Concomitant, these partnership agreements also shape the nature of how the recognition and facility time operate and what ends they are used for.

Joint Communications

In a significant number of employing organisations, unions and employers make joint statements to union members and employees after the conclusion of negotiations on issues of employment (which leads to the signing of agreements). This sometimes includes Unite at, for example, at AXA. Such a practice is further evidence of the architecture or furniture of partnership and mutual gains, and the desire for partnership *to be seen* to be working. Elsewhere, unions and employers traditionally issue separate statements (even if they include quotes from the other party in them).

Relations with Customers

Like other unions, financial service sectors have often sought to form real and virtual-based alliances with citizen customers in order to defend levels and standards of service and the resources they are dependent upon. The argument has run that reduced staffing levels and ill-rewarded employees do not make for the quality and quantity of service provision that customers should expect and receive. The riders here were that reducing staffing leads to inadequate levels of staffing as well as loss of skills and experience while ill-rewarded staff are also poorly motivated staff. Such an argument has been made by transport unions, especially the rail unions but little realised as passengers are relatively atomised and unorganised (see Gall 2017). In the case of financial services, the challenges to operationalise such an alliance are even greater. First, while potential affinity exists, the degree of empathy towards financial service sector workers is much lower than for rail workers because of the widely held perception of 'guilt by association' with the financial services companies. This is not counter-acted by the widespread existence of partnership between employers and unions—and which not a feature of the rail industry. Second, customers are even harder to organise because they seldom physically meet or congregate around common locations like rail passengers (with this being accentuated with the rise of electronic services). Third, customers can move between providers of services while passengers do not have this degree of latitude.

Consequently, the most that financial services sector unions have been able to do is raise issues and awareness, for example, by making public statements, carrying out surveys, and highlighting the view of others. In regard of Accord, it expressed concern that after the announcement of 9000 job losses and 150 branch closures in LBG in 2014 '… customer service standards and employee morale will suffer if all operations are not properly resourced' (Accord press release, 28 October 2014) and commented: 'The bank is singing the same old

song, Selling more is the number one priority. Whether or not customers want the products is another question' (*My Accord*, Summer
2011) while it also made much of a report in the *Times* (2 July 2011)
which stated: 'Quite how this squares with the bank's plan to improve
customer service and cut the number of complaints is anyone's guess.
Unless these 15,000 people are sitting around doing nothing, or Lloyds
thinks it can squeeze extra productivity from its remaining staff, both of
which seem unlikely, it is hard to imagine how this will not affect customer service, even if no branches are closed'. Meantime, LTU found
in its staffing survey of 2012 that '93% of respondents said that staff
shortages had an adverse effect on the service provided to customers'
(LTU press release, 28 September 2012) and publicised its submission
to the Financial Services Authority which advocated reforms to stop
financial services sector workers being given incentives to mis-sell financial products to customers (LTU press release, 26 November 2012). An
Advance survey of its members in 2011 highlighted that employees did
not feel they had sufficient time to serve customers, and were forced to
try to sell customers products that were unsuitable for them. Unite, in
nearly all of its voluminous number of press releases condemning job
losses and expressing concern for the consequences of these, conveyed
fears about their impact upon the provision of customer service, particularly in regard of the loss of experience and skills. For example, it
stated in regard of the RBS owners of NatWest: 'With job losses across
the country and surviving branches on reduced hours, there's no doubt
this latest round of cuts will hurt the bank's customers as well as our
members. With every branch closure NatWest is slamming its doors on
another community, dangerously undermining the bank's long-term
future' (*Guardian*, 15 April 2016), linked RBS's technical consecutive outages in 2012 and 2013 and its inability to rectify these swiftly
with loss of experienced staff (Unite press release, 3 December 2013),
and in regard of the Clydesdale/Yorkshire banking group: 'cutting costs
and eroding community banking … leaves customers with less choice.
Customers are being short changed by high street banks replacing counter staff with machines, yet our own poll showed nearly three quarters
of people want the human touch, not just a machine in their local bank
branch' (Unite press release, 25 March 2014). Lastly, in 2014, Unite

commissioned the Survation polling organisation to survey 1005 customers, finding that 62% wanted 'more staff in branches' (Unite press release, 27 January 2014). In all cases of union activity here, the practical outcomes have been some localised protests and petitions and national media campaigns. Yet, no discernible leverage has been created over employers to assist with gaining bargaining objectives.

Employers

Although employers are not the subject per se of this study, their importance remains for understanding the totality of the capital-labour relationship and its implications for the experience of employees. Consequently, there are a number of aspects of the behaviour of capital as employer which warrant consideration. This begins in this chapter with some consideration of their attitudes and behaviour in regard of non-union means of inter-action with their employees and in regard of the implications of niche market strategies for employment relations.

Alongside the dominance of partnership with labour unions, employers in financial services have also introduced forms of employee engagement separate form their relationships with recognised unions. Examples are to be found in the Allied Irish Bank (Burrows, n.d.), Bank of Ireland (Mears 2010), JLT Benefits Solutions, Nationwide, Prudential (Stevens 2005), RBS (Engage for Success 2012), RSA (Engage for Success, n.d.-a), TSB (IPA 2015) and Zurich Life (Sutherland 2015). Two other instances of (anonymised) employers using employee engagement also exist (Engage for Success, n.d.-b, c).

In some cases, these moves—when in the form of higher level institutional bodies such as company level staff forums or company level engagement committees—may be seen as posing a threat to the institutions and processes of union-orientated information exchange, consultation and bargaining. However, what transpires is that a key variable in explaining whether this does happen is the ability of unions to colonise these initiatives in employee engagement in order to either neutralise them and/or make them subservient to the aforementioned union-orientated institutions and process of information exchange, consultation and bargaining. Although various workplaces have been closed (such as branches and contact centres) with others opening up (contact centres) or work outsourced, there has never been an accusation from any union that this represented a tactic of 'double breasting' in order to engage in union avoidance. Only in the instances of offshoring has it been pointed out, almost in passing, that the workers carrying out the offshored work are not unionised. This is because the issue of the cost of labour has been far more important and this is not entirely synonymous with whether labour is unionised or not. Yet, there have been a small number of relatively large explicitly non-union operations in the financial services sector like the Egg bank and Norwich Union part of Aviva (see, inter alia, Butler 2009; Johnstone 2010; Johnstone et al. 2010a, b; Tuckman and Snook 2014) despite efforts of unions to organise some of these.

A number of new financial services companies entered the market over the last decade. Virgin Money expanded by buying Church House Trust in 2010 and Northern Rock in 2012. Santander bought into the British high street market through a series of acquisitions. Thus, it has its origins in three constituent companies—Abbey National, Alliance and Leicester and Bradford and Bingley which were all former mutual building societies. Abbey was bought in 2004, Alliance and Leicester in 2008 and the branches and savings business of Bradford and Bingley (which had been nationalised in 2008) in 2009. Most of GE Capital in Britain was bought by Santander in 2008. Santander UK as a rebranding of these operations was launched in 2010. By 2015, according to its annual report for 2016, Santander UK had 19,992 employees. With its acquired operations rationalised over a period of years in order to streamline high street presence (down to around 1000 branches) as well as integrated to end duplication of operations, Santander sought about building its market share and for a long while was known for having the worst customer service of any high street bank. Then it returned a number of offshored operations from India and launched its '123' customer account shortly afterwards, being able through such means to raise its customer satisfaction ranking quite dramatically. Meanwhile, Tesco Bank and Sainsbury's Bank were launched as joint ventures in the late 1990s but were bought over completely by Tesco (in 2008) and Sainsbury (in 2014) respectively. Marks and Spencer's financial services companies was started in the mid-1980s and sold off to HSBC in 2004. The only new full bank to be established was the Metro bank in 2010, being the only completely new retail bank to be set up in the last 150 years. Its branches are open 7 days a week, 362 days a year, creating 1700 jobs since its launch with a pledge to create 3300 jobs by the end of 2020 (*HR Grapevine*, 5 May 2015).

Virgin Money, Santander, Metro and a handful of others are known as 'challenger' banks. A 'challenger' bank is commonly defined as a relatively small retail bank, sometimes being a new entrant or player to the marketplace and set up with the intention of competing for business with large, long-established national banks, be it through offering superior service and/or better financial deals (see also Worthington and Welch 2011). The salience of the 'challenger' bank for employment relations is potentially two-fold. Profitability through higher levels of customer service may be believed to require higher levels of staffing and better motivated and retained staff (through better pay deals and working conditions). But the obverse is also true—in order to undercut the established players, such banks may seek profitability through competitive advantage by seeking to exploit its workforce at a greater rate than its rivals (albeit there are also other ways to also undercut rivals). In the former, relationships with unions are present and relatively positive while in the latter relationships with unions are absent or poor in the form of non- and anti-unionism. The cases of Santander and Virgin Money suggest that both strategies are used by challenger banks. In the case of Santander, the CWU believes it does not 'want to be seen to be courting controversy and is very concerned to foster good industrial relations and to reach agreement with unions on all issues' (John East, email correspondence, 3 September 2016). Added to, and underlining, this overt market strategy is that Santander as bank of Spanish origin has had considerable experience of negotiating with unions, and in particular negotiating with a multiplicity of often much more militant unions. In the case of Virgin, a more hostile attitude to Unite has been taken (see later). A much clear case of a challenger organisation is Capita's Life and Pensions division. It has rapidly expanded into the financial services sector since the financial crash, winning contracts to administer IT and processing systems for Abbey Life, AXA, CIS, Pearl/Resolution Life, Prudential and Zurich so that it employed some 12,000 staff in Britain (and some 4000 outside Britain due to offshoring) by the early 2010s. Its business model involves winning contracts and then reducing costs either through IT system improvements, offshoring and/or job losses. Frequent disputes with Unite (see Chap. 4) suggest that it has pursued even more aggressively the option taken by Virgin. However, by contrast and as with Santander, under Sabadell's entry into the British market through its acquisition of TSB, there was no attempt to erode terms and conditions upon the transfer, pay rises were more generous than in other companies (Accord press releases, 27 November 2015, 28 January 2016, *My Accord TSB*, June 2016)—although the terms of its SEA were not—and sales targets were not used.

Lastly, and in regard of the substance of the more accommodating position taken by Santander (but not as a result of a similar derivation), it maybe surmised that building societies would take a similarly helpful approach given their professed desire to put the interests of their members first. Indeed, given the turmoil amongst non-mutuals since the financial crash, it may have been expected that building societies would have sought to play up this strength at a time of difficulty and tarnishing reputations for these non-mutual competitors. There remain just under 50 building societies in Britain and in total, they employ some 40,000 staff and operate around 1500 branches. While with the largest by far is the Nationwide, the other sizeable building societies are the Yorkshire, Coventry, Skipton, Leeds, West Bromwich, Newcastle, Nottingham and Principality ones. Among these larger ones there is some considerable union presence (see above and Gall 2008) with just a smattering of presence in the smaller building societies. The picture is mixed in terms of the outcomes for employment relations that may be linked to employer perspective and strategy (see Chap. 4). In addition, there are a small number of other mutual organisations in the insurance sector such as NFU Mutual (which employs around 3500 staff).

European Works Councils

A number of companies like Allianz, AXA, Barclays, HSBC, Nationwide and Santander have European Works Councils (EWC) on which union members from Britain sit.[39] Although their remits are confined to the dissemination of information and consultation over the content of this information on a pan-European nature, unions have sought to use these resources to aid national collective bargaining and representation as well as to create inter-national linkages with fellow unions in order to exert influence over their common employer (see also Gall 2008: 152–153).

Conclusion

This chapter has mainly concerned itself with the players on the workers' side of the capital–labour relationship. Having examined the fate of both individual labour unions and labour unionism in general within the financial services sector, the next chapter examines the processes of interaction that comprise the dynamic relationship between capital and labour in the sector. The basis upon which the processes can be best examined is to appreciate the resource and policy bases of the unions and unionism in general. This means that it is not just a question of the resources that the unions have to deploy that guides their actions but also how and for what purposes the unions seek to deploy them. But, in any event, it is the case that the resources unions have to call upon, principally derived from their membership and activist bases, are not munificent. This paucity of resources does, however, influence what and how different unions seek to pursue in terms of policy objectives. Simply put, all other things being equal, a union with greater resources can consider being more ambitious in its policy bargaining objectives because this degree of resourcefulness can allow the enforcement of policy bargaining objectives. What has been revealed by this chapter is that all unions have experienced declining membership (albeit to different degrees and from different points or watermarks). The consequences of this for union density have been uneven. Equally importantly, the location of union membership has a bearing upon the ability to exercise strategic leverage over an employer. The movement of staff and functions from branches to back offices and call contact centres, alongside outsourcing and offshoring, has presented unions with considerable challenges of colonising newer workplaces where strategic functions are carried out and where employment characteristics appear less conducive to unionisation (for, example, younger workers on part-time and temporary contracts). Added to this is the age old challenge for labour unionism, namely, that unionising future members does not seem immediately to further the material interests of existing members.

Notes

1. This concerns not just the takeover of HBoS but also the selling off of the TSB retail bank (including Cheltenham and Gloucester branches).
2. Unfortunately, response rates were not available for membership surveys conducted to help formulate bargaining demands.
3. Outside of industrial relations *per se*, Accord's general secretary was a founding supporter of Stand Up to Racism in 2014 and the union supported the Justice for Colombia campaign, and was an affiliate of Trade Union Friends of Israel (as were Advance and BSU).
4. In relation to the CWU below, it uses the strapline: 'The only union dedicated to staff in Santander UK' (even though it is only recognised for the core bank and Geoban, albeit they are the major components of Santander).
5. The core bank is the customer facing part of Santander, Geoban covers its back office functions, while Isban covers IT and Produban is for IT maintenance.
6. UBAC originated in 1977 as the Bradford and Bingley Staff Association, changing its name in 2001. It affiliated to the TUC in 1998.
7. Staff numbers fluctuated from 20,000 in 2010 to 23,000 in 2011 and 26,000 in 2012 and then to 24,000 in 2013.
8. Aegon UK is a pension, insurance and investment company, owned by the Dutch Aegon parent company. In 1994, the Scottish Equitable Life

Assurance Society became Scottish Equitable with Aegon buying a 40% stake which was later increased in 1998 to 100%. It employs around 2100 staff working from its Edinburgh headquarters.

9. The Scarborough Building Society Staff Association (SBSSA) merged with the Skipton Staff Association (SSA) in 2009 following Skipton's acquisition of the Scarborough society. Shortly afterwards, the SSA became SURGE (Skipton Union Representing Group Employees).

10. An indication of this was that Britannia remutualised the Bristol and West building society when it acquired it in 2005.

11. The Leicester Permanent Building Society Staff Association was certified as an independent union in 1979 with around 1000 members at the time. It merged with the Alliance Building Society Staff Association in 1988 to form the Alliance and Leicester Building Society Staff Association. This was later renamed the Alliance and Leicester Group Union of Staff and affiliated to the TUC. At the point of transferring to the CWU, ALGUS had some 2098 members (of which 71% were women). Its membership in 2006 was 2300.

12. For a history of the IBOA—the finance union, see Rouse and Duncan (2012).

13. The recognition and procedural agreement sets out how both parties will work together and defines terms and conditions that are subject to 'negotiation' (including pay, working hours and holidays) and other issues over which consultation takes places.

14. Outside of the financial services sector, a number of unions like Community and Prospect increasingly emphasised the provision of their services like offering career/training/skills advice.

15. For example, UFS has agreements that allow its reps, on average, to spend about 5% of their working time carrying out union duties (*In Touch*, Magazine, Summer 2015).

16. Allianz in Britain comprises various companies, the largest of which is Allianz UK. Unite only has a recognition agreement with it.

17. This excludes a handful of other companies where Unite has a small number of members alongside members of another union.

18. It is also worth noting, according to Unite itself, that it is 'the only union negotiating for members in all areas of Lloyds TSB; ... the only union negotiating for members in Cheltenham & Gloucester; ... the only union negotiating for members in both Lloyds TSB and HBoS; [and] ... the only union negotiating for members in LBG and Co-op'

(Unite LBG newsletter strapline). Moreover, Unite agreed with Accord a demarcation of areas to avoid membership competition. It should also be borne in mind that facing multi-unionism is not the sole preserve of Unite for unions for in addition to Accord and LTU, the Advance and the CWU exist in Santander and where the CWU does not hold majority membership as a result of both the existence of Advance and its limited organising remit (stemming from the legacy of the Girobank and the Alliance and Leicester).

19. Indeed, when Unifi merged with Amicus in late 2004, Amicus' financial services sector membership was declared to be c. 200,000 (Gall 2008: 124) and by 2008, after Amicus had merged with the TGWU (which has negligible members in the sector), to form Unite, Unite had 167,674 members in the sector (based on the number of ballots papers sent out for the 2008 Executive council elections). The actual membership for Amicus including Unifi in 2004 was actually 161,269 (Gall 2008: 128).

20. However, membership figures deposited with the Certification Officer do not provide exact corroboration on this in terms of overall membership or numbers of members contributing to the general fund for the period 2012–2015 (where there is always a 6 month lag in depositing data and which means current figures are never available).

21. Figure computed from Unite Now! 'Executive Council Constituencies 2017–20', 2 October 2016. In this, it is stated: 'In relation to women members, it is proposed that an additional seat is provided for in each of the Health and Finance/Legal sectors, which have a density of 70.2 and 60.3% women members respectively, and in absolute numbers 64,831 and 46,964 respectively'.

22. See Unite Now! 'Executive Council Constituencies 2017–20', October 2016.

23. LBG was chosen because it had been subject to 'nationionalisation' and was the site of the largest non-TUC affiliated union in the sector. Funding for some 20 organisers as secondees from the bank was made available up to 12 months, and in many cases was extended thereafter.

24. The tendency for national company committees in banking to be more autonomous from their National Industrial Sector Committee than their counterparts in insurance results, in part, from the creation of Unifi where the maintenance of autonomy was part of the agreement with Barclays and NatWest staff unions to merge with BIFU. However,

as argued later, the tendency towards autonomy also has its roots in the orientation towards companies as a result of partnership agreements.

25. The allocation fell from four seats in the 2008 elections to three in 2011 and then two in 2014 (whereby one of the seats must be held by a woman) but was then increased to three for the period of 2017–2020, whereby at least two of the three seats must be women. In the event, all three seats were held by women after the Executive Council elections in 2017.

26. However, Unite also had a claim given it organises within RBS and it did secure a partnership agreement with RBS for its members in the joint-venture.

27. Affiliates were 17 in number in 2003, 16 (2004), 19 (2005), 18 (2006), 17 (2007), 15 (2008), 15 (2009), 14 (2010), 14 (2011), 11 (2012), 11 (2013), 11 (2014), 11 (2015) and 10 (2016). Accord, Advance, Aegis, CWU, Communication Workers Union (CWU), Leeds Building Society Staff Association, UFS, Unite, VIVO and the West Bromwich Building Society Staff Association are the ten affiliates for 2016.

28. The density figure for 2006 is lowered than that quoted in Gall (2008: 128) of 26.9% because the ONS has since revised upwards the number of employees for the sector from 1.092 million.

29. Individualisation is based upon the creation of differences between individuals rather than direct relationships.

30. Even where the provision of union support is not for appeals *per se* but mere preparation for performance appraisals, the effect is the same.

31. Unusually, Accord sometimes allowed non-members to vote in its ballots in order to engage with non-members and to increase the legitimacy of its view with the employer (but made clear it would not be bound by their (non-member) views if these contradicted members' views).

32. The use of surveys, as opposed to workplace or geographic branch/area membership meetings, to gauge member views has become increasingly commonly used by other unions.

33. Union conferences have traditionally concerned policy and perspective formulation as well as rallying activists and providing a platform for favoured politicians to speak from.

34. This was ascertained from reviewing the information of the number of officers and officer positions available on the websites of the main unions. Only in the case of Unite was this not possible.

35. In Unite, five women were national officers for the finance and legal section immediately before, during and after the financial crash out of a compliment of ten. However, the regional officials within Unite which had responsibility for the financial services sector were far more evenly balanced between men and women in relation to the proportions of male and female members in the sector.
36. For example, a report for the EHRC (2009: 10) reported: 'The gender pay gap for annual gross earnings (that is, all earnings, irrespective of hours) in the sector is 60%, much higher than the economy-wide gap of 42%. Based on mean full-time annual gross earnings, the overall gender pay gap is 55%, compared with 28% in the economy as a whole'. This was based upon an earlier report by Metcalf and Rolfe (2009). Evidence of the gender pay gap continued (see, for example, Perfect 2011; Fawcett Society 2016).
37. Provision of subsidy can also include the extensive time and resources put into creating and re-creating partnership agreements—see the case of LBG in Chap. 3 and RSA with Unite between 2007 and 2008 as a result of the deployment of the Questions of Difference consultancy.
38. The lowest level found was between 5 and 10% of working hours per week for a workplace representative with this rising to 25, 50 and 100% for senior lay representatives covering one (large) or more workplace.
39. HSBC was unusual in not having a EWC between 2012 and 2015. A voluntary agreement existed for a EWC between 1996 and 2012 but this was terminated by the employee side, representing some 270,000 employees, because of an inadequate provision of information and consultation by the employer. This came to a head over the closure of a shared service centre in the Czech Republic in late 2011 without any consultation with the EWC. The employee representatives then triggered the long formal process for a EWC to be set up under the EU directive.

References

Bain, P., Taylor, P., Gilbert, K., & Gall, G. (2004). Failing to organize or organizing to fail? Challenge, opportunity and the limitations of union policy in four call centres. In G. Healy, E. Heery, & P. Taylor (Eds.), *The future of worker representation* (pp. 62–81). Basingstoke: Palgrave Macmillan.

BIS. (2016a, June 21). *Table 2: Trade union membership as a proportion of employees by industry and gender, 1995 to 2014*. London: Department for Business, Innovation and Skills.

BIS. (2016b, June 21). *Table 1: Trade union membership by industry as a proportion of employees by gender, full/part time and permanent/temporary status, 2014*. London: Department for Business, Innovation and Skills.

BIS. (2016c). *Trade Union Membership 2015* London: Statistical Bulletin, Department for Business, Innovation and Skills.

Burrows, A. (n.d.). Making Allied Irish Bank a great place to work again' Engage for Success.

Butler, P. (2009). Non-union employee representation: Exploring the riddle of managerial strategy. *Industrial Relations Journal, 40*(3), 198–214.

Carley, M. (2012). *The representativeness of trade unions and employer associations in the insurance sector*. Luxembourg: EurWORK European Observatory of Working Life.

CWU. (2014). *Building tomorrow together—Getting women members active*. London: CWU.

EHRC. (2009). *Financial services inquiry: Sex discrimination and gender pay gap report of the Equality and Human Rights Commission*. Manchester: EHRC.

Engage for Success. (n.d.-a). *Evidence case study: RSA*. London.

Engage for Success. (n.d.-b). *Case study: Embedding customer centric behaviours in a financial services organisation*. London.

Engage for Success. (n.d.-c). *Evidence case study: Global financial services organisation*. London.

Engage for Success. (2012). *Evidence case study: Royal Bank of Scotland*. London.

European Banking Federation. (2005–2015). *European banking sector facts and figures*. Brussels.

Fawcett Society. (2016). *The gender pay gap: Facts, causes and solutions*. London: Fawcett Society.

Gall, G. (2008). *Labour unionism in the financial services sector: Fighting for rights and representation*. Aldershot: Ashgate.

Gall, G. (2017). *Bob Crow: Socialist, leader, fighter—A political biography*. Manchester: Manchester University Press.

Hall, M. (2004). Informing and consulting your workforce: Union-based arrangements at Abbey. *IPA case study number 6 series 4*. London: IPA.

IPA. (2015, June). *The inclusion network*. London: IPA.

Johnstone, S. (2010). *Labour and management cooperation: Workplace partnership in UK financial services*. Basingstoke: Gower.

Johnstone, S., Wilkinson, A., & Ackers, P. (2010a). Critical incidents of partnership: Five years' experience at NatBank. *Industrial Relations Journal, 41*(4), 382–398.

Johnstone, S., Ackers, P., & Wilkinson, A. (2010b). Better than nothing? Is non-union partnership a contradiction in terms? *Journal of Industrial Relations, 52*(2), 3151–3168.

Kirton, G. (2014). Progress towards gender democracy in UK unions 1987–2012. *British Journal of Industrial Relations, 53*(3), 484–507.

Koukiadaki, A. (2010). Informing and consulting employees: The VIVO Staff Association. *IPA case study 1/5*. London: IPA.

Mears, C. (2010, January 13). *Bank of Ireland employee forum drives engagement agenda*. London: IPA.

Metcalf, H., & Rolfe, H. (2009). *Employment and earnings in the finance sector: A gender analysis*. Research Report 17, Equalities and Human Rights Commission, Manchester.

NGSU. (n.d.). *Working with Nationwide—Working together*. Oxfordshire: Nationwide Group Staff Union, Cheney.

NGSU. (2016, April 27). *Nationwide recognition and procedure agreement between Nationwide and NGSU*. Oxfordshire: Nationwide Group Staff Union, Cheney.

Perfect, D. (2011). *Gender pay gaps*. Briefing Paper 2, Equalities and Human Rights Commission, Manchester.

Prosser, T. (2011). 'UK: The representativeness of trade unions and employer associations in the banking sector' European Industrial Relations Observatory On-line, Dublin, August.

Rouse, P., & Duncan, M. (2012). *Handling change: A history of the Irish Bank officials' association*. Cork: Collins Press.

Soriano, C. (2011). *Recession and social dialogue in the banking sector: A global perspective*. Dublin: Eurofound.

Stevens, R. (2005, October). *The high performance workplace—Prudential UK: The UK employee forum*. London: IPA.

Stuart, M., Martinez Lucio, M., & Charlwood, A. (2009). *The Union Modernisation Fund—Round one: Final evaluation report*. Employment Relations Research Series No. 104, BIS, London.

Sutherland, J. (2015, December). *Direct engagement of employees in change at Zurich UK life*. London: IPA.

Tarren, D. (2013). *Building trade union capacity for social dialogue through the provision and analysis of change within the European finance sector.* London: Syndex/Unite/UNI Global Union (Europa finance).

TheCityUK. (2014, January). *Key facts about UK financial and related professional services.* London.

TheCityUK. (2016, March). *Key facts about UK financial and related professional services.* London.

Traxler, F., Arrowsmith, J., Nergaard, K., & Molins López-Rodó, J. (2008). Variable Pay and Collective Bargaining: A Cross-National Comparison of the Banking Sector. *Economic and Industrial Democracy, 29*(3), 406–431.

Tuckman, A., & Snook, J. (2014). Between consultation and collective bargaining? The changing role of non-union employee representatives: A case study from the finance sector. *Industrial Relations Journal, 45*(1), 77–97.

Undy, R. (2008). *Trade union merger strategies: Purpose, process, and performance.* Oxford: Oxford University Press.

Unite. (2008, October). *Organising support Unite report—Stage 2 report: Banking and insurance.* London: Unite.

Unite. (2009, May). *Unite sector fact sheet.* London.

Unite. (2011, September). *Treasury committee—Written evidence submitted by Unite the Union.* London.

Unite. (2012, May). *Unite research fact sheet.* London.

Waddington, J. (2013). The views of members towards workplace union organization in banking between 1999 and 2008. *British Journal of Industrial Relations, 51*(2), 333–354.

Worthington, S., & Welch, P. (2011). Banking without the banks. *International Journal of Bank Marketing, 29*(2), 190–201.

3

Processes

Introduction

The workforces of the various financial services sector companies seldom have not been affected by job losses, outsourcing and offshoring. Indeed, some have been affected by successive waves of job losses, outsourcing and offshoring. Such processes of organisational restructuring have been occasioned by changes in the structure of capital ownership, namely, mergers and acquisitions, as well as by continuation of existing capital structures. For example, AXA life and pensions operations were bought by Friends Provident to create Friends Life in 2010, leading to issues for Unite of jobs cuts and harmonisation of terms and conditions (especially in regard of pensions). And after this, AXA restructured its own insurance activities by creating two divisions where redundancies were involved. The same degree of transformation has been true where, aside from programmes of job reduction and relocation, the tasks comprising different roles and posts have also undergone change, whether in situations of change in the structure of capital by way of inter- or intra-organisational restructuring. In this sense, change has been somewhat of a constant in the experience of employment in

© The Author(s) 2017
G. Gall, *Employment Relations in Financial Services*,
DOI 10.1057/978-1-137-39539-9_3

the financial services sector. Underlying these constant processes of aforementioned change has been the continued drive towards capital accumulation, whether this be returning to former levels or maintaining or increasing current levels. The strategic decisions made by companies to pursue profitability have led to the introduction of these processes of change. This chapter examines the *processes* by which the outcomes (detailed in the following chapter) have been arrived at. The significance of examining the processes lies not just in the manner by which they may influence the outcomes. It also lies in the sense that the issues of procedural justice and injustice are potentially on a par with the issues of substantive justice and injustice. In other words, the manner in which employees are treated can be as important as the end result of the treatment itself. For example, the perception or reality of an unfairly arrived at decision can be as critical to the employee as the nature of the decision itself. More widely, and given that labour unions remain the largest organisations of independent representation for workers in the sector, the manner of industrial relations is also an indication of the nature of the processes at work.

Although there is a potentially problematic sense of 'Which came first? The chicken or the egg?' in terms of order of causation with regard to seeking to analyse processes and outcomes separately, examination of the scale of events and phenomena across the entire financial services sector does require such a forced separation. However, it is recognised that some processes may also been seen as outcomes where there is a circularity of cause and effect. For example, a strike may be a *reactive*, after-the-event response to an occurrence, seeking to overturn the change like a site closure, while another strike may be take place in pursuit of a pay offer which has yet to be finally agreed. For this reasoning with most strikes being reactive, the few strikes that did occur are recorded and discussed in the following chapter on outcomes. Alternatively, sabotage or sickness absence may be responses to the process and outcomes of performance management. Evidently then, there can be a dynamic duality and inter-play to such phenomena.

The structure of this chapter is, thus, to begin by further developing the analysis of the process of partnership working, the impact it has had on the repertoire of union arguments made to employers and the effect of widespread redundancies on the process of partnership. Within LBG, partnership has suffered a severe setback in terms of the relationship between the employer and LTU and between LTU, on the one hand, and Accord and Unite, on the other hand. The origins of, and fallout from, this process are assessed. The chapter then moves to examine the process of performance management by which pay increases are made. Following this, developments in the institutions of industrial relations are reviewed with regard to union recognition and European Works Councils. Finally, issues of collective mobilisation and resistance, focussing on the prospects of industrial action, sabotage and grievance representation, are examined.

Partnership

The preponderance of partnership agreements and partnership working in the financial services sector has already been noted (Gall 2001, 2008) as has the high survival rate of these (Bacon and Samuel 2009). Since these observations, many partnership agreements in the sector have been updated and revised, in a process labelled, by employers and unions alike, 'modernisation' so the agreements are then said to be 'fit for purpose'. Examples are to be found at AXA, Barclays, LBG, Legal and General, RSA and Santander. A further indication of the extent and strength of partnership in the sector can be gleaned from government funding initiatives. The Partnership at Work Fund was, in essence, replaced by the Union Modernisation Fund (UMF) in 2005 (McIlroy and Daniels 2008: 105). While it was fundamentally a partnership fund, the partnerships primarily existed to varying degrees between various applicant unions and the then Labour government. However, the fund was used to promote partnership between capital and labour in the vein of its predecessor and this can be seen in the case of the funding to Accord and Amicus for HBoS and the PGSA for Portman Building Society. Of the total 93 UMF projects granted (matched) funding over three rounds just seven concerned the unions and staff associations of the financial services sector. Of these, only the aforementioned two concerned partnership working (with the others concerning the use of information technology to aid relations and communication between unions and their members). This has resulted primarily from the advanced and embedded state of partnership in the sector, and is further reinforced by only five of the 89 Partnership at Work projects, funded by the government's partnership fund, being found in the sector (Terry and Smith 2003: 28). This first section on partnership begins by examining one of the major and earlier agreements (at HBoS). It is followed by another considering the case of LBG where partnership has affected two quite distinct outcomes. Following that issues of ideological and institutional incorporation, victimisation, and implications for union organising are examined.

Partnership in HBoS

A major new partnership agreement was signed by HBoS, Accord and Unite in mid-2007 (Gall 2008: 149), right at the beginning of the process which led to the financial crash. The agreement took 7 years to develop and formally ran for only 15 months prior to the creation of LBG (*My Accord*, Summer 2010).[1] However, it was in the main continued with in practice thereafter until its replacement by a group-wide partnership agreement in LBG in 2015. As it contained a number of major new developments and was heavily supported and subsidised by the employer, it is worth examining in some detail (especially as a precursor to the new partnership agreement between LBG and Accord and Unite in 2015—see below). The rationale for new agreement lay in the employer and union desire to streamline the representation of employees into a 'single table' bargaining arrangement in order to end duplication and competition and to provide a more representative and authoritative form of worker voice for engagement in partnership (Jameson 2010). This rationale emerged from the experience of Accord and Unite in dealing with the consequences of the merger of the Halifax and BoS for their relationship and activities.[2] The new agreement was heavily backed by the employer, with senior executives recounting:

Last week, [we] met with our union reps for our quarterly partnership meeting. These sessions enable union reps and colleagues to get a real insight into our performance and offer me a chance to get some direct feedback on how colleagues are feeling across the business. The value of our local union partnerships is hugely important, and so thanks to all who participate in local site sessions. I would encourage all of our colleagues to join one of our two unions, and it is great to see the active role that all of our union reps play across all of our sites. It was very reassuring that no major issues were raised by the union in our session. (Tom Woolgrove, HBoS communication, 20 May 2008, quoted in Accord press release, 25 May 2008)

I value the informal meetings we have with reps. You help us to understand what is going on, especially in relation to the integration changes. (Michelle Boyd, quoted in Accord press release, 10 November 2010)

while Accord itself reported:

An article on HBoS GroupNet ... reported on the very positive responses to the questions about Partnership and union membership in a survey of nearly 8000 HBoS colleagues ... The findings were discussed at a joint Partnership meeting in Edinburgh on June 26 as were views on how the unions could use the survey results to grow membership further. (Accord press release, 21 June 2008)

Accord reps from throughout the Division met ... They were given an update on the current industrial relations agenda in HBoS by General Secretary, Ged Nichols, and had lots of opportunities to ask questions. Alex Harrison, Head of Investment Customer Service and Debbie England, the I&I [Insurance and Indemnity] Employee Relations and Reward Manager, joined the reps to give a business update and to take questions in what was a very positive session. There was a significant debate about how performance management was working in I&I which will be fed back to the I&I leadership team. (Accord press release, 2 July 2008)

Although not an overt overturning of collective bargaining, the agreement was more heavily tilted towards consultation, under which the previous scope and reach were extended, especially by way of earlier consultation and with lower and middle levels of management.[3] Part of he new agreement also saw the recognition of workplace representatives and funding of their facility time as well as a desire to increase union density. Initial progress was slow to fill the workplace representative positions (Gall 2008: 149) but from late 2008 to late 2011, 146 union reps (and 133 managers) were put through the training, paid for by the employer, for partnership (*My Accord*, Winter 2011, see also Stuart et al. 2010: 56). HBoS also agreed to provide access and resources to raise union density to 70% from its 50% level in 2007. Recalling the coverage of union densities in the previous chapter, the partnership agreement worked better for Accord that it did Unite, suggesting that the latter union which was perceived to be more independent minded and less of a finance sector union suffered while the former benefitted from a closer relationship with the employer (see Gall 2008: 149–150). Indeed, with an offer from HBoS to reimburse the first 6 months' cost of union membership for new starts, 80% joined leading to 3500 new members for Accord in first half of 2008 (BIS 2010: 8).

Despite the heavy backing of both unions and employer for the new partnership agreement, it was found that partnership working was slow to become operational at sub-national levels and slow to generate 'positive' results (Jameson 2010: 7). Consequently, UMF funds were applied for to help address these issues. The assessment of the operation of the UMF in HBoS found that: '62% of representatives felt their role was appreciated by management following the project compared to 42% beforehand; whilst 85% of management reported that union representatives understood partnership and the needs of the business following the project compared to just 22% beforehand' (Stuart et al. 2010: 56). Given the takeover by LloydsTSB, how partnership unfolded in HBoS is mainly covered in the next chapter.

Inset 3.1: Partnership in HBoS

The nature of the partnership at HBoS between the employer and unions was indicated by a Union Modernisation Fund (UMF) report (BIS 2010) under which the UMF funded a project to develop the partnership during 2008. Thus, through an existing partnership agreement:

Accord and Unite had been working on their business plans for ensuring that the bank maintained and improved its productivity and competitiveness in the global financial services market. Both unions needed to develop their capacity to support and train their reps in understanding the business and becoming more effective partners. UMF funding offered the ideal opportunity. The project provided consultancy, training and support so the two unions could create and embed a good practice framework in partnership working, by developing a partnership training programme to embed the partnership approach with its trade union reps for the benefit of their members and the business as a whole - which was key to both unions' modernisation strategies. (BIS 2010: 1)

Ged Nichols, Accord general secretary, believed:

The people strategy at HBoS is firmly focused on colleague engagement and there is a general consensus that wider cultural and behavioural issues need to change in order for colleague engagement to be embedded across the business. The joint training programmes and the wider roll out of the partnership agenda will help develop an environment where these cultural changes can be addressed and moved forward positively and constructively. There is no doubt that organisations that rank in the top 100 are employers that treat their employees well – which is good for employees and good for the business. Accord, Unite and HBoS see partnership working as extremely important but neither union had the capacity or the resources to cover new areas of training. In addition, partnership skills are a specialist area that neither union could deliver, so external experts were engaged to design and deliver the appropriate training and a training programme, so that the unions could be self-sufficient in the future. ... This is not just a union initiative but a joint approach to encourage collaborative approaches to problem solving, communication and the development of strong and effective relationships between unions and management. (BIS 2010: 1, 4)

He continued:

The resolve of HBoS, Accord and Unite to pursue partnership working through challenging times, a changing business and this project in particular, has not only remained steadfast but has been strengthened further on the basis of their conviction that the company is most likely to weather the tough market conditions by working in partnership across the business. There is clear evidence through the evaluation of the programme that the UMF grant has enabled Accord and Unite to make significant progress in developing and embedding the partnership approach with its trade union reps for the benefit of their members and the business as a whole. There is now a tried and tested partnership training programme in place, which has been rolled out to a number of reps and managers and which has been positively evaluated in terms of the improvements it has already brought to employee relations across the business. There is also clearly strong and unequivocal support for the partnership training programme to continue and compelling evidence already of the benefits that partnership brings to both the business and its employees. All the factors are therefore in place to build on the work already carried out, so that a sustainable partnership approach can be embedded even more widely, with the company joining the ranks of the many other organisations reporting tangible improvements in business performance. (BIS 2010: 8)

Partnership in LBG

Within LBG, two divergent outcomes have been arrived at under the auspices of partnership. The first was derecognition of LTU in 2015. The second is the partnership of the company with Accord and Unite, whereby the two unions work increasingly closely together (as they had begun to within HBoS). This section begins by examining the nature of the unfolding relationship between LBG and LTU, leading up to derecognition. It then moves to examine the relationship of Accord (as the larger of the other two unions) with LBG on job losses before considering inter-union relations in the light of partnership and, finally, the extent and nature of ideological and institutional incorporation of unions within partnership.

Acrimony and Animosity: LBG and LTU

From the points of the financial crash and LloydsTSB-HBoS merger onwards, LTU engaged in an increasing shrill and critical war of words with LBG. Accompanying these was a series of escalating actions.

Given that LTU's origins lay in being a staff association and one which spurned overtures to form a sector wide union (in the form of UNIFI), itself indicating the continuing hold of 'internalism', this was a particularly unusual outcome. The immediate origins of the antagonism of the LTU to LBG can be traced back to the issue of offshoring when, in 2000, LTU mounted a campaign based upon (i) customers not wanting to deal with overseas call centres; (ii) LloydsTSB having a social and corporate responsibility to the local communities from which it derived most of its profits; and (iii) operations overseas being generally less efficient than those centred on British-based staff. Its campaign involved a 500,000 strong petition and lobbying of MPs and government ministers. LTU claimed this led to the closure of the Mumbai call centre and return of 750 telephony jobs in 2007, along with the end to further offshoring (LTU *Newsletter*, 30 November 2009, 23 February 2011). Opposition to offshoring continued after the creation of LBG, with the LTU in mid-2009 commenting on a statement from LBG on offshoring of jobs: 'The Bank's so called 'commitment' is not worth the paper it's written on. What it says is that the Bank will keep operational jobs in the UK but will reserve the right to Offshore them whenever it wants to' (LTU *Newsletter*, 30 June 2009).[4] LTU also called for the return of some 5000 jobs from India which has been offshored given widespread labour shedding at the bank. At this stage, such an opinion was tempered by a wider perspective, with LTU stating: 'It's a fact of business life that when you bring together two large, overlapping organisations ... and ... commit ... of to making synergy savings of £1.5 bn over 3 years, there will inevitably be job losses. The key objective has to be to ensure that those that leave want to, on the agreed redundancy terms, and those who want to stay can' (LTU *Newsletter*, 30 June 2009).

The tempo and tone of LTU attacks on LBG were ratcheted up when LTU reported:

Now, in a move which shows just how desperate it is to get a clear run at ripping up staff pay and benefits, [LBG] has instructed HBoS managers to destroy communications from LTU. ... In a revealing insight the Bank has said: '... Any literature that is posted or faxed to our branches/sites from a union that is not recognised must be immediately destroyed (unless it is addressed on a personal basis) - and under no circumstances should be displayed'. (LTU *Newsletter*, 23 November 2009)

The reality is the consultation process has been a cynical sham from start to finish. [LBG] never had any intentions of listening to the views of their staff or changing its position regardless of the level of feedback. (LTU *Newsletter*, 18 March 2010)

[LBG] recently said that 'Colleagues are our most valuable resource' and 'Creating a great place to work is a core priority ...'. Those are just meaningless words. It's actions that are important and today's announcement tells staff all they need to know about the organisation for which they work. (LTU *Newsletter*, 18 March 2010)

[LBG] is quite happy to protect the interests of probably the top two earners and stick two fingers up to everyone else. The sheer level of arrogance exhibited by this decision will stick in the throats of all right-minded members of staff, regardless of what they think about the changes to pensions schemes. (LTU *Newsletter*, 26 April 2010)

The war of words continued throughout 2010, with LTU arguing LBG had no integrity:

[LBG] says that it 'supports the principles of equal pay and the elimination of any policies or practices, which may discriminate against men and woman either solely or partly on the grounds of sex'. Those are just words on a page ... (LTU *Newsletter*, 15 December 2010)

and

To say that [LBG's] new approach to the management of pay is intellectually bankrupt would give it a level of sophistication it doesn't deserve. There [are] ... just vague promises that add up to nothing worthwhile. (LTU *Newsletter*, 16 December 2010)

LBG responded by accusing LTU of being irresponsible and unconstructive by, in the words of its Group HR Director 'walk[ing] away' from ... talks ... despite the offer of further concessions to all unions, specifically to help us reach an agreement' (LTU *Newsletter*, 31 August 2010) and then 'consistently refus[ing] to work constructively with us' (LTU *Newsletter*, 17 March 2011). Following LBG's statement that staff would not be eligible for a pay rise or promotion if they did not sign the new terms and conditions contracts (LTU *Newsletter*, 7 September 2010), LTU repeatedly accused LBG of 'blackmail and bully[ing] them into signing new contracts of employment' (LTU *Newsletter*, 15 September 2010, 14 January 2011, 3 February 2011). In its campaign against the new contracts which embodied a reduction in the value of overtime (with core hours being extended) and sick pay and permitted an increase in flexible working (LTU *Newsletter*, 24 March 2010), LTU accused LBG of trying to intimidate it when LBG threaten potential legal action for inducing unofficial industrial action (LTU *Newsletter*, 4 February 2011). LTU responded by upping the *ante* in the form of organising a ballot on industrial action (see later). LTU was also compelled to apply to the state body, the Central Arbitration Committee (CAC), to gain information from LBG—which it refused to disclose—in order to conduct bargaining on pay (LTU *Newsletter*, 24 May 2011, CAC case DI/2/2011). LTU was successful.

Despite the fiery language, LTU had not come to adopt a militant, anti-capitalist stance for it still maintained in 2012 and 2014 that:

> There is no point being coy about it, Banks are in the business of making money. One of the ways they can do that is by selling financial services products to customers. The question is can they achieve that without a predatory sales culture and incentive and bonus schemes which drive short-term performance. We believe you can but it's not going to be easy. The Bank should scrap all of its current bonus and incentive schemes and start again. (LTU *Newsletter*, 18 July 2012)

and

> The Bank is a commercial organisation that's in the business of producing financial services products that customers want to buy. No one should be ashamed of that fact because the more successful the Bank is the better

terms and conditions of employment we should be able to negotiate for our members. However, that success needs to be built on firm foundations which means selling products that customers want and can afford to buy rather than just because the Bank has business targets it needs to achieve. (LTU *Newsletter*, 26 September 2014)

In the run up to derecognition by LBG, its Head of Group Employee Relations accused LTU of deliberately lacking transparency its communication with LBG and in explaining how LTU functions with the conclusion that: 'I am increasingly concerned … that your reluctance to be transparent on this issue underpins a more fundamental mindset that a relationship based on not working together, or with anybody else, is really what you want' (LTU *Newsletter*, 21 August 2014). To this, LTU accused LBG of being 'disingenuous' (LTU *Newsletter*, 21 August 2014) in stating that LTU was not employing the *modus operandi* of the Accord and Unite unions because they have a partnership agreement with LBG (via HBoS) and LTU did not. The notice to end the recognition agreement of LTU was explained by LBG: 'Disappointingly, following 3 years of discussions, Accord, Unite and the Group have concluded that LTU are not prepared to work in a collaborative and constructive way with our other recognised unions or with the group. As a result, we have decided to end our formal recognition agreement with LTU' (*Guardian*, 15 July 2015) with LBG further adding: 'LTU has continued to publicly attack and undermine the other unions' (LTU *Newsletter*, 24 July 2015). LTU responding by saying: 'Lloyds is paying us back for being a thorn in their side, but we are going to continue to be a thorn in their side' (*Guardian*, 15 July 2015), and 'we will continue to look after our members' interests both individually and collectively regardless of what anyone says … The bank wants weak and ineffective unions that agree with everything is says. We are not prepared to sacrifice our principles for the fig-leaf of recognition' (LTU *Newsletter*, 14 July 2015). LTU pledged to do this based upon its strength of membership, legal recourse and independence. It then revealed what it saw as the underlying motivations driving derecognition:

Since the merger, the Bank has wanted to recreate an HBoS employee relations environment in which the Unions did what they were told, never challenged key decisions and in exchange for weakness were rewarded with the occasional crumbs from the negotiating table. Staff in HBoS had weak, ineffective trade unions and that's what the Bank has wanted to recreate in Lloyds over the past few years. Under the new agreement the Unions would have been required to act with 'one voice' and that would have meant that the two smaller unions, who are in the Bank's pocket, would have been able to outvote LTU on all key decisions and the interests of our members would have been lost. That's what the Bank and the other two unions have really wanted from the beginning.

Let's take the imposition of the new harmonised contract of employment as an example. In the 'new world', [LBG] and the two smaller unions would have ignored our concerns on working hours and pensions, and simply reached a collective agreement, which would have been imposed over the heads of LTU and its members. We could never allow ourselves to be in that position. It also became clear that the two unions and [LBG] wanted to stop staff from joining a union of their choice. [LBG]'s concern was that with Group-wide recognition offered to all the unions, members of the other two unions would flock to LTU and that's what they wanted to stop at all costs. (LTU *Newsletter*, 17 July 2015)

The effect of derecognition was that LTU's formal relationship with LBG involving rights to information, representation, consultation and negotiation ended. This compelled LTU to rely upon its limited statutory rights (to accompany individual members in grievance and disciplinary hearings, to represent individual members, to be consulted on collective redundancies), to use Employment Tribunal claims and court action and to lobby and pressurise the company as best it could (including through the use of campaigns and industrial action). So, LTU was left in a position of trying to act collectively on behalf of its members but without much in the way of institutional rights to facilitate this. After derecognition, it claimed these methods were able to provide some effective representation within LBG. It also claimed the Accord and Unite unions prevented more fulsome effective representation of members' interests (see below). Of note is that the statutory right to union recognition, effectively re-recognition, was not available to LTU. Regardless of meeting membership and support thresholds, an application would be rejected by the Central Arbitration Committee because the employer already had existing union recognition agreements (with Accord and Unite) for the staff LTU would be seeking to gain recognition for. In order to manage these limitations, the strategy of LTU, therefore, has been to maintain its vociferous criticism of LBG and Accord and Unite as a way of justifying its existence and *raison d'etre*. This is explored below.

Tensions Over 'Nationalisation', Job Losses and Harmonisation

Accord greeted the proposed takeover by LloydsTSB of HBoS in late 2008 with initial dismay, believing that HBoS was sufficiently well capitalised to avoid such a government-inspired initiative and fearful of the consequences for members' employment security and terms and conditions of employment (Accord press release, 18 September 2008). It then moved to acceptance and support provided that certain guarantees were given about members' employment security and terms and conditions of employment. Indeed, it asked the then Labour government to use its influence to make sure terms and conditions were maintained but merely received platitudes about these.[5] Alongside this, it called for talks with LloydsTSB in order to discuss the union's 10-point plan on members' jobs, terms and conditions of employment and pensions. This was rebuffed. It took some solace from the statement on the vesting day of LBG on 19 January 2009 that: 'We intend to have constructive and meaningful dialogue with our unions throughout the integration process. Our aim is to reach agreed positions with all unions that take account of the needs of our business and our people' (Accord press release, 19 January 2009). This did not last long as it was also announced on vesting day that LBG was seeking to reduce operating costs by at least £1.5 bn per annum from 2011 and the first job cuts began in March 2009.

Accord did not flatly oppose job cuts, saying it was:

always unhappy at any planned reduction in the roles and opportunities available even when we fully understand what the bank believes to be the commercial need for the changes. The reality is that there will be a reduction in the number of employees in the Lloyds Banking Group as the new business takes shape and duplication is removed – nobody expected otherwise from the day that the takeover of HBoS was first announced. (Accord press release, 21 May 2009)[6]

and that it

remain[ed]committed to supporting members who are impacted by change programmes ... with advice [and] guidance ... and is opposed to compulsory redundancies ... [while] engag[ing] positively with the employers to test the commercial logic of any plans and to mitigate the negative impact on members in line with the Security of Employment Agreement'. (Accord press release, 21 May 2009)

In regard of the job security agreement, it sought to maintain its implementation in terms of setting out the processes for redundancy selection criteria, alternatives to redundancy (turnover, retirement, relocation and retraining) and severance terms as well as the timescales for collective consultation. It also sought to have the pledge from HBoS on not outsourcing or off-shoring its UK call centre operations maintained and extended to LBG.

Within a matter of months, Accord stated that while it 'has always accepted that there would be a reduction in the total number of employees' following the takeover, the manner in which the redundancy process was administered was far from satisfactory and that this was contrary to maintaining employee motivation and commitment, and thus, the success of LBG (Accord press release, 16 July 2009). To this end, it called for a halt to redundancies and restructuring. Accord them moved to add that with over 15,000 job losses announced with the first 9 months of the takeover that while '[w]e always recognised that some job losses were inevitable as Lloyds TSB integrated HBoS operations ... the scale of the changes announced today will leave many staff in shock' (Accord press release, 13 November 2009). Yet in late 2010, Accord believed: 'LBG has behaved better than we initially thought it would on job security matters [and] ... since we called for a temporary halt to job losses last summer, a better way to deal with organisational changes was developed. Since then job losses have been managed better and smarter with visible co-operation with the unions. The number of compulsory redundancies remains low' (Accord press release, 10 November 2010). By March 2011, 27,000 jobs were shed as largely as a result of redundancies (but also including outsourcing and sell offs). This was increased to 43,000 by June 2011, with 30,000 jobs shed and 13,000 more job cuts to come shortly.

Despite the ruptures embodied in the takeover of HBoS, Accord's Principal Executive Council proclaimed the purpose of the union's biennial delegate conference in 2010 was to 'discuss and reassert the strength of the Partnership approach and show how this sensible, mature trade unionism improves the working lives of our members [and t]o build on the successes within HBoS so we can apply it to the new working environment within LBG and prove that Partnership is the better way for our members' (Accord press release, 23 June 2010).

Accord not only supported partnership with capital but also, in the broadest terms, 'free market' capitalism whereby it believed that the deregulated form of finance capitalism worked to the advantage of its members. For example, it stated that it believed in '… more competition on the high street … [which] must be good for customers and for the economy more generally … [and that] … the prospect of any sale, as worrying as it might be for some, is surely better than the Lloyds Banking Group taking capacity out of the industry in pursuit of its own cost reduction agenda … New entrants into the market may also require the skills and expertise of the some of the specialists and other staff who have become 'surplus to requirements" (Accord press release 2 November 2009).

Whilst there were some compulsory redundancies since 2008 in LBG, their number has remained relatively small throughout the sector. The estimate of around 10,000 jobs out of between 250,000 and 300,000 shed overall by 2017 in this manner appears as quite an achievement on behalf of the unions involved. For example, Accord stated: 'we have seen compulsory redundancies kept to a minimum' (Accord press release, 14 July 2016). However, whilst this is an achievement, it is less of one when recognition is made of, on the one hand, the number of staff wishing to leave and, on the other, the relatively generous severance terms available (as a result of the consecutive renewals of Security of Employment Agreements (SEAs)) in most companies. For example, in LBG the SEA was extended from 2012 to 2013, from 2014 to 2016, and from 2016 to 2017 (even though in the first extension the severance terms for new starts were reduced [*My Accord*, Winter 2012] and the period of consultation was reduced following the reduction in statutory period from 90 to 45 days [Unite LBG newsletter, May 2013]). Thus, the vast majority of redundancies have been achieved through voluntary means. For example, LTU commented in 2012: 'The current Lloyds TSB terms have been in place for a number of years and are amongst the best in the financial service industry. It is those severance terms and the Job Security Agreement which have enabled the Bank to reduce its staff numbers significantly over the last few years without having to resort to wholesale compulsory redundancies' (LTU *Newsletter*, 1 December 2011). The issue of compulsory redundancies is returned to in Chap. 4.

One of the other early major consequences of the takeover of HBoS by LloydsTSB to form LBG was the harmonisation of terms and conditions of employment between the staffs of the two former constituents. Accord made no recommendation in its consultative ballot to accept or reject the terms it was party to negotiating, saying, essentially, that its members 'know best' when in possession of the full information. Thus, 'we] will not be recommending members to vote in one way or another in the ballot. We know and respect our members and trust them to make the right decision for themselves and their colleagues' (Accord press release, 3 December 2009). This could be seen in at least three ways, namely, an act of extreme democracy, an abdication of national leadership or an indication of a divided membership. When members voted, only 27% did despite repeated urging, with 84% finding the proposed terms and conditions unacceptable and 80% supporting a further ballot if Accord could not make progress in further negotiations (Accord press release, 1 March 2010). Further talks, aided by ACAS and carried out jointly with Unite (following Unite rejecting the proposed terms and conditions), did not lead to any improvements. The offer was then imposed but then revised to which its terms were balloted upon by Accord. The offer, including a 1.5% pay rise, saw different parts rejected (pensions) and accepted (pay, terms and conditions) but overall 56% voted for the terms on a 41% turnout (Accord press release, 23 June 2010). On the issue of pensions 'a narrow majority of the members of the FSPS [final salary pension scheme] who voted saying they would be prepared to take action in an attempt to get negotiations reopened' (Accord press release, 23 June 2010). Further talks took place on pensions but without any concessions.

By late 2013/early 2014, Accord showed signs of losing some patience with LBG and its proffered form of partnership. It said:

> [We] believe in working people standing up against injustice. That time is fast approaching. We will do everything we can to negotiate a fair outcome on the pensions that our members and their families have spent their working lives building and relying upon. But if the employer won't listen and won't change its current proposals then all employees in the bank, whether they are in defined benefit pension schemes or not, have a decision to make. Do you trust an employer which breaks its promises or not? If not, what are we going to do to change things? (*My Accord*, Autumn 2013)

and in a perceived breach of the spirit of partnership, Accord questioned whether '[w]e all in this together... aren't we?' over reductions in the worth of defined benefit pensions schemes when the chief executive of LBG was awarded a £2.3 million bonus (Accord press release, 22 November 2013). Then it gave the company notice that had it engaged an independent scrutineer to supervise a consultative ballot regarding industrial action (and any statutory ballots that may be needed then to authorise action) in response to continuing job losses, outsourcing and off-shoring, the imposition of a 0% cap on increases in pensionable pay in its defined benefit pensions schemes and the imposition of a below inflation pay rise whilst paying increases to executives in the form of allowances to circumvent the EU rules on bankers' bonuses. Accord stated:

> [T]he cumulative effect of the incessant bad news is corrosive. Members have reached a point where they will be prepared to say 'enough is enough' because the management of the bank is losing the trust and

confidence of the people who loyally serve its customers. The bank is also endangering its ability to meet the future needs of its customers and the communities it serves because it is pushing loyal staff to the point where they will no longer care. (Accord press release, 8 April 2014)

On a 32% turnout in the consultative ballot, 85% of respondents said they had lost trust and confidence in the capability of the bank's management to run the bank in the interests of all of its stakeholders including customers and employees, and nearly 80% responded that they would be prepared to vote for and participate in industrial action, up to and including strike action, to say to the Lloyds Banking Group that 'enough is enough' and to demand a better deal for bank employees (Accord press release, 12 May 2014).[7] Given that the level of support for action was deemed by Accord to be insufficient to move to a statutory ballot for industrial action, it sought to leverage what it could with the result as it stood (*My Accord*, Autumn 2015), given the turnout was 'not as high as it would have liked' (Accord press release, 12 May 2014). The leverage resulted in LBG agreeing to extend the lifeline of the existing job security agreement to the end of 2016 (Accord press release, 15 July 2014). The willingness to engage in membership mobilisation had significant limits for Accord told LBG: '… if we were to take industrial action, the objective would be to get the bank to return to negotiations on the cap it has imposed on the defined benefits pension schemes and a range of other issues which affect all employees in the bank. If you are prepared to undertake such negotiations without us having to resort to action then that is clearly better from all perspectives' (Accord press release, 13 June 2014) and that 'There are, inevitably, differences and complications [on the salient matters of] … pay and reward matters, the future of the performance management system and dignity at work issues … but, at least we are engaged in discussions that are focussed on making employees better off and improving the quality of working life in the bank more positively than we have been at any time since the financial crisis of 2008 … [even if] things take time to deliver and we are yet to make progress on the key issue of the 0% cap on the growth of future pensionable earnings in the bank's defined benefit pension schemes' (Accord press release, 15 July 2014).

The prospects for partnership appeared to have been revived from 2015 onwards judged by Accords' attitude. In addition to pay deals being jointly agreed (see later), a new recognition agreement was signed in 2015 and the outcomes of the 2015 pay deal were viewed as positive. These included measures concerning the way pay was structured and progressed so that 17,500 lower grade staff received an uplift after allowances were consolidated into their salaries or their minimum grade salaries, and 'pay clusters' were removed from the Retail Division in line with the policy set by Accord members through the union's Biennial Delegate Conference in 2014, 'demonstrat[ing] that our new agreement with [LBG] delivers positive results through a constructive approach to engagement and negotiation' (Accord press release, 12 August 2015). Accord then stated: 'We and Lloyds Banking Group have a good record of managing these issues through turnover and voluntary redundancy …' (Accord press release, 3 February 2016), suggesting that the removing the Senior Personal Banking Adviser role out without compulsory redundancies 'demonstrated the value of positive engagement between unions and management' (Accord press release, 24 February 2016). Indeed, a year after signing the new recognition agreement, Accord released a statement asking 'So, what has been delivered?' since then, and listed 13 minor improvements (Accord press release, 14 July 2016).

Inter-union Relations at LBG

Traditionally, there had been considerable enmity between Accord and Unite (and its predecessors) in HBoS and between Unite (and its predecessors) and LTU in LTSB (and its predecessors) but the unfolding processes of financial crisis, company merger and the embedding of partnership saw these enmities change substantially. The new enmity that emerged was principally between Accord and LTU (with Unite cast as a minor accomplice to the villainy of Accord according to LTU). Accord and Unite were pitched in one corner and LTU in another because of their attitudes to LBG, and much of this was coloured by the nature of competition between the unions. As a non-TUC affiliate, the LTU was not bound by TUC rules on competition for members but by the same token as LTU was not a TUC affiliate neither Accord nor Unite were bound by TUC rules in relation to LTU either. Following the takeover of HBoS by LloydsTSB to form LBG, Accord and LTU faced each other as the principal protagonists. Because of Accord's willingness to work in partnership with LBG and it being far bigger in membership numbers than Unite, LTU increasingly cast itself against Accord as the only independent union for staff within LBG (and then TSB once it was sold off). Thus, as part of its positioning strategy in relation to competing unions, LTU decided not to take any form of subsidy from the employer (LTU *Newsletter*, 28 September 2010, 14 July 2015).[8] It promoted this as part of its independence, being also neither affiliated to the TUC nor any political party. It was for this reason that Accord often stated it was 'funded by members' subscriptions only' (*My AccordTSB*, May 2015; *Accord Mail (Lloyds)*, October 2016), and in a reference to LTU's trading activities, 'We do not receive funding from any other organisations and we have no related businesses or other business interests' (*Accord Mail (Lloyds)*, September and October 2016).

Tensions between Accord and Unite and LTU were evident from early on from the creation of LBG. LTU accused Accord of being ideologically craven and strategically spineless in the face of the employer's will and power as well as being duplicitous, opportunist and recidivist (LTU *Newsletter*, 3 September 2015, 8 September 2015, 28 September 2015). It accused Unite of the same 'sins' but for reasons less of ideology and strategy and more over numerical membership weakness. Such accusations are laid out in full in the Insets 3.2 and 3.3 on LTU's pronouncements against Accord and Unite. The hostility was mutual although not expressed in anything like the same qualitative or quantitative terms by Accord or Unite. For example, Accord stated that while it had 'been negotiating alongside the Unite and GMB unions … LTU has continued to refuse to work with any of the other unions and this has not helped matters' (Accord press release, 23 August 2010); 'The Lloyds TSB Union (LTU) has refused to work with any of the other three unions recognised by LBG throughout the integration talks. Instead, it chooses to attack us and seems to be dedicating an awful lot of its members' hard earned subscriptions on attempts to poach members from the other unions' (*My Accord*, Summer 2010); and 'Why hasn't LBG set up its own group-wide partnership agreement? Accord and Unite both believe that partnership's good for them and good for the company. A win:win. The other union in heritage LTSB [i.e., LTU] has a different approach to industrial relations, preferring to shout and oppose rather than talk intelligently' (*My Accord*, Winter 2011). Following derecognition of LTU by LBG, inter-union competition increased with Accord seeking members in the areas of LBG in which LTU has been traditionally dominant (*My Accord*, Autumn 2015). Accord reported that: 'LTU has accused Accord of being too 'cosy' with the company, warning that 'he who pays the piper plays the tune'' (*My Accord*, Winter 2011). With derecognition of LTU, it retorted: 'LTU isn't going to go away. It will have opinions but no influence' (*My Accord*, Autumn 2015), frequently stressing that, along with Unite, they were 'the ONLY recognised Unions' [emphasis in original] (Accord press release, 12 January 2016). Over the personalised attacks on its general secretary, Accord responded by saying: 'Just because they [LTU] shout louder does not mean that they are any more effective', dismissing LTU's claims about the prowess of the industrial action it initiated as 'willy-waving' (*Guardian*, 15 July 2015). Later, Accord's general secretary stated his personal view was that LTU was a body 'howling at the moon ... [and its] criticis[m] of other legitimate, TUC affiliated, unions [was] to try to deflect attention from its own deficiencies' (Ged Nichols, email correspondence, 28 October 2016). It is, thus, apparent that while Accord did make some response to—and criticism of—LTU, this was of a rather limited amount relative to the criticism and castigation of it by LTU. The reason for this was the view that engaging in an equal measure of tit-for-tat in the past was an onerous task which left workers feeling that each union was 'as bad as each other' and neither should be trusted' (Ged Nichols, email correspondence, 28 October 2016). Moreover, Accord decided that:

> Our strategy when HBoS was taken over by LloydsTSB was to 'circle the wagons' and do everything we could to secure our members' jobs and terms and conditions of employment in the most difficult period that the financial sector had ever experienced. We didn't think they would think

it a wise or productive use of our time and resources to be rebutting the attacks from LTU. Not least because our members knew what LTU was saying was untrue and LTU was not attracting people from Accord in any significant numbers despite their claims. We haven't been 'dragged into the gutter' by LTU up to now so I'm not going to respond to their vitriol [at your request] ... What [LTU] publishes in its 'Wizard of Oz' style makes little or no practical difference to Accord, our members or the employers that we engage with on our members' behalf. (Ged Nichols, email correspondence, 28 October 2016)

Unite decided that responding to LTU's accusations about it would only give the accusations more publicity and fan the flames of inter-union strife. With the enmity between Unite and LTU predating the financial crash, especially in the form of membership recruitment competition and different industrial stances, the further ratcheting up hostilities by way of Unite responding was not viewed by Unite as being worthwhile. Unite national officer, Rob MacGregor (interview, 7 September 2016), asserted that such open rivalry was 'often seen to be counter-productive, especially in the eyes of members so that a public slanging [match] was kept to a minimum'. However, this did not come without consequences. According to Unite: 'LTU continues to issue newsletters which are either lies or incorrect about Unite. Unites' decision to ignore the jibes is however becoming frustrating to reps as the LTU newsletters are becoming more frequent and more vicious' (Unite *Finance Sector Update*, 5 June 2013). However, MacGregor did recount that 'something of a rapprochement was achieved [with LTU] during the period 2012–2015 when the three unions worked together towards signing a new single agreement on an industrial rela-tions framework with bank. The sticking issue was that LTU wanted to maintain its own independent position. It was not opposed to part-nership with bank but it didn't want to lose its independence vis-à-vis the other two unions [Accord, Unite] under a process of single-table bargaining' (interview, 7 September 2016). Under single-table bar-gaining, LTU as the larger union risked being outvoted by Accord and Unite when acting in unison. MacGregor (interview, 7 September 2016) went on to characterise LTU as 'a financial services company

that offers trade union services', with the offers of services and dis-
counts being over and above those traditionally offered by the bank,
and to opine that the 'rationale for LTU becoming pseudo- militant
[was] that it needs to protect its membership base'. Relations between
Accord and Unite have been increasingly cordial and business-like
as they operate within a single table bargaining forum, have found a
common opponent in LTU and call each other partner unions within
the partnership framework (even though there remain some tensions
over demarcations of areas of influence). Joint working, for example,
led to the carrying out of a joint survey in LBG on stress in 2012 and
on pay in TSB in 2015 and occasionally one union would stand in for
the other one on consultations.

Inset 3.2: The War of Words—LTU Attacks Accord and Unite, Part 1

The open and public vitriol of LTU against Accord and Unite is almost
unknown within contemporary inter-union relations. Historically, the
intemperate language used by LTU is reminiscent of a militant, left-led
TUC-affiliate attacking a moderate, right-led TUC union (as at the time of
the 1984–1985 miners' strike) or a TUC-affiliate attacking a non-TUC affiliate as a yellow union which is the pocket of the employers. Because of
this, it is worth laying out some of the examples of these words.

Initially, there was a certain degree of coyness by omission whereby
LTU said it's 'job was to protect the long term interests of staff by ensuring that they were not hurt in the rush to squeeze the maximum out of
the takeover. ... The proposed new terms and conditions we have seen are
so completely unacceptable that no independent Trade Union, worthy of
that title, could ever accept them. LTU will not accept terms that are so
fundamentally detrimental to the long-term interest of our members and
their families' (LTU Newsletter, 19 October 2009), 'LTU is the only trade
union operating within the Lloyds Banking Group that is actively oppos-
ing the Bank's Offshoring Policy' (LTU Newsletter, 30 November 2009),
and 'Unlike other Unions, LTU is not prepared to sell out its members for
the sake of some shabby agreement or enter into a game of charades
whereby the proposals are put out to consultation and the Bank follow
that consultation with some prearranged changes, which are then heralded by a Union as a major victory. The issues would then be put to bed
and the Bank and the Union then do a Morecambe and Wise style dance
off into the sunset their hands held high whilst staff pay and conditions
are torn to shreds. That may be the way things were done in HBoS but LTU
will never enter into those kinds of games' (LTU Newsletter, 23 November
2009).

Then, the attacks became more specific when the names of the other two unions began to be used as well as being increasingly frequent. Thus, in an article entitled 'Crossing the Rubicon?' in 2009, LTU said:

In recent years HBoS has enjoyed a very close relationship with both Unite, who have become notoriously ineffective and Accord, the Union representing most union members in HBoS. Just how close becomes clear when one realises that: HBoS set a target for Union membership of 70% of staff. Many companies would like to have a target of 0% but I have only ever seen this sort of policy in companies determined to support Unions who say little and do even less; To help achieve its policy HBoS even paid for the first 6 months of Accord members' subscriptions. One is bound to ask how independent a trade union can be if it becomes that close to and dependent on an employer? LTU neither seeks nor accepts favours or financial support from the Bank. Our view is quite simple: you can't have effective independent trade unions without paying for them but you definitely won't get independent trade unions if the employer pays for them. (LTU *Newsletter*, 23 November 2009)

Soon after, LTU variously charged in 2010 alone that:

UNITE have at least rejected the Bank's proposals and they should be commended for at least being prepared to defend their members. However, time will tell whether they run for cover when the bullets start flying. ACCORD [is] a lost cause and are looking for an agreement, any agreement, whatever the cost to their members. (LTU *Newsletter*, 6 January 2010).

Unite, which represents less than 2000 members in Lloyds TSB and less than 10,000 across both Lloyds and HBoS and is the least capable of mounting any credible resistance to the Bank's proposals, is already setting out the terms under which it will sell its members down the river. And those terms are very cheap. Members will recall that a few months ago we said … that when the going got difficult other Unions would seek to try and negotiate some minor concessions from the Bank, claim them as some sort of major victory, announce the end of terms and conditions discussions and then with the Bank do a Morecambe and Wise style dance off into the sunset … We fully expected Accord to do that because that's been the basis of their relationship with Senior Management in HBoS for a long time.

Unite on the other hand at least showed some signs of having a backbone, when they rejected the Bank's proposals, but it now seems that they are reverting back to their usual behaviour. (LTU *Newsletter*, 12 March 2010)

Unite also rejected the proposals but they have still failed to publish actual voting figures which is not surprising given that, according to the Bank, they have only 10,000 members in the two Banks combined. We think that overstates Unite's membership and certainly in Lloyds their membership is well under 3000. With their Union failing to oppose anything, members of ACCORD (the largest Union in HBoS) accepted the proposals and said that they were happy for the Union to sign a collective agreement to bring the new terms and conditions into effect. Accord, however, realising that going it alone would destroy their so called Partnership Agreement with the Bank and Unite and the fact that they would be isolated, have sought to cling on for a bit longer. (LTU *Newsletter*, 30 July 2010)

LTU's Executive Committee still wants to reach a collective agreement with the Bank but not at any price, unlike Accord and Unite. … if it wasn't for LTU's complete and unwavering opposition to the Bank's proposals there would have been no discussions at ACAS at all. Unite have been irrelevant to this process, given the fact that they have so few members. Meanwhile, Accord had given up the ghost before the meetings at ACAS took place. In fact, they told staff that the last set of proposals were the Bank's final offer and encouraged their members, with help from the Bank, to support the revised terms and conditions. Many Accord members, realising that they were being sold down the river, voted against the terms and conditions and made it impossible for Accord to sign up to a collective agreement. Having suffered such a humiliating snub, Accord then sought to piggyback on our discussions at ACAS in the hope of getting some extra titbits which would enable them to announce a victory and then reach an agreement with the Bank. And that's exactly what they have done. (LTU *Newsletter*, 31 August 2010)

It's no good Unite and Accord saying [they] will continue the fight because as soon as they put pen to paper the fight was over and done with. Accord and Unite have fallen into that trap and tens of thousands of staff are going to see their final salary pensions wither on the vine. And lest we forget the Bank has admitted that the pension changes will save £1.1 billion and what did they give up for that saving [?] [A]n extra year's protection. (LTU *Newsletter*, 2 September 2010)

Last week Unite announced that it had accepted the Bank's new terms and conditions on behalf of their small number of members ... When announcing its consultative ballot result a few weeks ago, which overwhelmingly rejected the Bank's proposals on terms and conditions and pensions, Unite said that its members "deserved better". According to the results 86 and 66% of Unite members said they opposed the Bank's proposals on pensions and on terms and conditions. However, despite the overwhelming rejection of the Bank's proposals, Unite attended the ACAS talks with the specific intention of agreeing to whatever the Bank proposed. And all the Bank offered was extra protection of a year for loss of holidays, overtime and medical insurance. Unite asked members for their views and then ignored them completely. It seems that the Unite leadership have taken the cynical view to look after the interests of their members in HBoS and simply forget about their members in LTSB. Those members have been mugged and Unite are fully responsible. (LTU *Newsletter*, 7 September 2010)

The Bank has granted many Unite Representatives up to a month off their normal work duties to assist it with pressurising Lloyds TSB Staff into signing the new Contracts of Employment [so that] ... Unite [is] now effectively becoming an additional arm of the Bank's Human Resources Department, assisting it with pressurising staff into forfeiting their existing rights. (LTU *Newsletter*, 28 September 2010)

... with the connivance of Accord and their junior partner Unite, who both agreed to the new terms and conditions and pensions cap, the Bank was allowed to get away with not carrying out an Equality Impact Assessment on the new terms and conditions before they were introduced, something which is essential in a large organisation. (LTU *Newsletter*, 15 December 2010)

Inset 3.3: The War of Words—LTU Attacks Accord and Unite, Part 2

In 2011, LTU alleged that Unite and Accord consented to LBG 'stitching up' the process of nomination, selection and election for Member-nominated Trustee Directors (MNDs) on company pension schemes (LTU *Newsletter*, 24 October 2011, 23 November 2011). In 2013 and 2014, during an Employment Tribunal case on pay discrimination against women for not signing new contractual terms, LTU personally attacked the Accord's general secretary for appearing as LBG's 'star witness' (LTU *Newsletter*, 30 October 2013, 6 January 2014), saying:

We would be the first to admit that we criticised Accord for accepting the new terms and conditions of employment and through its actions allowing the Bank to divert attention from the pensions cap issue. However, that's completely different from siding with the employer in a legal case being taken by another Union, on behalf of its members, against that employer. (LTU *Newsletter*, 30 October 2013)

What we could never understand is why the General Secretary of Accord (the main union representing HBoS staff) would be supporting the Bank in a case LTU was fighting for so many staff?

There is no love lost between LTU and Unite but one can't help thinking that they would never have done such a thing. Siding with an employer on a legal case being taken by another Union is crossing the Rubicon for which there is no going back. Whatever his reasons, that decision will come to haunt the General Secretary of Accord for a long time to come, irrespective of the outcome of the case. (LTU *Newsletter*, 6 January 2014)

In a departure from standard accusation of being feckless, it charged that:

Debating motions calling for the nationalisation of Lloyds Banking Group which [Accord] did at [its] conference last week is a complete waste of time. The time for talking is over; the Bank has made its position clear. Whilst no one wanted to be in this position, the fact is we are and it's a case of fight or flight. Accord needs to decide whether it's a proper trade union or some modern day offshoot of the Tooting Popular Front, endlessly debating motions which nobody cares about. (LTU *Newsletter*, 31 March 2014)

But Accord was not the only target of criticism for LTU asserted that:

Accord and Unite have said very little following [LBG's] imposition of the freeze on pensionable pay. Unite, to quote a recent commentator, 'continue their vow of silence'. That's understandable given that they have very few members in HBoS and even fewer in Lloyds. Carrying out an industrial action ballot would require them to publish their membership number which is the last thing they want to do. Even if they did take industrial action, no one would notice. (LTU *Newsletter*, 31 March 2014)

It called the two unions 'HR approved unions' (LTU *Newsletter*, 12 August 2015, 3 September 2015, 28 September 2015, 21 October 2015,14 November 2016, 14 December 2016), 'bank approved unions' (LTU *Newsletter*, 6 April 2016), 'HR approved staff unions' (LTU *Newsletter*, 17 January 2017), 'favoured unions' (LTU *Newsletter*, 8 September 2015), 'in-house staff unions' (LTU *Newsletter*, 31 March 2017), and 'in-house unions' (LTU *Newsletter*, 28 July 2015) suggesting this 'demonstrat[ed] their total lack of independence' (LTU *Newsletter*, 28 September 2015). However, it was not long before LTU returned to concentrate its fire on Accord:

To sell your own members down the river is one thing but to then try and undermine a union that is fighting tooth and nail for its members is something completely different. … LTU's position may have been 'willy waving', to coin the phrase used by Accord, but you've got to be able to find your willy to wave it in the first place and they have shown consistently that they can't. (LTU *Newsletter*, 24 July 2015)

[W]hat favours did the Bank get in return for distributing the magazine and how can Accord, whose membership is significantly smaller than LTU's across the Group, ever claim to be an independent trade union if it takes financial handouts from the Bank? … Accord has had to produce literature that the Bank has approved. But it gets worse. Not content with using the Bank's resources to support what is supposed to be an independent union, the HR Director, Rupert McNeil, has written a letter accompanying Accord's magazine that reeks of desperation [to help Accord]. unions' (LTU *Newsletter*, 8 September 2015)

Ideological and Institutional Incorporation

On part of employers, partnership seeks to inculcate unions and workers with a particular version of a managerial ideology as part of a process of attitudinal restructuring whereby early incorporation of union representatives into company-initiated forums of consultation and social dialogue with management allow unions to better be able to understand how and why management acts as it does—with a view to gaining consent and agreement to these actions (see also Johnstone 2011). The most obvious evidence of the manifestation of this process at work is to consider the kind of arguments that unions make to management within these forums. Before doing so, and in order to avoid ahistoricism and decontextualisation, it is worth recalling that such arguments existed before the era of partnership (when staff associations, internalism and moderation were very influential), and these arguments are not the preserve alone of unions in the financial services sector. That said, the heightened centrality of what can be called 'business friendly' arguments to union orientations towards management, along with the frequency with which they are made, suggests that a new era may have been entered, especially with regard to Unite. Whether the use of these arguments is ideological, that is made out of conviction, or instrumental, that is made as a result of weakness, and what the balance between the two is will be addressed in the concluding chapter.

For the time being, some examples of the presence of an ideational influence of partnership can be found in Unite in insurance. So, at AXA, there was a fairly explicit acceptance by Unite that market conditions generally and specifically to AXA required only making reasonable demands and being sensible:

> We are under no illusions that these talks will be easy given the economic climate and the impact that it has on both employees and employer. However, we trust a pragmatic approach to the talks will allow us to reach a mutually acceptable agreement. ... The economic situation and the depressed market the company is trading in is such that costs are a major concern and will come under intense scrutiny and pressure to be reduced to ensure AXA remains profitable in the UK. (*Unite in AXA*, November 2010)

Yesterday's announcement of the Commercial Lines organisation review has a definite 'Back to the Future' quality about it as the company turns back the clock and reverts to a de-centralised branch structure for its Commercial Insurance organisation. Unfortunately the decision is not without a negative impact on employees as a number of jobs lost, many in management grades,. However, the restructure and empowerment of staff should see AXA able to regain its position in a highly competitive market and secure employees jobs for the future. Clearly a number of you will be very frustrated by the volte-face and angry about the impact has on colleagues who have worked hard for AXA in recent times. We share that frustration, least of all because we were never convinced with the previous Branch Transformation Project which closed a number of branches, increased the number of managers compared to staff and centralised work. However, it is pointless engaging in a blame game, the situation is now that AXA Commercial's gross written premium has fallen sharply and costs risen so action has to be taken to secure the long term viability of the commercial operation. (*Unite in AXA*, November 2010)

Outside of insurance, Unite (Unite press release, 8 July 2008) stated in 2008 of 300 job losses in Barclays that: 'Whilst the union understands that the market conditions mean that the 'First Plus' product is no-longer viable, we wholeheartedly condemn the decision to run down the Cardiff site' while of LBG job reductions in 2009, Accord (Accord press release, 15 June 2009) commented: 'We are always unhappy at any planned reduction in the roles and opportunities available—particularly in the current economic environment—even when we understand what the bank believes to be the commercial need for the changes. Accord challenges the rationale for every initiative to establish that the changes are focused on building a better bank for the future and not just cutting costs in a way that may undermine the business in the medium to long term'.

In regard of HBoS, Stuart et al. (2010: 56) reported: 'Accord and Unite have been working in partnership with the company on its business plans for ensuring it maintains and improves its productivity and competitiveness in the global financial services market. Both unions were looking to train and upskill their representatives in business understanding and the methods of partnership working' while Jameson

(2010: 11) noted: 'The business acumen of senior officials meant that unions were able to put forward a robust challenge which was valued by the business in confirming that they had considered every option' and quoted Accord's general secretary as saying: 'We certainly didn't get our own way all of the time and we weren't running the organisation … [but] I think we had real influence and I think we used it in a responsible way'. At CBG, in consulting its members on their pay demands in 2014, BSU commented: 'Obviously we cannot make any promises and, in light of the financial state of the company, we are not sure what can be done …' (BSU Newsletter, July 2014).

In Chap. 2, the depth of the implantation of the partnership ideology was evident. Yet, the limits to this were also apparent as already recounted in this chapter. The depth of the implantation of partnership ideology was evident for Advance and NGSU but the aforementioned limits to this were not. This was related to, in the former case, the status and practice of Santander being a 'challenger' bank, and in the latter case, the Nationwide remaining a building society. The earlier part of this section on partnership within LBG demonstrated the commitment of LTU to a particular form of partnership with capital allied to a general perspective of moderation. But with the absence of such partnership from the employer, LTU reacted by engaging in something more approximating to a 'hot' war of words and limited mobilisation. Ultimately, through derecognition LBG responded by, in effect, saying neither the partnership LTU sought nor how it responded to its absence were deemed acceptable.

The limits to partnership—or the limited influence of partnership—can also be found by virtue of many unions showing themselves to be adept at turning the 'business case' argument around and using it against management and employer—albeit often without much discernible effect on employer practice (see Chap. 4). Thus, Accord often made the argument that management actions were 'bad for business'. For example, it stated: 'The constant flow of job cuts across LBG must now be halted and staff be allowed to get on with delivering the high quality and impressive service they are so good at providing. The Lloyds management pursuit of this cuts' agenda is counter-productive in their aim of a successful business' (Accord press release, 12 October 2016) and 'This 'death by a thousand cuts' approach does nothing to give confidence to those who will be staying with the business, trying their best to meet customers' needs and help to sustain the group for the future' (*Guardian*, 13 October 2016). Meantime, LTU (*Newsletters* 10 November 2016, 23 March 2017) proffered that: 'cost reduction through shrinkage is largely a one-way street. It's the easy route to short-term profitability but there is a serious risk that a smaller community footprint, with reduced visibility, will cause damage that will be difficult to reverse. The current management team won't be around when any chickens come home to roost but most staff will be'. Indeed, from 2013 onwards, the argument that remaining workers were putting the banks back on the road to recovery and should be rewarded was frequently made but cut no ice as there were no mutual gains to be had it seemed. Unite has sought to do similarly as a selection of its headlines to its press releases indicate (see Inset 3.4). However, Unite also made the argument that employers were being incompetent and short-sighted in pursuing their own interests by 'losing' necessary skills and experience as a result of redundancies (Unite press releases, 27 November 2013, 2 September 2014).

Inset 3.4: Selection of Headlines to Unite Press Releases

Lloyds staff deserve recognition for putting the bank on the road to recovery (1 March 2013)

Reward Lloyds staff for putting the Horse back in the black (1 August 2013)

Profitable RBS should end the jobs 'slash-and-burn' culture, says Unite (2 August 2013)

Staff should share in HSBC's jump in profits, says Unite (5 August 2013)

Aviva profits boost case for greater job security, says Unite (8 August 2013)

Lloyds must ensure staff contribution recognised as profits increase (29 October 2013)

Confirmation of over 1000 job cuts at Lloyds Banking Group is further blow for staff (28 January 2014)

Barclays boosts bonuses while slashing staff (11 February 2014)

Reckless incompetence cost 1000 jobs at the Co-op Bank (30 April 2014)

8000 job cuts at HSBC show staff are being punished for boardroom misconduct (9 June 2015)

700 job cuts at Lloyds 'exposes the myth' that we're in this together (1 July 2015)

Capita urged to drop 'derisory' pay plans as profits surge (27 July 2016)

Lloyds accused of cutting 'too far too fast' as Unite demands jobs guarantees (28 July 2016)

The peril of ideological incorporation outlined above is complemented by the peril for unions of procedural or institutional incorporation, whereby unions become something akin to subcontracted resolvers of managerially created problems. This is not to suggest that they become dependent appendages of management, for to do so would undermine their own *raison d'etre* and membership support base (notwithstanding any management subsidy). Yet it is to indicate that once inside the various fora of micro-social dialogue, there is—as Unite national officer, Rob MacGregor (interview, 7 September 2016) commented—'a danger of too much involvement to extent that we can end up doing the employer's job for them—but the bind is that it is also in members' interest for us to try to mitigate the impact of employers' action—so it can be a difficult tightrope to walk'. Recalling the analysis of Accord and Advance in Chap. 2, there was evidence of this sub-contracted function. Fellow Unite national officer, Dominic Hook (interview, 6 September 2016), recounted that at Barclays the union 'had been drawn into the minutia of decision making, which can have 'good' and 'bad' outcomes [because] we are part of the decision-making process. This means we have to take responsibility where the outcomes are not seen to be 'good' by members but where they are seen as 'good', it shows that we got in early to influence things and make them better'. Unlike some other unions, Unite did not issue joint statements with employers, with Rob MacGregor (interview, 7 September 2016) stressing that despite the aforementioned danger, Unite maintained its independence as evidenced by its membership communications in regard of their tone, content and emphasis of communication, stating that the union would only issue an erratum if 'a fact was wrong … the banks don't like being badly portrayed and they have their sensitivities such as being described as [internationally] offshoring of work without the loss of jobs [domestically]'.

Whilst different unions can be placed at different points on a spectrum with regard to the extent to which they were subject to, and subjected themselves to, ideological and institutional incorporation, the general extent of both was limited by the continuing and underlying conflict of interests between capital and labour over the division of the fruits of their joint endeavours (and which itself had not been eradicated by partnership). Indeed, the expressions of this sharpened in the post-crash period as the abundance of fruits and any associated munificence declined sharply. For example, as the next chapter demonstrates, maintaining one's employment came at an increasing cost in terms of longer working hours and harsher performance management regimes.

Velvet Gloves and Iron Fists

One indication of the prevalence of partnership within the financial services sector in both *de jure* and *de facto* terms has been that there were only three instances of victimisation of union activists (see Gall 2013 for an overview). The first was a senior Unite representative working for Steria in Barclaycard. In late 2008, the rep was sacked for the inappropriate use of an internal telephone line. While accepting this wrongdoing, Unite believed his summary dismissal for gross misconduct was disproportionate and sought his re-instatement on a reduced punishment. The second was another Steria Unite rep working in Cooperative Financial Services in late 2008, where he was selected for compulsory redundancy. The third was at HSBC between 2013 and 2015 and concerned a senior lay Unite activist who was a member of Unite's Executive Council and the chair of its national company committee in the company. Therefore, the need on the part of the employers to decapitate oppositional workplace unionism though such victimisation—as a part of a strategy of 'forceful opposition' (Bain 1970)—was not perceived to exist to any great extent, although it should be noted that two of the cases of victimisation took place within a part of the financial services sector where strategic leverage is easier to generate and exercise though industrial action (see Chap. 4). Moreover, the limited development of oppositionalism per se within the trajectory of growing 'unionateness' can be read as both a cause and consequence of partnership. Indeed, many of the staff associations that transmogrified into independent unions sought to encourage members to come forward to take up positions of being workplace representatives with arguments about developing their skills, careers and understanding of the business they worked in albeit these were made alongside other arguments above achieving fairness and justice for colleagues (see Chap. 2).

Partnership and Organising

As alluded to before, both the strength and ideological disposition of union organisation have strong bearings upon the ability of labour unionism in the sector to provide effective representation for members' collective interests. A key foundation for union strength is to be found in the practice of union organising. Partnership has a number of implications for union organising, some of which may be seen as positive and others as negative. For example, access to staff at induction for recruitment, legitimated status with and within the employing organisation, provision of facility time and so on may be seen as some of the more positive aspects (although critical voices may suggest they are equally indicative of an overly close relationship). The tension there is over the (ideological) nature of partnership. However, the structure of partnership itself is equally important and, in this respect, it has strong parallels with the impact of traditionally centralised company-level bargaining upon local bargaining and the opportunities for workplace unionism and workplace organising. In the context that pay and conditions of employment could not be bargained over at the local level given that these were set at the national company level, the issues for bargaining were largely confined to interpretation of these or matters with a local complexion over which local management had discretion. The impact of this was to limit the extent to which workplace unionism could develop and concomitant re-inforce tendencies for members to see their relationship with their union as a servicing-orientated one (see also Gall 2008). Where this was not so resulted from identifying, via members and workers, issues of grievance which could then lead to agitation and mobilisation. For example, a former Unite shop steward (interview, 19 September 2016) reflected of his workplace:

> Our campaigns were relevant to our members as it was them who mostly informed us of the issues they faced. When it was required, I certainly agitated the membership over issues to develop a sense of collectivism. For me campaigns do not have to have a material win, it is about being realistic [and] educational campaigns are just as important ... There are definitely some local issues which can be bargained over but this depends

on the management style and approach on a site to site basis and the strength of the union. Locally, we won a number of issues on site such as improved facilities for staff ([like]... vending machines), the removal of 'name and shame' boards, the scrapping of local policies implemented by management etc. ... What we achieved was not done through 'partnership' meetings but rather the mobilisation of the membership. It was clear to me at the start that local partnership where a complete waste of time as there was no capacity to negotiate. Local partnership served the interest of the business not the union. If there was an issue that needed negotiated in would be on the terms set by the reps, we would call the meeting and control the narrative.

Process of Pay Determination: Performance Management

Previous research identified the widespread use of PRP to determine the pay increases of individual employees (see, for example, Marginson et al. 2008). Indeed, Van Wanrooy et al. (2013: 24), surveying the results of the 2011 *Workplace Employment Relations Study* (WERS6), found the usage of payment by results was higher in the financial services sector (65%) than elsewhere in the private sector overall (25%). However, union influence still existed. For example, Arrowsmith et al. (2010: 2735) commented: 'Unions retain collective bargaining over the aggregate 'pay pot' and in many cases the actual distribution, with most employees getting much the same pay award' with Marginson et al. (2008: 337) stating: 'In all but [one of our six case studies in finance] unions are able to negotiate over the actual percentage allocations attached to appraisal ratings or across a pay matrix, in addition to the broad parameters of the pay pot. In this way unions are able to secure at least RPI for employees rated average or above in their appraisal— in other words, most of the workforce' while Gall (2008: 7) recorded: 'Collective bargaining on annual pay rises has been replaced by individual performance-related pay where the union/staff association role is relegated to trying to influence the size of the total sum available to fund performance related increases and the implementation of the schemes, i.e. assessments'. Since those studies were conducted, the situation has worsened considerably for the collective determination of the process of deciding pay rises. This has occurred as result of (i) employers increasingly playing hardball in negotiations over the size of the 'pay pot', and (ii) the increasing use of tighter and more rigid performance management system which deploy 'forced distribution' and 'market matrices' where unions have almost no influence on the distribution of pay awards to individuals.

This section examines how unions have responded and often sought to contest the process of pay determination in the form of performance management systems vis-à-vis the processes employed, concerning issues of transparency and fairness, while the next chapter examines the outcomes and impacts of performance management. Performance management systems were introduced in the 1990s and 2000s in the financial services sector and constantly refined as a result of economic and sector shocks as well as mergers and acquisitions (Taylor 2013). In a study including fieldwork between 2010 and 2011 and covering five banks and three insurers, Taylor (2013: 42) argued: 'The recession subsequently provided the context and justification for organizations to accelerate and intensify existing programmes and practices of intensive micro-measurement and management'. Among the most detested components of the post-crash performance management systems used by employers in the financial services sector (especially in banking) are 'forced distribution' and 'market matrices', while others have been the use of sales targets, ranking against colleagues and customer satisfaction surveys. The result of 'forced distribution' by using a standard bell curve in performance rankings leads to (i) the assessments of ratings arising from annual appraisals being subsequently fitted into a set of pre-ordained categories (such as Top performer/Strong performer/Good performer/Developing performer/Under-performer) either by those carrying out the appraisals or by managers senior to the appraisers where each category has already been determined to contain a set number of staff; and (ii) the bottom 10% of performers are put on performance improvement plans (PIPs) as a prelude to being 'managed out' of the business. Once these are 'managed out', the 10% above them become the new next worse performers even though the average of performance may have been improved. In terms of determining the actual pay award for each individual, the categorisation such as Top performer/Strong performer/Good performer/Developing performer/Under-performer (or see Table 4.1) is then mapped onto a market matrix whereby depending upon the assessment of where an individual employee's existing salary (grade and spine point) sits, the category rating will be applied differentially. It is these two combined components which differentiate performance management systems from the PRP which existed before in the sector.

In LBG as elsewhere, Unite's policy position on the PRP that resulted from performance management was that it 'opposed to this form of reward. We do not believe that, whatever good intentions … [LBG] may have, this means of reward can be operated entirely fairly or transparently. We know, from the evidence of many studies and the experience of our members, that PRP does not promote overall business performance' (Unite LBG newsletter, May 2016). Earlier it argued:

An enforced bell curve in Performance Management occurs when a company insists that the performance ratings are forced into predetermined performance distribution approach. This requires a specific percentage for each rating category to be achieved – through ranking techniques that lead to people being moved up/down rating categories – regardless of whether people have achieved the standards expected. (Unite Barclays *newsletter*, January 2015)

The big problem is that score card reviews rank you against your colleagues rather than considering you on your own merits. This leads to what's known as the 'bell curve' which produces artificial winners and losers even if everyone is performing well. This happens when companies insist on fitting everyone's rating into a predetermined range, where only a certain percentage of us can achieve top ratings. This creates an artificial top and bottom 10%, so even if you've hit all of your goals for the year you may lose out just because other people in your department have performed just as well or slightly better. (Unite LBG magazine, *The Spark*, Autumn 2015)

This resulted in Unite calling for the abolition of performance management systems altogether (as it did at AXA in 2013 even where forced distribution was not used). However, given that it was the smallest of the three unions within LBG and that financial services sector workers were difficult to mobilise, Unite was in practice forced to deal with the actuality of performance management, deprioritising its principled opposition to the system of performance and instead dealing with its symptoms and consequences. (However, in a small number of other companies like Prudential, Unite did act upon its policy by every year asking for an across-the-board rise plus merit even if the result was the same as elsewhere, namely, trying to negotiate effectively upon the size of available pay pot and the principles by which it is distributed so that most employees receive a minimum rise.)

So Unite, like Accord and LTU, campaigned against the application of performance management in terms of its transparency and fairness with regard to process and outcome. Two of their particular campaigning aims were to end the use of 'forced distribution' and to delink performance measures from targets (whether sales or customer ratings). LTU expressed concerns that so-called 'poor performers' could be managed out of the door and increasingly quickly (LTU *Newsletter*, 6 March 2012). Given that 'forced distribution' occurs when employees are placed into performance categories which have already been assigned to hold a set proportion of staff, leading to individual assessments being changed in order to fit the assigned proportions, Accord, for example, argued: 'The performance management, recognition and reward systems have to be aligned to ensure that some staff are not rewarded for 'pushing products' whilst others are threatened about poor performance if they are genuinely committed to customer service and only sell to customer needs' (*My Accord*, Summer 2011). And, as far back as 2008, Accord was seeking to end the use of league tables and their open publication (Accord press release, 13 July 2008). Meantime, just prior to the creation of LBG, LloydsTSB signed a three-year pay deal with LTU (in 2008), with an agreed pay formula of market movement plus 1% for performance and a joint review of the performance management system with the aim of producing a clearer link between pay and performance and the most appropriate pay distribution process. Overall, the unions in LBG (Accord, LTU, Unite) called for the performance measurements, and the organisational culture surrounding them, to be less output based and to take cognisance of the behavioural inputs so that the outcomes were fairer to workers and more ethical in terms of preventing mis-selling. To this end they took the opportunity to lobby the Financial Services Authority (FSA)[9] which was tasked with regulating the financial services sector's use of incentives in the wake of the personal protection insurance (PPI) mis-selling scandal (see, for example, LTU *Newsletter*, 26 November 2012).

Years of unions' dialogue with LBG on performance management finally led in 2013 to minor improvements in regard of fairness and transparency of ratings whereby (i) the distribution curve was not to be 'forced' but rather 'expected' so allowing more capacity for 'good performers' to be rewarded as such (60 up to 70%) and fewer to be forced into the 'developing' category (15 down to 5%); (ii) the re-introduction of the previous emphasis on how staff achieve their objectives and not just a focus upon how much they achieve in terms of targets; and (iii) enhanced training and support for line managers carrying out the performance reviews to reduce bias (including the provision of 150 coaches) (Unite LBG newsletter, May 2013; *My Accord*, Spring 2013). However, Unite, for example, did not make progress on a range of its other demands such as abolishing the calibration process whereby distant senior managers made final decisions on performance ratings; introducing 360° feedback for managers to ensure greater accountability; and reducing the time and resources spent upon performance management so that customers could be better served. And, a harmonised performance improvement policy was imposed unilaterally in 2012 (Accord press release, 6 March 2012). A similarly limited delinking of performance measures from targets was achieved in TSB in 2015 (*My AccordTSB*, December 2015). Union action took the form of lobbying the employer in meetings and negotiation by deploying mutual gains arguments underpinned by the number of individual appeals against ratings. LTU continued its campaigning as it became apparent that a high level (in excess of 60%) of different staff groups not meeting targets indicated the targets were unrealistic (LTU *Newsletter*, 9 April 2014), and that new targets of meetings/calls with customers to review their banking needs became more pronounced (and were used in office and regional league tables) (LTU *Newsletter*, 26 June 2014). Towards the end of 2014, LBG also removed income, products and customer needs targets and ended peer comparison in order to focus upon customers, people and risk measures (LTU *Newsletter*, 26 September 2014). Concomitant, the variable pay system was changed to become based entirely on customer feedback measures, although the policy of asking customers in branches to rate staff in 2016 was ended (Accord press release, 22 July 2016). While welcoming this, LTU stated it was:

> not about to get dewy-eyed about any of these changes and the proof of the pudding will always be in the eating but the move from outputs to inputs, if that's what happens in practice, is sending the right messages about what's going to be important in future. However, if we start to see activity or customer service league tables being produced or emails from RDs criticising staff for not having enough lending appointments in their diaries then we will have no hesitation in publishing those in future Newsletters. (LTU *Newsletter*, 26 September 2014)

Unite believed that 'new 'customer needs' targets ... are nothing more than a dressing up of sales targets for frontline staff and could lead to scandals similar to PPI and mortgage endowments', adding '[i]n response, LBG undertook to make scorecards balanced to avoid this'(Unite LBG newsletter, June 2013). Indeed, Unite stated in late 2015 that:

> Major employers elsewhere in the finance sector are now moving away from PRP, most recently RBS. Unite will continue to argue that the best way for Lloyds Banking Group to deal with performance is through managing exception [presumed to mean 'expectations'] with support and training. However, while we have not been able to achieve the removal of PRP in LBG, we recognise that progress has been made and we will continue to work with the Bank to replace performance pay approaches with coaching and team-working. (Unite LBG magazine, *The Spark*, Autumn 2015)

This remained true despite in 2016 LBG standardising the way in which staff were paid under the variable pay schemes by basing variable pay on an individual's balanced scorecard rating, rather than solely on customer feedback. And, LTU believed that its similar warnings were validated with evidence of the continued use of targets (LTU *Newsletter*, 4 February 2015), 'unrealistic and irreconcilable targets' (LTU *Newsletter*, 30 August 2016), and 'forced distribution' (LTU *Newsletter*, 8 May 2012)[10] afterwards.

Turning to other employers, in Barclays campaigning by Unite led to the company issuing a statement in late 2013, saying 'we will not 'force' the distribution of a performance curve' (Unite Barclays newsletter, January 2015) and followed by an instruction to managers, stating: 'Last week's message from our Group Executive Committee highlighted two important changes to the Performance Management process: we will not 'force' the distribution of a performance curve within Barclays; and no manager will be asked to change the rating of an individual's performance to achieve a 'forced curve'' (Unite Barclays *newsletter*, January 2015). By early 2015, Unite reported to its members:

[we have] had only a small number of managers contacting the union in situations where they have felt they were being pressurised to reduce the ratings of their team to conform to a 'Bell Curve', as opposed to altering individual ratings as part of the consistency process. We have responded by pointing them to the statements from the Group Executive and supporting them in arguing their case. Happily they have been successful in challenging the position and maintaining the ratings for their staff. (Unite Barclays *newsletter*, January 2015)

Prior to this, Unite had some success in Barclays, CBG and HSBC in reducing the dependence of performance criteria upon meeting sales target and replacing these with customer satisfaction ratings. This was also true in RBS (see Chap. 4). However, as Unite national officer, Dominic Hook (interview, 6 September 2016), acknowledged the move away from such sales and target regimes was the result of political pressure from the FSA, itself acting under pressure from the government which needed to be seen to be compelling the financial services sector to 'get its house in order' after its role in creating the financial crash. In late 2012, the FSA (2012: 5) stated: 'We know that the way sales staff are paid influences how and what they sell to consumers and can encourage a culture of mis-selling'. In Zurich, UFS campaigned to increase the levels of transparency on salary ranges and the process by which staff were assigned to these within the company's performance management system. Even in 'challenger' bank, Santander, with quite a supine bargaining partner in Advance, there was a high level of membership disquiet and concern over the use of performance management and the use of disciplinary procedures to deal with alleged under-performance (*Advance* members' magazine, Summer 2012 and Spring 2015). Thus, a 2014 Advance survey showed on an 80% response rate considerable overall levels of disquiet and concern over the pay system while in 2012, Advance argued there was an increasingly common but unjustified and unnecessary use of disciplinary measures to deal with mistakes. It lamented that this is no way for management to get the best out of people in order to create a successful business.

Bonuses

Running alongside the use of PRP to erode the significance of collective bargaining over pay has been the rise of the 'bonus culture'. For the overwhelming majority of staff, bonuses at between 5 and 10% of salaries became significant and integral parts of overall earnings or remuneration. In many cases, unions can—as with the PRP pot—negotiate over the size of the bonus without being able to influence its distribution thereafter, which is based on performance criteria. The move towards PRP and bonuses underpins the use of the language of 'reward' rather than wages or salary.

Union Recognition and Derecognition

Until 2007, unions had shown an ability to gradually extend their organisational rights by gaining new union recognition agreements on the periphery of their main and longstanding agreements (see Gall 2008: 115, 132). Between 2000 and 2007, 36 new recognition agreements were gained to add to the 31 secured between 1990 and 1999. Although derecognition was not unheard of it, it was not prevalent in any significant measure. However, this still meant that there were many newer areas of operations, particularly with regard to investment banking and new players, which employers kept 'union free' using union avoidance methods or for which there was no latent demand for unionisation. Yet the tendency for gradual extension of recognition has since 2007 rather been thrown into rather sharp reverse for few new agreements have been gained, some of the new agreements were essentially re-affirmations of existing agreements following outsourcing, and there were proportionately more cases of derecognition (including the major case of LTU in LBG) than before. This section charts these developments. But before moving to this, it is worth stressing that these developments in recognition, derecognition and non-recognition have a part to play in accounting for the fall in the percentage of staff whose pay is determined by collective bargaining from 31% in 2007 to 23% by 2015 (see Table 2.3). This is the case even if it is difficult to be precise given the impact of performance management and management intransigence in negotiations upon the existence and practice of collective bargaining. In the wider sense, the means of co-determinating the terms of the employment relationship have contracted even further since the financial crash so that employer power is ever more in the ascendancy (notwithstanding that partnership working can also be viewed as extending employer power). For many observers, the continued contraction of collective bargaining (as per the proxy of bargaining on pay) will seem highly paradoxical in that the period since 2007 has been a time when collective bargaining has been most needed to protect the pay and conditions of workers in the financial services sector.

Accord signed its first union recognition agreements outside LBG in 2011 (Equitable Life Assurance Society) and in 2014 (Communisis). Both were formerly linked to the pre-merger constituents of LBG. Just before its formal acquisition by Sabadell in early 2015, Accord and Unite signed a new recognition agreement with TSB, taking the form of a partnership agreement. LTU was not party to this agreement so was effectively derecognised. This was a result of its increasingly fraught relationship with LBG and LTU's demand that the union with the largest membership, namely, itself, have more influence in negotiations than the other recognised unions, namely, Accord and Unite. Later the same year, Accord and Unite also signed a new partnership-based recognition with LBG. It was the result of 3 years' discussions which sought to design a new agreement to replace that of 2008 (Accord press release, 14 July 2015). According to Accord, it sought to 'build a collaborative and co-operative relationship with the other unions … [with t]he objective was to enable all of the unions to enhance their combined influence with the Group in the interests of all employees, increase total union membership and effectiveness, cut out wasteful rivalry and promote trade union solidarity. … The relationship between [LBG] and [Accord and Unite] is underpinned by a commitment to joint problem solving, meaningful dialogue and an agreement to seek viable solutions in support of the Group's strategy. This collaborative approach continues to recognise the independence of Accord and Unite and their objectives of protecting and promoting employment across the Group' (Accord press release, 14 July 2015). Critically, the new agreement meant that 'from now on, [Accord and Unite] will negotiate on behalf of all employees in [LBG]' (Accord press release, 14 July 2015). Unite heralded the new agreement in similar terms as 'an important milestone in our long relationship with LBG … provid[ing] a clear framework for LBG and Unite to work together positively on a wide range of issue to reach mutually acceptable outcomes—that's good for our members and it's good for LBG. The Group have committed to negotiating and consulting with Unite on issues including pay, grading and salary structures, job security, holiday entitlements, core hours of work, overtime and performance management' (Unite LBG magazine, *The Spark*, Autumn 2015). Unite was also keen to stress that LTU 'can no longer represent you on any collective issues such as pay, terms or conditions' (Unite LBG magazine, *The Spark*, Autumn 2015). Following the agreement, Unite reported that five workplace reps have been elected by the membership to work for Unite in LBG full-time (Unite LBG magazine, *The Spark*, Autumn 2015). A year later, Unite reported: 'Unite and Accord have been engaged in discussing … changes with the Bank in a collaborative, open and frank manner over an extended period, which has been a step forward in our engagement with [LBG]. The Bank has given commitments to working closely with Unite and Accord on monitoring how these changes work in practice. We expect to continue our engagement with [LBG] throughout 2016' (Unite LBG newsletter, Summer 2016). The response of LTU to derecognition by LBG was laid out earlier in this chapter.

As alluded to above, cases of derecognition were not unheard of in the financial services sector. For example, in 1989, the Midland derecognised MSF so that BIFU became the sole recognised union, MSF was derecognised by Abbey when it acquired Scottish Mutual in 1992, Amicus was derecognised by Abbey when took over Scottish Provident in 2001, and ANGU derecognised by General Electric when Abbey sold it First National Bank in 2003. These cases and others were either instances of the 'streamlining'—from an employers' point of view—of recognition and collective bargaining arrangements or complete derecognition of any union. In all cases, the numbers affected were relatively small. It is this context which makes derecognition of LTU by LBG so unusual in terms of being carried out by one of the biggest employers in the sector and affecting so many workers. The explanation for this idiosyncrasy was to be found in the particular context of partnership and inter-union relations within LBG. First Direct, owned by HSBC, also derecognised Unite in 2016.

Meanwhile, in 2015, Unite gained recognition for staff in Cofunds following its acquisition by Legal and General, where it already had recognition. Recognition in Cofunds replaced a staff forum. However, Unite was unsuccessful in 2008 in gaining recognition through an application to the Central Arbitration Committee for its members at Capita Life and Pensions, the former Scottish Amicable/Prudential Craigforth site, in Stirling, where a staff forum served as a non-union form of collective representation. The application was rejected for not providing evidence of majority support for collective bargaining (Central Arbitration Committee TUR1/648/2008). Yet Unite continued its campaign and won voluntary recognition covering the 750 workers in 2010 after persuading the company to concede to an ACAS conducted recognition ballot which it won with a 97% vote for on a 60% turnout. Just prior to this, in 2007, Capita and Unite signed a

partnership agreement for the sites where Unite already had union recognition. Meanwhile, in 2007 Unite signed a new recognition agreement with AXA, encompassing AXA Insurance, AXA Life, AXA Shared
Services and AXA UK so that there was just one agreement for AXA.
On the back of this, Unite was able to gain recognition for AXA's Derry
Service Centre in Northern Ireland. And, in 2008, Unite secured recognition for former Cap Gemini staff which were TUPE'd into Prudential,
and recognition for Steria workers working in Cooperative Financial
Services in Skelmersdale in 2008. As a result of organising LBG's Speke
contact centre, Unite gained recognition for the site in 2012. Using
the Central Arbitration Committee statutory route, Unite won recognition at the National Bank of Greece in 2016 with an automatic
award, given that of the 30 staff 70% were union members (CAC case
TUR1/962/2016). By contrast, and as with its predecessor, Amicus,
Unite was unable to make inroads into Standard Life, this being all the
harder with the revitalisation of VIVO from 2008 onwards. The same
was true at Direct Line Insurance Group (which also owns Churchill
and Green Flag insurance companies) and the FSA until its abolition.[11]
Finally, in 2010, Unite sought union recognition for the middle managers at HSBC following imposition new contractual terms but recorded
no success in this.

Aegis, in 2013–2014, was unsuccessful in gaining union recognition
through a Central Arbitration Committee application at JLT Benefit
Solutions for around 100 ex-Aegon employees who transferred across
(CAC case TUR1/862/2014). When the bargaining unit was determined, it was wider than that of the former Aegon employees and in
this situation the application did not then pass validity test of membership and support thresholds. JLT operated a staff forum as an alternative to union recognition. Elsewhere, the CWU has been able to extend
its recognition rights into Santander subsidiaries, namely, ISBAN
(2013), Geoban (2014) and Produban (2014). In 2013, recognition
was gained for ISBAN after the CWU made a request for recognition
under the statutory procedure managed by the Central Arbitration
Committee. After talks with the CAC and the assistance of ACAS, the
CWU reached a voluntary agreement which provides that all ISBAN
staff, numbering around forty, that transferred from the Alliance and

Leicester under TUPE now have collective bargaining rights. In the other two cases, recognition was agreed without recourse to the CAC. In the case of Produban, the bargaining unit was just 14 members of senior management staff. It should be noted here that there is no evidence of ballots for industrial action—or their threats—being used to try to exert leverage over the bank.

Finally, it is important to cover the aspect of non-recognition in addition to movements in recognition and derecognition. Recalling the decline in the coverage of collective bargaining on pay in the financial services sector in Table 2.3, and using this as the best available proxy for the extent of union recognition, it becomes clear that the largest part of the sector is that without coverage of union recognition. Unite's (2008) Organising Support Unit report highlighted that such areas within banking include the specialist, non-retail banks and within insurance the newer entrants to the marketplace. For all the unions—but especially Unite as the only substantial example of a sector-wide, multi-institutionally organising union—the scale of the organising challenge (see Chap. 2) is again indicated by the extent of non-recognition, particularly given its association with non-unionism. There is no evidence that employers have created substantial alternative means of collective interest representation in these non-union organisations.

European Works Councils

Like other unions elsewhere, unions in the financial services sector have sought to augment their national bargaining and representational resources with the assistance of those resources gained from participating in EWCs. However, while seen as beneficial and useful, there has been no sense in which these additional resources have made a crucial or critical difference to the balance of power or to prevent employers from proceeding as they originally intended. A very small number of exceptions to this 'rule of thumb' exist whereby, as a result of the greater familiarity of domestic unions with their continental counterparts, British unions have been able to persuade their European sister unions to lobby on their behalf with employers which are based in mainland Europe.

Collective Mobilisation

The premise for examining the nature of the challenges facing unions which seek to collectively mobilise their membership in order to try to co-determine the terms and conditions of the employment relationship through collective bargaining is that political and legal methods—as alternative means of action—are of limited utility to them. The vast majority of unions organising in the sector are not affiliated to any political party and those that are (Community, CWU, Unite and USDAW) faced a number of difficulties in exercising political power. First, and notwithstanding that common cause can be made with other sections of memberships within their unions, the financial services sector memberships of these unions are not in commanding positions to influence union policy and priorities with regard to a number of specific issues affecting the workforces within the financial services sector (such as performance management, and 'nationalisation'). Second, and setting that aside, in any case the exclusion of the Labour Party from government since 2010 and its inability to act as an effective opposition, has not provided these affiliated unions with much in the way of political leverage. This situation had not changed with the election of Jeremy Corbyn to the leadership of the party from September 2015. Third, and notwithstanding that change in party leadership, the Labour Party has not been a social democratic (let alone socialist) political party which has been open to overtures to control and regulate the behaviour of employers over and above certain minima and basic standards. With regard to legal means of redress, the Employment Tribunal system remains the main tool available to workers and their supporting unions. Despite some changes (such as the introduction of fees for making applications and the requirement of using ACAS early conciliation prior to making applications), the Employment Tribunal system continues to be predicated upon delivering restorative justice in a reactive manner and is not generally amenable to being used as a means of pro-active, pre-emptive bargaining. Other than disclosure of information to undertake collective bargaining—subject to a successful application to the Central Arbitration Committee—there are no legal recourses to assist unions in bargaining. Even where statutory union recognition has been granted, there is neither a duty to bargain nor a duty to bargain fairly obligation, and statutory union recognition is limited to a small number of issues. More pertinently, the overwhelming majority of union recognition agreements in the sector are voluntary ones. Therefore, in the same vein as European Works Councils, both political and legal means should at best be viewed as compliments to collective bargaining rather than alternatives or substitutes to it. This section now turns to examine the nature of the challenges for membership mobilisation to underpin the pursuit of union demands within the process of collective bargaining.

Given the prevalence of partnership working, it is worth re-iterating that membership mobilisation (especially in the form of industrial action) does not sit well with the spirit and letter of partnership. In terms of obstacles and barriers to mobilisation, certainly of a more deep-seated and extensive kind, this must be considered to be one of the first, and primary, ones. In addition to the influence of partnership on union arguments which may have a demobilising impact in terms of their appeal to reason (see earlier), it is worth recalling the comment of the NGSU general secretary: 'We have never called a ballot for industrial action and our relationship with Nationwide is such that I can't imagine the circumstances when we would' (*Rapport* magazine, Winter 2015). This perspective is salient for unions like Advance, Aegis, BSU, LBSSA, LUBBSA, SUWBBS and UFS (see Chap. 2) as well as the sections of Unite membership in building societies as a result of mergers and transfers of engagements through its predecessors, BIFU and UNIFI (see Gall 2008). It may also be more salient for some of Unite's national company committees (see Chap. 2). Accord, LTU and Unite appear to be less influenced in this way given their limited attempts at collective mobilisation.

Moving on from this, there are factors separate from, and not directly linked to, the influence of partnership which account for and explain the paucity of collective mobilisation in the post-financial crash period. These can best be examined by considering how the development of grievances was affected by the cost/benefits analyses of union members especially with regard to job cuts and severance packages, and recalling the discussion in Chap. 2 concerning the impact of atomisation and fragmentation.

While Unite continued to object to the unfolding development of what it saw as the deleterious policies of LBG, it often found it was unable to make substantial progress in delaying, stopping or reversing them because its membership was unprepared to act collectively in the desired manner of mobilisation. Of course, its absolute and relative numerical weakness was a factor. The Organising Support Unite report in late 2008 put Unite membership at c. 11,000 (19%) in LloydsTSB and c. 6000 (11%) in HBoS (Unite 2008: 4), and thus 13% in what would become LBG in 2009. So, for example, in early 2013, it called upon LBG to review its job loss strategy and cease the continuous stream of job losses, extend the current JSAs, give staff the confidence and security that 'they won't be next', and end the increasing use of agency staff to fill needs whilst redundancies continued. In doing so, it argued the LBG's growth and success could not and would not be achieved by continuous and damaging job cuts and the loss of hard-working and loyal staff as well as that casualisation of the workforce and undermines colleagues' future job security. Here, it was deploying arguments concerning the independent interests of workers as well as those of mutual gains.

But when it came to putting pressure on LBG to these ends, Unite was without much in the way of leverage as a result of the resource of its members. Its members did act but not as was needed or wished for. An indication of this was the 2013 pay settlement. In early 2013, Unite registered a second failure to agree following the outcome of its consultative exercise where members rejected LBG's final pay offer of 1.75% (which was the lowest of all the pay offers made by the major financial services sector employers and financial losses were incurred as a result of PPI misspelling fines) when Unite made a claim for 4%.[12] Unite then sought the option of ACAS conciliation. Although it was likely to have taken this particular course anyway, Unite was unable to do much more given that, although in the consultative exercise of members, 91% of those taking part rejected the final offer and 69% stated they would consider industrial action on the matter, the turnout was 'extremely low' (Unite LBG newsletter, May 2013). No progress was made at ACAS on any parts of Unite's claim for LBG insisted that it believed that the current offer was reasonable after posting a loss and that 96% of staff would receive a pay increase. The pay rise was then imposed. In this example, the membership did act *en masse* by not participating in the consultative ballot. There may have been a number of reasons for the decision to behave in a manner of collective inaction but it was unlikely that they did not include reasons of cost-benefit analysis (such as not being prepared to lose pay to gain a small increase) and opportunity to act (pay not being seen as a significant grievance). In terms of deleterious changes to final salary pensions in LBG, 93% of respondents believed that 'an attack on one set of colleagues is an attack on all' (Unite LBG newsletter, January 2014) but this did not lead to any collective mobilisation on the issue. Again calculations of cost and benefit to action as well as the impact of the fragmentation of the membership played their roles.

In LBG, as elsewhere, Unite was, at best, able to 'knock off the rough edges' of company policy by engagement through the institutions of partnership by using a mutual gains agenda, and internal and external campaigning to affect corporate reputation (see Chap. 3). Where management practice diverged from company policy, its role was to gain enforcement through lobbying (see Chap. 2 with regard to the same role for other unions). The (internal) institutions of partnership comprised the rights to information, consultation, negotiation and social dialogue. Unite, like other unions, had little in the way of external resources to draw upon such as political support (see earlier) or legal regulation or redress. Pursuit of a mutual gains agenda saw Unite try to convincingly align company objectives with employee interests (see above). The arguments concerned providing good pay and conditions as well as satisfying jobs to recruit, retain and motivate staff. For example, Unite policy was that PRP, such as performance management, does 'not promote overall business performance' (Unite LBG newsletter, May 2016). But given the clash between these and the primacy given to those aims and objectives of the company by management and which could be enforced as result of the imbalance in power and resources, progress was slow and limited, often representing compromises where Unite gained some of but very far from all it wanted. Moreover, in a period when cost reduction through redundancy was at its keenest, the argument over recruitment and retention was not a powerful one. Indeed, the threat of redundancy was of use to the employer as a 'stick' (and not 'carrot') to compel performance. The combination of membership weakness regarding mobilisation and incorporation into the ideology and institutions of partnership compelled Unite to operate in a technocratic manner whereby it used membership surveys as a way of getting information from members on their views on issues and which was then presented to management as a force to limited compel to action with.

Despite approaching the issue from a different perspective (see earlier), LTU found it had similar problems. It encouraged oppositionalism amongst its members by saying, for example: 'The thing that is going to have to change is the feeling amongst staff that they are passive bystanders and the Bank has some inalienable right to walk all over them whenever it chooses to do so. It doesn't and 'things can stay the way they are' but for that [change] to happen staff are going to have to be prepared to look the Bank in the eye and say: 'No you can't change my contract of employment without my agreement and if you do then I will defend myself and my family" (LTU Newsletter, 6 January 2010). In terms of collective mobilisation to support this, LTU organised a membership ballot in 2010 where it gained a 99% rejection of LBG's terms for harmonisation of conditions but on a 25% turnout (LTU Newsletter, 19 February 2010). The 99% rejection comprised 10,339 voting members, which translated into 10,000 non-signers in mid-2011 (LTU Newsletter, 7 June 2011), then 8441 by the end of 2012 (LTU Newsletter, 16 November 2012), most of whom were part-time women workers (LTU Newsletter, 4 October 2013, 26 November 2013) and some 6000 by late 2015 (LTU Newsletter, 16 September 2016) in spite of the aforementioned alleged 'blackmail' by LBG. Such opposition led to the delay of the implementation of the new contracts by 8 months.

LTU also moved to a ballot for industrial action in 2011 on the issue of working hours (LTU Newsletter, 4 February 2011), which produced a 32% vote for on a 47% turnout amongst the 1200 members in the two regions affected by the pilot on this (LTU Newsletter, 6 April 2011). LTU was unable to take action on this basis so it pursued legal redress (see below). In early 2014, LTU organised a consultative ballot of 13,000 members, producing on a 74% turnout a vote of 98% against cap on pensionable pay and 93% for a ballot on industrial action short of a strike, namely, an overtime ban and work-to-rule (LTU *Newsletter*, 22 January 2014). Although LTU had taken care to reduce the possibility of a legal challenge to its ballot by LBG (with regard to membership details), the ballot was suspended after a challenge (on notification details) which may have led to an application for an injunction (LTU *Newsletter*, 23 May 2014). LBG continued to challenge LTU's balloting and governance processes (LTU *Newsletter*, 21 August 2014). The ballot result returned an 89% vote for action on a 37% turnout (LTU *Newsletter*, 18 November 2014), with LTU 'reluctantly com[ing] to the conclusion that there was too low a level of support for us to instigate action confident that it would succeed' (LTU *Newsletter*, 5 December 2014).

Alongside the limited movement towards industrial action after failing to secure satisfactory collective agreements with LBG, LTU also employed the tool of legal action on the issue of pensions, new employment contracts and related issues of discrimination. For example, in a test case it won a legal victory against LBG on indirect discrimination against women for not signing the new contracts and where the effect was to deny them a pay increase in 2013. This led to the pay rises being paid (LTU *Newsletter*, 9 January 2013). In 2014, it then took a similar case for those 800 non-signers which were being transferred to TSB. And in 2016, LTU launched a legal test case on behalf of three female members of LBG's defined benefit pension schemes, claiming sex discrimination because the pensions of female members of staff increase at lower rates than male members (LTU *Newsletter*, 7 August 2016).

Accord, like other unions, faced an increasingly fragmented membership (in terms of the ramifications of length of service, pension entitlement, grading and so on), making collective mobilisation difficult. For example, Accord found that in a consultative ballot in 2014 on pay and pensions members in the lower grades were much more willing to take action than those in higher grades while the highest proportion of members willing to take action were those employed for 10 years or less (Accord press release, 12 May 2014). This suggests, on the one hand, the lowered paid felt more aggrieved while, on the other hand, those members not in defined benefit pension schemes also felt more aggrieved. Indeed, there is likely to have been a large degree of overlap between the lower paid and those not in the defined benefit pension schemes. However, it was not the case that part-time workers were unwilling to take action for 85% of part-timers said they would be willing to take action compared to the 77% of full-timers (Accord press release, 12 May 2014).

Strikes, Industrial Action and Leverage

As recounted in Gall (2008: 87), the sense of a growing trend towards workers in the financial services sector undertaking strike action was one which peaked in 1997 and declined quite sharply thereafter. By 2007, there had been 6 years without any strikes (see Table 3.1). This trend towards quiescence has continued and deepened since 2007, with only six strikes and a lesser number of instances of industrial action short of striking, all taking place within the insurance sub-sector, being recorded from 2008 to 2016, representing the financial and post-financial crash periods (see next chapter). This observation and conclusion

Table 3.1 Strike activity in the financial services sector, 1999–2015

Year	Number of strikes	Days not worked ('000s)	Workers involved ('000s)
1999	0	0	0
2000	0	0	0
2001	1	200	100
2002	0	0	0
2003	0	0	0
2004	1	Negligible	Negligible
2005	2	3000	2300
2006	0	0	0
2007	0	0	0
2008	0	0	0
2009	0	0	0
2010	0	0	0
2011	0	0	0
2012	0	0	0
2013	0	0	0
2014	0	0	0
2015	0	0	0

Source ONS annual articles

is arrived at by using different sources of evidence. Prior to 2010, the Office of National Statistics (ONS) produced annual analyses which clearly showed the levels of strike action in the financial services sector. But since 2010, the ONS changed the Standard Industrial Classification categories—by reducing them from 27, dating from 2003, to just 12—so that the financial services sector now falls within the 'Financial and Insurance' component of the 'Financial and Insurance, Real estate, Professional, Scientific, Technical and Admin Activities' category. Strikes have been recorded in this broader category as the annual analyses produced by ONS, for the years 2009–2015, indicate. There have been 95 strikes involving 31,400 resulting in 46,000 days not worked for these years, suggesting that these have been small and short strikes. However, analysis of the industrial relations of the sector since the financial crash, which is based upon union and newspaper reporting, shows that only a very small handful of these strikes (as per above) have taken place within financial services.[13] And, the two strikes of 2016 (see Chap. 4) were not due to be reported until the annual analysis for 2016 was to be published in mid-2017. The situation with industrial action short of a strike is that only a tiny number of instances have taken place, being fewer than the number of strikes.

Data provided by the main balloting organisation, the Electoral Reform Services, since 2002 indicates that the number of ballots for strikes and industrial action short of striking had fallen to its lowest ever level in 2015 since its high point of 2006. Prior to 2007, the unions in the financial services sector did not manifestly engage in the common tactic of other unions of using industrial action ballot results to strengthen their hands at the bargaining table—or get back to the bargaining table—without the certainty of following through with industrial action if necessary. What was more common was to use membership consultative ballots on initial offers to seek to gain revised offers.

Immediately following the financial crisis, Unite attempted to create usable leverage over a number of employers in the sector via the influencing the investment decisions of local authority pension schemes. As local authorities routinely invest their pension funds in financial institutions, and as an affiliate of the Labour Party , Unite sought to organise the sizeable number of Labour-controlled councils. The objective was to use the ethical concerns of such councils to move investments away from employers with poor records of treating their employees to those with better records. However, this leverage strategy had no obvious impact, largely because councils sought to maximise their financial returns and the form of pressure was too dissipated to lead to changes in employment practices. However, Unite was far more successful with another innovative attempt in its leverage strategy. This concerned campaigning to halt offshoring whereby members refuse to cooperate in the transfer of the knowledge required to undertake the work to the new operator, specifically in regard of the training of the workers of the new operator (see Chap. 4).

As the next chapter shows, where actual industrial action (strikes and industrial action short of striking) have taken place since 2007–2008, these instances have occurred within Unite and within the pensions and insurance sub-sector. Recalling the discussion of union organising propensities in Chap. 2 as part of the examination of common characteristics across and within unions in the sector, there is little surprise to find that there appears to a positive association between this and the ability to organise industrial action in the pensions and insurance sub-sector and a negative association between this and the ability to organise industrial action in the banking sub-sector. This was not always the case though (see Gall 2008: 80–89). Unite national officer, Dominic Hook (interview, 6 September 2016), primarily attributed the relative preponderance of industrial action to the insurance sub-sector to the result of being 'easier to organise a small number of larger sites' and the strategic leverage developed over offshoring (see above). This perspective was confirmed by a senior Unite Capita shop steward (interview 10 October 2013, email correspondence 8 November 2016).

Individual Representation and Actions

This section considers an array of individually-based actions as part of the processes by which employees have responded to changes in their terms and conditions of employment. As stated elsewhere, these processes may have a collective character in terms of whether the resource base upon which they are founded is of a collective derivation, or whether the actions are part of a more common pattern.

Individual Casework

In the vast majority of the magazines and newsletters of unions in the sector, there was a consistent and constant appeal to members to avail themselves of the representational services they provided. This ranged from advice on how to prepare for an annual appraisal to how to appeal against an appraisal rating and how to undertake a grievance on issues of conduct and performance. It also included appeals against being selected and not being selected for voluntary redundancy and advice and guidance on the application of terms for leaving to specific individual situations. So, like other unions operating in environments of performance management systems, LTU found that its resources were increasingly being taken up with individual casework. Thus, in 2009, it stated: 'At the end of June 2009, LTU had represented more members [in hearings] than we did in the whole of 2008, and 2008 was itself a record year' (LTU *Newsletter*, 27 August 2009) albeit it added:

> It's only when you look closely at these cases that you realise many of them could be dealt with informally without the involvement of the Union or HR. But it seems that the first reaction of many Line Managers when confronted with a member of staff who has made a mistake is immediately to reach for the Disciplinary Policy. We don't blame Line Managers for that reaction because that's what they have been told to do by HR but they are implementing a flawed approach that is damaging morale and diverting energies unprofitably. (LTU *Newsletter*, 27 August 2009)

In 2014, LTU supported 'over 3100 members in cases of different types and everyone was represented by an official or one of our lawyers' (LTU *Newsletter*, 14 July 2015), representing about 8% of its total membership. For Accord, in August 2016, it represented 82 members in cases (*Accord Mail (TSB)*, September 2016). Extrapolated to a twelve month period, this means just under 1000 cases per annum, equivalent to around 5% of its membership. In 2010, Unite (2010: 2) reported 'an increase in the level of performance based disciplinary hearings which Unite has been involved with', and a number of its officers reflected that often during periods of redundancy exercises, there was too much concentration of resources upon those that were leaving and much less on those staying. Meanwhile, the BSU reported: 'We have noticed an increase in misconduct cases in the branch network' (BSU newsletter, July 2014) and 'Partly due to the business seeking to tackle poor performance and sickness issues, we have noticed an increase in members contacting us for help' BSU newsletters, July and October 2015). Forced distribution in CBG led in 2015 to BSU having 'nearly 50% more appeals [than for 2014]' (BSU newsletters, March 2015) when previously CBG denied that it used forced distribution (BSU newsletters, November 2014). Finally, and whilst the NGSU did not stress the serviced-orientated benefits of membership to the extent of the UFS, it is worth noting that a large part of the NGSU's resources were devoted to individual casework, whereby the proportion of formal hearings that the union supported members in was 5% per annum. Thus, in 2010, there were 608 instances, with 501 in 2011, 507 in 2012, 486 in 2013, and 510 in 2014 (*Rapport* magazne, Spring 2015). And when the annual totals of disciplinaries and grievances are combined, there were around 1000 conduct and performance cases per year from 2008 to 2010 (*Rapport* magazine, December 2010).

Sabotage

Sabotage by workers is not widely known of in the financial services sector. This is probably for obvious reasons, concerning the secretive nature of carrying out sabotage, the wish by saboteurs to be cautious in publicising their acts, and the desire by employers to avoid publicising instances of sabotage lest it encourage others or cause reputational damage. It may also arise from measures taken by employers to prevent sabotage or at least identify the saboteurs for subsequent disciplinary action, dismissal, criminal action and damages. Additionally, the tradition of this form of direct action has not been strong in Britain or the financial services sector in the last generation so there is little in the way of previous history and experience to draw upon for potential saboteurs (see Brown 1977). Nonetheless, one might have expected examples to have occurred like the downing of Citibank's ATM system in the USA in 2013 by a disgruntled worker who believed he was about to be fired after a performance review (LibCom 2016). Indeed, the catastrophic information technology failure at RBS in 2012 as a result of human error and where redundancies had eliminated staff with the experience to quickly resolve the problem (*Guardian*, 26 June 2012) indicated the potential for this in Britain.

Of the instances that could be identified, one was at Scottish Widows (LibCom 2013). The recounting of the acts of what are best described as 'organisational misbehaviour' rather than sabotage as such—by which is meant destructive behaviour outside of organisational rules—took place in 2013 at the company but referred to 'some years ago' and, therefore, are likely to have predated the 2007–2008 financial crash. Alongside some semi-collective action to place pressure upon management to gain protection for two co-workers from high pressure call handling, the instance of 'misbehaviour' concerned a group of workers for over a period of a year delaying dealing with certain calls by putting them on hold in order to provide the time to then help customers recoup forgotten pension benefits in response to a regime of performance management based upon targets, disciplinaries and bullying. Some others included individuals and small number of workers working to contract—taking breaks and starting work and leaving work on time—as a direct challenge to management's policy of understaffing and over-working (LibCom 2012). Lastly, it is worth noting that there have been no workplace suicides or acts of protests through suicide (like self-immolation), whether individual or in groups, as there have been when repressive management regimes have taken place or mass redundancies have been made (as in China, France or South Korea). There have been many cases of financial service sector workers stealing from their employers and defrauding customers, under the nomenclature of 'white collar crime', since the crash but it is not known whether there have been more or less cases since the crash and whether, or what proportion of, these are related to acts of resistance against employers. Certainly, no claims were made by those convicted of fraud and theft that their actions were acts of resistance. Rather, the cases continued to be those for funding lavish lifestyles or gambling additions.

Sickness Absence

Although the long running annual Confederation of British Industry (CBI) surveys on sickness/absence included respondents from 'banking, insurance and finance' (albeit a very small proportion), no sectoral breakdown was available. However, of note was that the trajectory of overall levels of absence was downwards. By contrast, Chartered Institute of Professional Development (CIPD) surveys covered 'Finance, insurance and real estate' but only for a short longitudinal period, including on average a similarly low level of respondents from this sector to the CBI surveys' parallel category, and showed that within the private sector, absence was in the mid-range and falling in the sector. Yet, quite apart from there being no detailed breakdown of sickness absence levels for the financial services sector, within the data that is available it is not possible to determine what the respective proportions of genuine and non-genuine sickness/absence are, much less whether non-genuine sickness/absence is related to some form of resistance to management and employers or whether, for the purposes of the next chapter, sickness absence is related to stress result from the pressures of lower staffing, increased workloads and performance management systems. Additionally, no company data (of any kind) on sickness/absence was available. Yet it can be reasonably suggested, based upon somewhat anecdotal evidence from unions, that sickness absence as a resistive and reactive response to performance management system was unlikely not to have occurred more widely (see also Taylor 2013). However, it is unwise to try to estimate its prevalence and extent. That said, no evidence was found of collective or mass 'duvet days' or 'blue flu'.

Conclusion

The evolution of employer strategy towards labour unionism in the financial services sector has moved from union substitution and 'peaceful competition' (Bain 1970) in the form of promoting and sustaining internalism and staff associations against independent labour unionism (see Gall 2008) to peaceful co-existence through partnership as staff associations transmogrified and became less ideologically and organisationally dependent upon employers. The only obvious instance of 'forceful opposition' (Bain 1970) in the post-crash concerned LBG derecognising LTU, and the tipping point for this was LTU mobilising to undertake industrial action in 2014 after a long period of increasing tension with the company. Indeed, the decline of single institution-based unionism as a result of company and union mergers meant that multi-unionism was not so extensive as it previously and there is cooperation amongst a number of unions (Accord and Unite, Advance and CWU).

Notwithstanding paucity of data on parts of the financial services sector outside of banking and insurance, the main institutional process by which employment relations are organised and conducted is through partnership between capital and labour. This is as a consequence of the largest employing organisations recognising unions in this manner and all companies which engage in partnership applying its outcomes to all their employees (notwithstanding the declining propensity to holding union membership in the sector). Despite the repercussions of the financial crash, partnership has continued. Indeed, one could go as far as to plausibly say that partnership has continued because of repercussions of the financial crash. It has proved useful to capital because capital has sought to manage the processes of labour shedding, reducing pension entitlement and performance-managing employees in an organised way where it is the most powerful player. But an organised way also comprises the processes coming with some consent of the representative organisations of labour, namely, the labour unions in the sector and without disrupting the process of capital accumulation by industrial action of any kind (including sabotage) or by unforeseen and uncontrolled labour turnover. For labour, there was no obvious alternative to partnership because of its weakness judged by membership density and members' propensity to mobilise collectively. Overall, partnership at least guaranteed 'a seat at the table' so that unions could have some small level of input into the aforementioned processes by which flight, fright and falling-in-line took place. But they did so knowing that the subterfuge of partnership was, nonetheless, the reification of the managerial prerogative.

Whilst employers and their managers kept the upper hand, as this chapter shows, it was not all plain sailing for them despite the prevalence of partnership. Indeed, partnership gave unions the ability to ask awkward and difficult questions even if they did not like, and could do little about, the proffered answers they received back. The most obvious absences of plain sailing were to be found in LBG where the employer faced dealing with three unions (which negated the portent of the highest combined union density in any major employing organisation) and over the issue of performance management in most employing organisations throughout the sector. Performance management took on an added significance because of the changed context in which it operated, namely, since the financial crash. With an economic situation depressing demand for financial services products, employers sought to use performance management to get more out of those remaining employees in order to try buck the market trend for their own individual company. The way in which the particular components of performance management developed or were applied reflected this. With regard to labour shedding, it was a measure of the employers' desperation to quickly and extensively reduce their headcounts—as a route to cost cutting and a return to former level of profitability—that explains why they were willing to maintain the JSAs/SEAs in their current form (which dated from before the financial crash and when considerable numbers of voluntary redundancies were made in the 2000s). With a worsening work experience, thousands of workers were keen to take the opportunity to leave (see also Chap. 4).

The relative calmness by which the processes of labour shedding, pension impoverishment and performance management took place is worth pondering a little more given the extent of the number of workers deleteriously affected by these phenomena. Unlike in France, there were no 'bossnappings', occupations, sit-ins or suicides to try to resist and subvert the redundancies and ever harsher working conditions in the financial services sector in Britain. This was no different to rest of Britain (see Gall 2011). Even in Eire, with a greater preponderance of occupations (see Cullinane and Dundon 2011), the financial services sector saw no replication of this. Its construction sector saw more instances of direct action than any other sector in its economy in response to the repercussions of the financial crash (see Gall 2017). Some of the calmness in the financial services sector in Britain can be attributed to the impact of partnership whereby an acceptance of management actions was generally affected, with unions then cast into the subordinate role of seeking to manage the process to ensure as much procedural fairness as possible. For example, in essence redundancies were accepted so long as they were carried out fairly in terms of the process and the provision of an element of choice. The case of UFS (*Zurich Newsletter*, 20 January 2016, 7 March 2016) in this respect is but just one example of a less critical acceptance while Unite engaged in harsh condemnation but was not able to go beyond this in terms of giving effect to its criticism. Aviva's takeover of Friends Life was but one example of this (Unite press release, 2 December 2014, 19 January 2015, 26 March 2015). Indeed, one of its senior lay activists (interview, 18 October 2016) commented: 'the big banks are just slaughtering us at every turn and we've no coherent response'. Thus, as the next chapter shows, unions were rather less able to ensure substantive fairness with regard to the outcomes of management actions whereby redundancies increased the workloads of remaining staff (see also, for example, Accord press releases, 24 February 2016, 3 March 2016, 24 June 2016).

Notes

1. Jameson (2010) believed the process to reach the agreement started in 2005.
2. Jameson (2010) noted there was some resistance from Unite national leadership but sector officials won their case to pursue the partnership.
3. Jameson (2010) noted the *quid pro quo* of recognising legitimate difference of interests between capital and labour concerned recognition of the unions' aims of employment security, dignity at work and fair rewards in return for unions' constructive engagement in delivering success for the company and its change programmes.
4. This was also the view of Unite although it was expressed in less vitriolic language (Unite LBG newsletter, May 2013).
5. However, Accord opposed the motion passed at the TUC congress in 2012 which called for the full nationalisation nationalisation of the banking sector, calling it 'a utopian position that is never likely to be

realised' (*Guardian*, 11 September 2012). It did, however, support Unite's motion at the 2013 congress to create a British investment bank.

6. This line was repeated in subsequent communications like its press release of 15 June 2009.

7. The questions asked were: 'Have you lost trust and confidence in the capability of the bank's management to run the bank in the interests of all of its stakeholders including customers and employees?' and 'Would you be prepared to vote for and participate in industrial action industrial action, up to and including strike action, to say to the Lloyds Banking Group that 'enough is enough' and to demand a better deal for bank employees?' (Accord press release, 16 April 2014).

8. Whilst it was clear this concerned secondments to working for a union, it remained unclear if that also included facility time.

9. The Financial Services Act 2012 abolished the FSA from 1 April 2013 and its responsibilities were then split between two new agencies: the Financial Conduct Authority and the Prudential Regulation Authority of the Bank of England.

10. In this newsletter, LTU quoted the Head of Business Unit saying in an email to his Line Managers: "We are failing in our efforts to agree a distribution curve … I have therefore taken the liberty of forcing a distribution curve on the attached'. [he then sends them a list of names before and after he forces the distribution] He says that the Line Managers should have the debate about those he has moved but 'we need to hit the numbers so the principle we should agree up front is that if we move a colleague out of a section then they need to be replaced".

11. The FSA established a staff consultative council for its 2500 staff (*Financial Adviser*, 26 January 2012). Following its abolition, the Prudential Regulation Authority part the former FSA was transferred to the Bank of England so that union recognition was gained.

12. The full claim included a 4% across the board increase, an underpinning minimum rise of £800, a 5% increase to minimum and maximum of salary bands, attainment of 95% market pay within 6 months in role, attainment of midpoint of market zone within 3 years in role, removal of pension cap, and a full Equal pay Audit.

13. Previously, it was the case that ONS data under-represented strike activity in the sector (see Gall 2008: 86–87) but this now does not

appear to be the case as with so few strikes it is relatively easier to measure them by incidence, numbers of workers involved and days not worked.

References

Arrowsmith, J., Nicholaisen, H., Bechter, B., & Nonell, R. (2010). The management of variable pay in European banking. *International Journal of Human Resource Management, 21*(15), 2716–2740.

Bacon, N., & Samuel, P. (2009). Partnership agreement adoption and survival in the British private and public sectors. *Work, Employment & Society, 23*(2), 231–248.

Bain, G. (1970). *The growth of white collar unionism*. Oxford: Clarendon Press.

BIS. (2010). *Accord and Unite: Developing union reps within a partnership framework at HBoS*. London: Union Modernisation Fund Report.

Brown, G. (1977). *Sabotage*. Nottingham: Spokesman Books.

Cullinane, N., & Dundon, T. (2011). Redundancy and workplace occupation: The case of the Republic of Ireland. *Employee Relations, 33*(6), 624–641.

FSA. (2012). *Guidance consultation: Risks to customers from financial incentives*. London: Financial Services Authority.

Gall, G. (2001). From adversarialism to partnership? Industrial relations in the finance sector in Britain. *Employee Relations, 23*(4), 353–375.

Gall, G. (2008). *Labour unionism in the financial services sector: Fighting for rights and representation*. Aldershot: Ashgate.

Gall, G. (2011). Contemporary workplace occupations in Britain: Stimuli, dynamics and outcomes, *Employee Relations, 33*(6), 607–623.

Gall, G. (2013). Employers against Unions: The British experience of union victimization. In G. Gall & T. Dundon (Eds.), *Global anti-unionism— Nature, dynamics, trajectories and outcomes* (pp. 104–120). London: Palgrave.

Gall, G. (2017). Injunctions as a Legal Weapon in Collective Industrial Disputes in Britain, 2005–2014, *British Journal of Industrial Relations, 55*(1), 187–214.

Jameson, H. (2010). *Partnership at HBoS*. London: IPA.

Johnstone, S. (2011). Partnership working in UK financial services. London: IPA, 25 March.

LibCom. (2012, January 23). *Credit crunched—Working in financial services during the 2008–2009 crash*. London.

LibCom. (2013, October 23). *Worker sabotage in a financial services call centre*. London.

LibCom. (2016, August 1). *Revenge of a Citibank worker*. London.

Marginson, P., Arrowsmith, J., & Gray, M. (2008). Undermining or reframing collective bargaining? Variable pay in two sectors compared. *Human Resource Management Journal, 18*(4), 327–346.

McIlroy, J., & Daniels, G. (2008). An anatomy of British trade unionism since 1997: Strategies for revitalisation. In G. Daniels & J. McIlroy (Eds.), *Trade unions in a Neoliberal World* (pp. 98–126). London: Routledge.

Stuart, M., Martinez Lucio, M., Tomlinson, J., & Perrett, R. (2010). *The union modernisation fund—Round two: Final evaluation report*. Employment Relations Research Series No. 111, London: BIS.

Taylor, P. (2013). *Performance management and the new workplace tyranny—A report for the Scottish Trades Union Congress*. Glasgow: University of Strathclyde.

Terry, M., & Smith, J. (2003). *Evaluation of the partnership at work fund*. London: DTI. (URN 03/512).

Unite. (2008, October). *Organising support unite report—Stage 2 report: Banking and insurance*. London: Unite.

Unite. (2010). Unite the Union response to the FSA Consultation paper 10/27 Implementing CRD3 requirements on disclosure of remuneration, Unite, London, December

Van Wanrooy, B., Bewley, H., Bryson, A., Forth, J., Freeth, S., Stokes, L., & Wood, S. (2013). *The 2011 workplace employment relations study—First findings*. London: ACAS/BIS/ESRC/NIESR.

4

Outcomes

Introduction

This chapter considers the outcomes of the employers' actions upon
workers' material interests in the formers' pursuit of seeking to advance
profitability in a period of economic and financial instability and overall decline in the wake of the financial crash. The chapter, thus, concerns surveying the outcomes of flight, fright and falling-in-line
following the examination of the processes and institutions that gov-
ern employment in the previous chapters. Therefore, the main components of the attack upon workers' material interests which are examined
are job losses, immiseration of pay, heightened pressures of work and
impoverishment of pensions. If a table was to be constructed of each
company in the sector in terms of whether performance management
systems operate, job cuts were made and the worth of pensions reduced,
then nearly all the boxes of the table for each company would feature
a 'tick'. That said, not every employer action should be viewed solely
through the lens of the financial crash for, counter-intuitively, even
if the crash had not taken place, it would have been more than likely
that many of these same outcomes would have been sought and, in all

© The Author(s) 2017
G. Gall, *Employment Relations in Financial Services*,
DOI 10.1057/978-1-137-39539-9_4

likelihood, achieved in some measure. The difference between the crash and the non-crash scenarios is that the crash provided an additional edge or special contemporary character to an otherwise more general historical process of capital accumulation. In this sense, it changed the conditions for the drive to accumulate but not the rationale or motivation per se. Thus, the pace and extent of the flight, fright and falling-in-line are likely to have been greater than would have normally been anticipated for the period studied. Indeed, one of the most obvious phenomena in the period was the spate of takeovers occasioned by the market volatility in the financial services sector, whereby companies were placed in the position of being either 'the hunters' or 'the hunted'. The profit enhancing rationale for every takeover included cost reductions and this primarily focussed upon job cuts. Another of the major changed conditions which the crash brought about, as Chap. 3 demonstrated, was to weaken workers' collective ability to resist, through their unions, the employers' terms for seeking to advance profitability. So, it can be said with certainty that the outcomes explored in this chapter are those of 'after' the crash if not necessarily all 'of' the crash itself.

This chapter begins by setting out the scale of reductions in jobs and posts before dealing with the aftermath of the conditions experienced by the remaining workforces in terms of their working time, pay and pensions. To give an initial sense of the scale of the reduction in posts, on the third anniversary of the beginning of the financial crash, Unite compiled figures showing that 100,000 jobs had been 'lost' since the run on Northern Rock on 13 September 2007 (Unite press release, 14 September 2010).[1] The 2011 WERS6 Survey noted that the financial services sector was one of the four most affected sectors by employment and output since the recession (Van Wanrooy et al. 2013a: 6). And, by the fourth anniversary of the beginning of the financial crash, Unite calculated that 100,000 jobs had gone by mid-2011 in retail banking alone with 150,000 jobs lost overall in the sector (Unite press release, 7 September 2011). The thrust of this chapter is then to argue that the impact of job shedding in the context of the continued desire of the employers to cut costs and increase revenues in order to boost profitability has led to the remaining workforces being caught in a pincer movement of being forced to increase productivity and to do so with fewer staff. This had led to deterioration in working conditions. To give an initial flavour of this, the 2011 WERS6 Survey noted that in the financial services sector one third of respondents in sector reported an increase in workloads (Van Wanrooy et al. 2013a: 8) while Unite characterised the situation in RBS as a 'pressure cooker environment', citing that in a members' survey, 68% of staff reported work-related stress, 62% have considered leaving the bank and 85% are having to work unpaid overtime every week (Unite press release, 21 March 2016). In Barclays, Unite reported:

> Reorganisation of work in branches in Barclays along with reduced staffing levels has result in intolerable pressure on staff leading to '[p]oor customer experience leading to anger, abuse [and] threats [of] … violence being directed at staff … [m]anagers … fire-fighting every day just to help deal with the flow of customers, often to the detriment of their substantive role … [s]taff regularly having to work their rostered day off and work significant overtime … [with] only the goodwill of staff working flexibly, outside their contractual requirements that is keeping the network operational'. This end Unite lobbied the company to act, calling for an emergency meeting with management. (Unite 2014)

In late 2016, a LTU survey of its members in commercial banking found: '63% … said that the demands the Bank places on them are unrealistic; 72% said they struggled to deal with their daily workload; 90% of staff said agreed that 'long working hours are an integral part of the culture in Commercial banking' [with] … 34% either disagreed or strongly disagreed with the suggestion that their latest performance rating was a fair reflection of their overall performance … [and o]nly 19% of respondents said that they were confident that the performance management system was being managed in the correct way' (LTU *Newsletter*, 2 November 2016). Meanwhile after admitting 'We lost our way…', the chief HR officer at RBS then stated: '… 'Determined to lead' is our new common plan for leading teams … If anyone didn't 'get' the new regime, they had to go …' (*People Management*, 7 March 2016). This gave an indication of the increasingly authoritarian organisational culture of employers in the sector with a 'shape up or ship out' attitude underpinned by systems of performance management (see also Martin and Gollan 2012). This is reinforced by Joris Luyendijk's 'banking blog' for the *Guardian* (see Chap. 1) where the picture that emerges is one of an increasingly authoritarian organisational culture where senior executives rule the roost not just through a regime of performance management but also through institutionalised bullying.

Although the components of employment, remuneration and working conditions are considered separately for ease of presentation and analysis, it should be borne in mind that financial services sector workers seldom viewed each component in isolation. This is particularly true in three aspects. First, pensions are generally viewed as being more important than pay—not in the sense of being deferred pay but rather that the relatively generous pensions are seen as a trade-off for relatively less generous pay and increasingly intolerable working conditions. Indeed, they are often seen as a reward for making it through a working life in a financial services sector organisation. Second, the hegemony of performance management systems has created the widespread view that the conditions under which employees work and are assessed have increased in importance relative to the monetary value of the pay rises employees receive. Third, the ability to either move upwards through the grading structure or gain promotion in order to escape relatively poorer pay and conditions is still a major objective for many. Therefore, employees view matters of remuneration and working conditions in the round.

The final parts of this chapter present, firstly, an assessment of the extent and impact of union influence in ameliorating and mitigating the deterioration in the conditions of employment; secondly, the voice of workers whereby they tell of their experiences in their own words; thirdly, an examination of the sparse evidence of fight; fourthly, an assessment of the impact of challenger and mutual status upon employment relations (especially in terms of job cuts, pay, pensions and working conditions); and finally, an overview of the comparable situation in Ireland (the Republic of Ireland or Eire, and Northern Ireland).

Job Reductions

This section examines the flight of many tens of thousands from the financial services sector since the financial crash. It does so on the basis of the discussion in Chap. 2 on overall employment levels in the sector and the maintenance of JSAs and SEAs in Chap. 3. The two main points that arise from this previous discussion are that (i) since the crash, there has been an internal reconfiguring of the balance of employment between the sub-sectors within the sector such that overall employment levels have remained relatively stable[2]; and (ii) the ability of employers to reduce their staffing levels without recourse to compulsory redundancies strongly reflects the relatively 'generous' severance terms of the JSAs/SEAs.[3] Nonetheless, flight in the sector can still comprise a considerable element of compulsion, if not force, for staff may opt for redundancy because they believe working conditions have become intolerable (see later and the workers' testimonies in particular) and they believe they are being 'managed out the door' under performance management systems.

Although a sense of the extent of reductions in jobs and headcount has already been given in previous chapters and culminating in an estimate of between 250,000 and 300,000 by early 2017, it is worth putting some flesh on the bones of these figures by examining the situation in a number of individual instances. The job reductions have primarily taken place through redundancies rather than offshoring and outsourcing. So since the financial crash (from 2007 until 2017), Aviva has reduced its workforce in Britain from around 21,000 to around 15,000, Barclays from c. 103,000 to c. 71,000, HSBC from c. 67,000 to c. 43,000, LBG from c. 140,000 to c. 73,000, Northern Rock from c. 6500 to c. 2500, RBS from c. 170,000 to c. 80,000 and Zurich from c. 10,000 to c. 4000. Other significant job losses have also taken place at AXA, Bank of England, Diligenta, Friends Provident, Legal and General, NAG and RSA.

Given that some of the biggest (in absolute and relative) labour shedding exercises took place under state control, it is worth examining the process in LBG in more detail. By early 2017, a total of 67,000 jobs had been removed from LBG since the takeover of HBoS, bringing the size of the workforce down to around 73,000. These took place in a number of waves of 30,000 (2009), 15,000 (2011), 9000 (2014) and 3000 (2016). The majority were eliminated as a result of voluntary labour shedding but offshoring, outsourcing and sell offs also played their part too.[4] Not all reductions in jobs led to redundancies, given not just the offshoring, outsourcing and sell offs but also the availability of redeployment and non-replacement of vacant posts as a result of natural wastage. For example, LTU observed in 2011: 'Based on our integration experience we would expect approximately half of the 15,000 job losses to result in redundancy' (LTU *Newsletter*, 7 June 2011) while LBG stated in 2014: '... since the strategic review in 2011 only around a third of role reductions have led to people leaving the group through redundancy' (*Guardian*, 10 July 2014). In line with the discussion of limited compulsory redundancies in Chap. 3, the *Guardian* (29 October 2014, 14 November 2014) then reported LBG stated: 'more than 90% of the jobs lost since 2011 had been managed through redeployment, voluntary redundancy or not replacing people who resigned' and '1000 redundancies out of 15,000 in the last 3 years had been compulsory'. However, as the number of jobs shed rose, increased concern was expressed that a greater proportion of compulsory redundancies would be required as the latitude for voluntary redundancies declined following the reduction in the number of the remaining staff willing to leave by such means. Thus, for example, Unite 'demanded guarantees of no compulsory redundancies' (Unite press release, 21 May 2014), stated that it 'opposes all job losses and demands that senior management guarantee that all staff impacted by this latest round of cuts are offered genuine and realistic alternative job options within LBG' (Unite press release, 1 July 2015) and called for a 'no compulsory redundancy guarantee' (Unite press release, 28 July 2016) to supersede LBG's policy that '[c]ompulsory redundancies will always be a last resort' (*Guardian*, 10 July 2014).

Turning to the level of compulsory redundancies, there are some indications that their numbers rose as the scope of voluntary redundancies and other means of job shedding (retraining, redeployment, non-filling of vacant posts etcetera) declined in relative terms. For example, with HBoS's abolition of 4800 posts only 63 compulsory redundancies were made (Jameson 2010: 11). From 2013, Aviva, CBG and NAG were amongst a small handful of companies that made compulsory redundancies while in RBS in 2016, Unite sought to 'hold the bank to its promise to avoid compulsory redundancies' (*Guardian*, 15 April 2016). At a time of continuing redundancies, offshoring ICT jobs to the likes of India, China and Poland became more of a political 'hot potato'. For example, by 2015 RBS had some 12,000 employees in India and 1500 working for it in Poland (Unite *Finance e-bulletin*, March 2015). Unite, for example, condemned this in the strongest possible terms, believing RBS in 2016 to be committing the 'ultimate betrayal of [its] loyal workforce' (Unite press release, 20 July 2016) and that HSBC was being 'as ruthless as it is reckless' (Unite press release, 16 May 2016). Meantime, LBG was heavily criticised by Unite for employing 4000 agency workers while continuing with redundancies (Unite press release, 13 March 2013). The manner of redundancies was not of the most brutal nature as experienced elsewhere in post-crash Britain, namely, being sacked by text without any period of notice or forewarning. But there was one occasion within LBG when 'staff were told that the retail protection business was closing with the loss of 700 jobs by DVD' (LTU *Newsletter*, 21 November 2014) and the year before, in 2013, the 2134 CIS financial advisers were dismissed and required to re-apply for jobs as a result of the takeover by London Mutual.

The sense in which some of the job reductions would have taken place regardless of the financial crash can be most keenly seen in the programme of branch closures, offshoring and automation. Driven by changes in customer behavior, as a result of developments in ICTs, and set within the context of employers seeking to cut costs and achieve competitive advantage in order to advance profitability, many functions have been taken out of branches and automated into centres within or without Britain. For example, in 2011, LBG 'had no customers using mobile technology, yet it estimates 5 million did so this year, while 14.4 million customers have chosen to go paperless. The bank expects branch transactions to halve in the next 3 years. The internet has already had an impact on the call centres banks set up to stop customers calling their branches—call volumes are down 10% year-on-year since 2012' (*Guardian*, 29 October 2014). Meanwhile, RBS 'said branch counter transactions had fallen by 43% since 2010, while digital usage had jumped by 400% over the same period' (*BBC News*, 12 May 2016). Overall, the *Guardian* (17 October 2016) reported: 'In 2011 there were 478 million 'customer interactions' in Britain's bank branches. This year [2016] it will be less than 280 million'. Meantime, around

3000 branches were closed in Britain in the last decade, according to the Campaign for Community Banking Services, leaving around 8000 by 2016 (*BBC News*, 13 May 2016). The pace of closures appeared to increase with over 1000 branches closed between January 2015 and December 2016 (*BBC News*, 14 December 2016). This formed part of a wider European trend, whereby some 5500 bank branches (or 2.5% of the total) were closed across the European Union in 2012 according to the European Central Bank, compared with 7200 branch closures in 2011, so that the European Union had 20,000 (or 8%) fewer outlets at the end of 2012 than it had when the financial crisis began in 2008 (*Reuters*, 11 August 2013). However, the use of ICTs to replace the traditionally more conventional means of delivering financial services (through tellers in branches) appears to have accelerated in response to the deleterious impact of the financial crash on company profitability, and there also seems to have been a touch of taking advantage of the weakness of those social forces against branch closures to press ahead with even more. Future predictions were equally significant with the *Guardian* (17 September 2016) suggesting there were 3200 too many bank and building society branches based upon a 650 branch model for each major operator (and reporting the Campaign for Community Banking Services has closed down its website as it was unable to stem the flow of branch closures). And, in 2016 RBS began automating increased numbers of low value face-to-face transactions in 2016 using advanced artificial intelligence (*Observer*, 13 March 2016; *Guardian*, 14 March 2016). *The National* (15 March 2016) reported that after an investigation by the FCA into 'the market for financial advice, which stated that automated services—or 'robo-advice'—can deliver a 'cost-effective' service … the FCA said it would launch a unit to help firms develop more automated advice models'.

Impact upon Union Organising

Recalling the issues of dislocation and disorganisation, one of the outcomes of the programmes of job reductions has been that large numbers of workplaces have been shut down by employers. Amongst the many examples are not just the branch closures but also closures of large workplace such as call/contact and processing centres with between several hundred to several thousand workers. Examples are three of Aviva's Manchester centres and its Bristol centre too; Barclays' Peterborough, Manchester, Coventry, Glasgow, Liverpool, Cardiff and Dartford centres; Friends Life's Preston, Basingstoke, Coventry and Manchester centres; Friends' Provident's Manchester site; Intelligent Processing Solutions' seven sites; LBG's Bridgend, Warrington, Manchester, Southend and Chester centres; Legal and General's Ipswich and Surrey centres; RBS's Bristol, Plymouth, Telford, Farnborough and two London centres; RSA's Bristol and Birmingham centres; and UK Asset Resolution's Newcastle centre. The closure of these 39 centres is not an exhaustive list of large site closures since the financial crash. The salience of this for union organising is that it exerts a heavy toll on union resources. While organising in larger sites is relatively easier (see Chap. 2), given the lower levels of work affinity and identity (in relation to traditional occupations of banking and insurance) and considerable staff turnover, this still requires the expenditure of considerable resources. For such sites to be closed in such numbers represents a destruction of union organising resources, especially when one considers that union membership is not generally maintained afterwards as workers do not necessarily regain employment in the sector and union membership does not aid with regaining such employment (see also Gall 2008).

The Aftermath

This section now examines the working experience of those 'left behind' after the labour shedding exercises. The logic of this ordering is to allow the scene to be set so that the working conditions of those remaining in employment could then be properly situated. Of course, given that the labour shedding was not a one-off process at the outset of the crash, this separation is a little artificial. It must also be borne in mind that the data deployed for this study is not able to lay out a sequential analysis in terms of measuring the experience of work every 2 or 3 years after the financial crash. Rather, and as stated in the introductory chapter, this study seeks to provide an overview of what has happened across and throughout the whole period since the crash. Nonetheless, there was a pervasive sense that 'things were getting worse' as time wore on. Beginning with issue of trust and respect, the section then moves to examine working time, performance management, pensions and other terms and conditions.

As with the introduction to this chapter, it is worthwhile giving an early indication of the perceptions and experiences of the changes working conditions. In its 2012 submission to Parliament on Banking Standards, Unite included a number of comments from its members. These were: 'Too many privileges for higher levels and not enough credit to lower levels who keep the bank running on a daily basis'; 'Targets are not realistic and we are not rewarded fairly for the things we are achieving';'Too much work with not enough time to do it, resulting often in unpaid overtime'; 'Constantly feel worried about my job as everything is being 'looked at' and trying to juggle all the balls with not enough hours in the day to do everything'; and 'We have not learnt from all the mis-selling in the past!!! Recent changes to the system etc. have not been fully implemented'. Meanwhile a UFS member complained: 'Staff reductions mean we are working harder, doing more with less people' (UFS *Report*, Summer 205). In its evidence to the same parliamentary investigation into banking standards, LTU observed:

> Now staff in Lloyds Banking Group don't generally wake up in the morning thinking: 'How many customers can I fleece today?" but they do wake up worrying about how many loan appointments they've got in their diaries or how many sales they need to make to hit their insurance targets and preserve their jobs. That is the predatory sales culture that exists in most banks today and banks have devised ever more complicated and esoteric bonus and incentive schemes to drive that short-term sales culture. ... The vast majority of bank staff want to do the best for their customers but can't because they are under constant pressure to hit ever-demanding targets, which increase every year. A failure to hit those targets can result in staff being subject to performance improvement plans and in some cases being dismissed for under-performance. A number of management practices we have been dealing with are based more on humiliation than on positive motivation. (Affinity 2012)

Trust and Respect

Surveys of employee attitudes concerning the trust and confidence held in their employers indicated that, not unsurprisingly, levels of these were in decline in the period since the financial crash as well as being a result of their employers' chosen means to deal with the effects of the crash upon their levels of profitability. Historically, employee levels of trust and confidence in employers within an ideological and institutional framework of *de facto* partnership and mutual gains were relatively high and were reified by a model of employment based upon secure employment, career advancement and a panoply of non-wage benefits (like pensions as deferred wages and extensive holidays). Nonetheless, they served to obscure and mask the *realpolitik* of superordinate and subordinate relations between capital and labour. The effect of the employer responses to the consequences of the financial crash has been to undermine these foundations of previously held trust and confidence (albeit in a more attitudinal than behavioural sense).

So, in a survey of more than 3000 Accord members in LBG called the Quality of Working Life survey in 2011, 32% did not think LBG was 'a good employer' with 58% feeling 'it's probably no better or worse than others' (*My Accord*, Summer 2011). The same survey revealed 65% felt put under pressure to complete LBG Colleague Engagement Survey, 61% did not think any action would be taken as a result of the survey, over half also thought the results were manipulated to show the situation was better than it actually was, and 57% said morale in their workplace was low (*My Accord*, Summer 2011). A 2012 'Pulse' survey of employees undertaken by LBG and with a 55% response rate made uncomfortable reading for the employer (where conventional assumptions are used). Thus, job satisfaction and pride in working for the bank fell to 44%, down 8% from the previous year while trust and confidence in leadership and the bank's future has dropped by 10–39% (*My Accord*, Summer 2012). The results of a joint Accord-Unite pension survey of their members in late 2013, and ahead of the 0% cap on pensionable for the final salary scheme saw '79% of respondents [saying they] did not trust the Group to reinvest a significant amount of the savings into the overall reward package', as LBG stated they would be, and 'over 99% of respondents believe[d] that [LBG] should be committed to genuine consultation and make the decision based on the feedback received from colleagues' which it did not (Unite *LBG Newsletter*, January 2014).

Overtime

The phenomenon of unpaid working of overtime became increasingly widespread as existing staff were implored or felt compelled to take up the extra work as a result of reduced staff levels.[5] On top of this, new forms of the micro-regulation of work, sometimes the result of internal company initiatives to create new products or services and sometimes the result of external regulation after the mis-selling and excessive risk taking scandals, led to an increasing sense of overload and over work. Staff responded to this by work more extensively (as well as intensively). Thus, in 2011, with the aforementioned Quality of Working Life survey, Accord found 88% of members worked unpaid overtime every week with almost 30% doing more than 5 hours (*My Accord*, Summer 2011). One of the reasons for this was that 37% reported constant under-staffing with a further 40% responding they had the right number of staff unless a colleague was off sick (*My Accord*, Summer 2011). Then in a survey of members in 2013, Accord found 88% reported they worked unpaid overtime regularly (*Accord Mail (Lloyds)*, October 2016). Accord's general secretary opined in late 2016: 'I know that some people are more than happy to leave [LBG] on the voluntary redundancy terms that the unions have negotiated. But for those left behind, working life seems to get ever tougher and [LBG] really needs to address the issues and concerns of the remaining workforce' (*Accord Mail (Lloyds)*, October 2016).

For its part, Accord sought to convince LBG that 'More cannot always be achieved with less!' (Accord press release, 24 February 2016) and 'There comes a point where it is not possible to achieve more with less; only less can be achieved with less' (Accord press release, 3 March 2016). An earlier indication of the consequences was given by the responses to a joint Accord/Unite survey on stress in LBG in 2012 which gained 11,000 respondents (*My Accord,* Spring 2012). 85% reported being 'stressed by their work' with 75% suffering symptoms including headaches, depression, anxiety attacks and sleeplessness. In terms of the perceived causes, 82% reported being 'stressed about an uncertain future', '77% worrying about job security' and 80% felt 'over-worked, ha[d] unrealistic targets and objectives, too many objectives, tight deadlines and [we]re under pressure to perform well' (*My Accord,* Spring 2012). Meanwhile, a survey by LTU in 2011 reported that:

[o]ne of the most disturbing findings of our survey is the amount of unpaid overtime that continues to be undertaken in Branches. In the pilot region, 26% of staff do 5+ hours of unpaid overtime every week. Nearly 50% of staff do 3+ hours overtime per week … We carried out a survey on staffing levels a few years ago that produced very similar figures to those we are publishing today. Assuming there are 20 k staff in the Network and 50% of those are doing 3 hours of unpaid overtime every week that equates to some 30,000 hours per week. Over a year that equates to some 1,560,000 hours per year or 857 full time members of staff. (LTU *Newsletter,* 16 August 2011)

LTU's staffing survey the next year found '91% of members … said … staff in their branch are routinely asked to work in the evenings' and '83% of respondents said … neither overtime pay nor Time Off In Lieu was offered to staff working overtime' (LTU *Newsletter,* 28 September 2012). Then in 2016, LTU opined:

Bank Managers are under pressure like never before. Staffing levels are being cut to the bone and that's going to continue if the current CEO has his way. But the Bank's expectations about what must be delivered with fewer resources remains undiminished. As we've said before, for many Bank Managers it's often a battle just to get the branch staffing to a level where they can open the doors safely. Everything thereafter is a bonus. And let's be clear Bank Managers can only do that in most cases because they themselves are spending more and more time on the counter and that's confirmed by the results of our survey. (LTU *Newsletter,* 25 August 2016)

In 2014, Unite questioned 'whether LBG is living up to its own job security agreements as it would appear that an extraordinary number of colleagues are working overtime to make ends meet which, at a time of job losses, should not be happening' (Unite press release, 9 July 2014) and stated in 2016 that it 'has made it clear that 'efficiency' cannot simply mean axing more jobs while expecting the same work to fall on fewer shoulders. The bank forgets that these relentless cuts have a human cost. Unpaid overtime and work-related stress are already at endemic levels across the bank and this will reach a crisis point if Lloyds continues to swing the axe' (Unite press release, 21 April 2016). In a newsletter to members in early 2016, Unite reported:

> It is clear that across the Group workloads continue to rise, leading to a sharp increase in work-related stress. However, for many colleagues this increased pressure is going unrewarded, with unpaid overtime remaining an endemic problem. 67% of members said they had considered leaving the bank to join a competitor, with 46% citing pay as the reason for moving. That's no surprise when 49% are borrowing money just to see them through the month. This has a clear impact on members' health with 74% reported having experienced work-related stress within the last year. Perhaps the biggest cause of this stress is the endemic culture of unpaid overtime, with a staggering 80% of members reporting having to work additional unpaid hours in an average week. 70% of members feel forced to work these hours because of rising workloads. Examples of extra work range from coming in early to be ready to take customer calls, to skipping lunch breaks in order to complete work. Over time all those extra minutes and hours add up to significant unpaid overtime. (Unite *LBG Newsletter*, February 2016).

Across the financial services sector, in a poll of 3841 Unite members conducted by polling organisation, Survation, in 2015, of the 74% that reported there had been job losses in their branch or department, 60% also said they had to work longer hours as a result; 76% reported that there were situations when they were asked/required to start earlier or finish later than their contracted hours, and of these, 77% said the additional hours they worked here were not recognized via overtime payments; and 63% said they take less than their contracted time for breaks and lunch (Unite 2015).

A 2016 poll of some 2000 Unite in Barclays found '79% said they do unpaid overtime and additional hours and of these 69% said this was due to increased workload [with] 69% report symptoms of stress caused by their job' (Unite Now! Executive Council report, September 2016). Meanwhile in HSBC, a survey by Unite's members in mid-2016 indicated that '58% do more than 2.75 extra unpaid hours a week [and o]f those 65% say it is because of pressure due to workload [with] 78% report[ing] symptoms of stress at work' (Unite *HSBC Newsletter*, September 2016). Elsewhere, a survey conducted by BSU in early 2015 showed that nearly 74% of the 321 respondents in braches were performing at least 1 hour unpaid overtime per week (BSU *Newsletter*, March 2015). In response to AXA Group CEO, Paul Evans, stating a restructuring called Project Falcon was 'not about doing more with less or across the board cost reduction', Unite retorted: 'Tell that to those who are losing their jobs, or those remaining to pick up the pieces!' (Unite in AXA, 14 May 2013).

Pay and Performance

The determination of pay rises in the financial services sector is now governed almost without exception by performance management systems.[6] While still continuing to constitute a form of PRP, the PRP under performance management systems is of a more total nature, covering a wider range of assessed attitudes and behaviours than before as well as being measured by a harder range of quantitative criteria (like targets) than before. In this sense, performance management systems can be characterised as somewhat totalitarian and authoritarian and, thus, oppressive to workers and their experience of employment. Laaser (2016: 1010, 1014), deploying data gathered between 2010 and 2012 through interviews with managers and workers in bank branches, observed:

- With the rise of [performance management systems] and the marketization of the employment relationship, low-trust and conflict ridden engagements between branch management and employees increased significantly, shaping everyday interactional realities. Low-trust relationships were enmeshed in [branch workers'] perception of [branch managers] as the personalization of a system that subordinates them under the dictate of performance expectations. At the heart of these sentiments are [branch workers'] evaluations of the [performance management systems] as a workplace regime that treats employees as factors of production, narrowing their multiple interests and concerns down to those that are essential for meeting market demands.

and

By arguing that the [performance management systems] driven workplace regime prioritizes market needs over human needs and strips many of the human and social texture out of the workplace, an ample warning is provided regarding the impact a purely target and marketized workplace regime has on people and, ultimately, the society.

Indeed, Taylor (2013) characterised the move as one from performance appraisal to performance management, with performance improvement being used as a disciplinary tool. Added to this transition has been the injurious issue of calibration resulting in 'forced distribution'. Thus, individuals are assessed in appraisals on an annual basis by line managers based upon unilaterally determined criteria. They are then ranked as fitting into set, pre-arranged and pre-apportioned sized categories as a result of 'forced distribution' and then mapped onto a matrix based upon what are held to be market rates. Market rates exist to reflect not just regional differences in the labour markets for pay but also where an individual is within their grade or pay range. Thus, for a particular grade or level, an individual is assessed leading to a rating which is then applied depending on their current market pay position as Table 4.1 demonstrates. Consequently, *de facto* pay freezes are possible under 10 categories (in Table 4.1) while below inflation pay rises, leading to *de facto* pay cuts, are possible in six categories if inflation (based upon the retail price index) was at 2%. Failure to evade performance rating categorisation as 'Partial Achieved' or 'Unacceptable' results in being placed

Table 4.1 Performance pay matrix determination

Performance rating	Position in market pay range guide				
	<80%	80–90%	90–110%	110–120%	>120%
Outstanding	6.50	5.00	4.00	2.50	£200
Exceeding	5.00	4.00	2.50	1.50	£150
Achieved	4.00	2.50	1.75	1.00	£100
Partial achieved	0.00	0.00	0.00	0.00	£0
Unacceptable	0.00	0.00	0.00	0.00	£0

upon performance improvement plans (PIPs). Failure to improve within PIPS can result in being 'managed out the door' in the words of a Unite finance union officer (in Taylor 2013: 58).

Significantly for the purposes of this study, performance management systems have become more pervasive and persuasive since the financial crash—as a result of capital seeking to deal restore levels of profitability through heightening levels of labour exploitation via the wage-effort bargain. In particular and notwithstanding the outcomes of union pressure and external regulation on the matter, the criteria used have become tighter and the thresholds to be passed higher in order to gain desired ratings. Along with the issue of the use of 'forced distribution', the pay rises and performance consequences of PIPs have become one of the main sources of discontent and grievance for workers in the financial services sector. Thus, a senior Unite activist recounted that:

> Since the crisis began and certainly following all the redundancies there has definitely been a significant increase in the use of so called performance improvement plans (PIPs), a new tool that management use to deal with performance and training issues through 'coaching plans'. There has been a significant number of people put on PIPs for failing to meet targets and it is clear that despite the rhetoric of support and development available this is disciplinary action in all but name. The heightened focus on performance is a result of Lloyds' attempt to do more with less, and people who aren't meeting targets are identified and go speedily through the PIP process and out the door on capability charges if their performance does not rapidly improve. Performance also typically plays a role in determining who gets a zero pay increase so you can see another reason for the extra interest. (in Ellis and Taylor 2010: 807–808)

Meantime, Unite finance sector research officer, Liz Cairns, noted:

> Many members initially took performance management on board and were able to identify opportunities which could reward them for their hard work. [But] following the financial crisis, with bonuses cut and an increasing gap between inflation and real wages, a failure to acknowledge the contribution of a significant majority of the workforce and a widening gap between the pay at the top and those further down the ladder, it is no longer delivering for them. ... We need alternatives to performance-based reward, which are fairer and more transparent where successful companies reward the workforce more equitably. ... I do think it has reached a turning point and there is more recognition that the system needs to change; but we need to be able to provide alternatives to make that change. (in LRD 2013: 24)

LRD (2013: 24) also observed that: 'Unite's perception is that people are managed-out of organisations on the cheap on the back of so-called underachieving and poor performance. ... Unite believes that this process is a strategic exit policy to avoid paying redundancy pay in some companies' while one of Unite's senior activists believed: 'In reality, performance management schemes provide a route for managers to push workers who don't meet their targets out of a job. The crisis in the banks has seen an increase in staff being squeezed for not meeting imposed targets' (Somerville 2009: 15). And, drawing on the experience of Unite members in five banks and three insurance companies by 2010–2011, Taylor (2013) recorded an intensification of work, reduced porosity of the working day, staff being more managed and being more visibly managed, with managed exits becoming prevalent, especially where sickness absence records were used against staff in this process.

Before examining the outcomes for pay of the performance management systems since the financial crash, it is worth observing that PRP—as a form of payment by results—in the financial services sector has a higher prevalence than in any other sector of the economy (Van Wanrooy et al. 2013a: 24), and that Barclays was the last major employer to introduced PRP (in 1998) so that since the mid-1990s the vast majority of companies in the sector have operated PRP systems which determined all of an individual's pay rise (rather than just a proportion as with the prior situation of the additional use of merit pay on top of across-the-board rises) (see Gall 2008: 80–88, 116–117). The EHRC (2009: 40–41) had already noted evidence of unfairness of process and outcome in the use of PRP in the sector while Traxler et al. (2008: 422–423) noted that PRP mapped on to market rates led to real wage cuts, not inflation proof pay rises, in the 2000s in their six case studies. It is also worth observing that, unlike parts of manufacturing or the public sector, pay freezes per se were relatively unusual in the financial services sector since the crash. For example, the few instances comprised pay rates frozen in 2010 and 2011 at Allied Irish Bank with 2500 staff in Britain while AXA Life instituted a pay freeze in 2010 for its 8700 staff as did Smith and Williamson in the same year for its 1500 staff. As part of the public sector, the Bank of England froze pay rates in 2010 and 2011 for all but the lowest paid. HSBC announced a pay freeze in 2016 for 28,000 staff but then ignominiously reversed this. Indeed, the 2011 WERS6 survey recorded that the financial services sector was the least affected by wage freezes and pay cuts of any sector in the economy (Van Wanrooy et al. 2013b: Table 5.6) while IDS (*Pay Report* 1058, October 2010) recorded most pay freezes were found in manufacturing and the public sector. At first sight, and given the scale of the crisis in the post-crash financial services sector, this might seem strange until one recognises that what was a much more common phenomenon in the sector was that large swathes of staff based did not receive pay rises as a result of PRP, with no major employers in the financial services sector not using some form of PRP, and in particular most used those based upon rating outputs from performance management systems.

As pay rises for individuals are (nominally) determined by individual assessment under performance management systems, the most appropriate ways to assess the value of pay rises overall are to examine the percentages which they add to the total pay bill, the average pay rise and the perception of the processes that led to these outcomes. In the section below, entitled 'Rough edges and minor victories', analysis of the size of the pay pot settlements shows that only minor concessions were routinely made in the process of collective bargaining. To put some flesh on this, the experience of Accord in LBG is instructive.

LBG's 2010 proposed pay pot rise was rejected by its members in a ballot but with a low turnout. A further balloted on a revised offer resulted in a slightly higher turnout with an acceptance of an average 1.5% rise. Accord members narrowly rejected the pay pot offer of 2.5% for 2011 by 50.6% on a 27% turnout (Accord press release, 28 January 2011). It then called for further talks and following small changes with regard to reaching market rates and reviewing performance management, the offer was accepted by Accord (Accord press release, 21 March 2011), especially as reps thought 'there wasn't a realistic prospect of members taking industrial action to try to secure a better deal' (*My Accord*, Winter 2011).[7] There was no agreement over the 2013 pay deal (of 1.75%), with Accord reporting that there was less anger from members overall than expected (*My Accord*, Spring 2013).[8] The offer of a 2% pay rise in 2014 was rejected by Accord (*My Accord*, Winter 2014). However, following a union recommendation, the 2015 pay offer was accepted by 94% of members in a ballot with a low turnout, making it the first agreed pay deal since 2009 (Accord press release, 6 January 2015). The assessment of Accord with this pay deal was that 'one decent pay deal doesn't restore what has been lost in recent years. But it is a step in the right direction as we work to ensure that employees share fairly in the rising prosperity of the bank' (Accord press release, 26 October 2015). The pay deal for 2016 of 2% was accepted by 80% (Accord press release, 11 December 2015) of the Accord members but on a 'disappointing' turnout (*My Accord*, Winter 2016). It was greeted in the same terms as the 2015 pay deal (Accord press release, 4 November 2015).

Turning to Unite's experience, it remained the only union to continue to demand, in the age of performance management based PRP, across the board pay rises. For example, in LBG in 2013, it demanded a 4% pay increase for all staff. As a result of the imposed pay pot deal that year, Unite estimated that 4300 employees received no pay rise (Unite *LBG Newsletter*, October 2013). In RBS, in 2011, 68% of staff received a 1% or more rise, 39% received 2% or more, 24% received 3% or more and 12% received 4% or more (*IDS Pay Report* 1076, August 2011). This meant that 32% of staff, numbering some 21,000 received no pay rise, while in 2012, Unite estimated that '[s]ome

28,000 RBS workers will receive no pay rise this year' (*uniteWORKS*, March/April 2012), equating to 61% of the bargaining group. Of the remainder '[s]ome 28% of staff received an increase of 1% or more; less than 7% of staff received 2% or more; and less than 2% of staff received 4.8% or more' (*IDS Pay Report* 1097, May 2012). Given this, there was significance to Unite gaining a pay rise in 2013 for those staff who did not receive a pay rise in 2012 and securing in late 2015 an end to the use of sales-led performance related pay for retail staff, number-ing some 20,000 employees. The corollary was that these staff gained an increase in fixed base pay. Unite national officer, Rob MacGregor, called upon '… other banks to follow suit and end the hard sell' (*Guardian*, 20 November 2015) but this fell upon deaf ears.

Polling of its members by Unite found that in LBG, widespread dis-satisfaction and discontent with the company's performance manage-ment system existed.[9] Thus, in late 2013, nearly 80% of respondents believed that the performance management process was 'not fair and/or consistent'; over 85% did not believe that the performance manage-ment system motivated staff; and nearly 70% want a move away from a performance-related pay system (Unite *LBG Newsletter*, October 2013). Another survey in the summer of 2015 revealed that 96% of respond-ents said they would 'like to see the back of performance reviews' (Unite LBG magazine, *The Spark*, Autumn 2015). The same article stated '87% sa[id] annual reviews should be scrapped entirely' and added 'LBG is far from alone, with 63% of Unite members in HSBC agreeing that it's time for annual reviews to go and 83% in RBS'. In a 2016 newslet-ter, Unite reported of a further membership survey: 'The results were stark with only half of members surveyed believing that meetings to dis-cuss their performance at work were of any use, while 81% claimed that reviews are neither fair nor consistent. 88% believed that ratings are being forced to fit into a pre-determined range, with 90% saying that this type of review system does nothing but demoralise' (Unite *LBG Newsletter*, February 2016). A 2015 poll of some 2000 Unite members in Barclays found: '61% don't feel that Barclays recognise staff efforts in pay; 54% said that they don't feel Barclays operate an effective or fair performance development system [and] 85% of respondents believe that minimum rates for each grade should not be less than 90% of the market rate' (Unite Now! Executive Council report, September 2016). In 2016, a poll of Unite members in HSBC found: '64% support across the board pay rises, i.e. a set percentage for all colleagues; 82% believe ratings are being forced to fit with calibration; 80% believe that the performance management process does not work in a fair and consistent way [and] 83% believe that the performance management system does not motivate colleagues' (Unite *HSBC Newsletter*, September 2016). Finally, a motion to Unite's (2015) Finance and Legal Industrial Sector Conference, submitted by both the National Industrial Sector Committee and a number of Regional Industrial Sector Committees said of performance management: 'As a snapshot of our members' views, 96% of respondents to a survey in the sector e-bulletin supported the abolition of annual reviews. This was echoed in surveys of the sector's largest employers; with 88% of members in Lloyds Banking Group and 83% of members in the Royal Bank of Scotland supporting the demand'.

Pensions

The worth of pension schemes in the financial services sector has been degraded quite extensively since the financial crash albeit the direction of travel, especially with the closure of new entrants to final salary schemes and the closure of final schemes, was underway already. Final salary schemes were increasingly replaced by less generous defined benefit schemes, and defined benefit schemes of whatever nature by defined contribution (or money purchase) schemes which had no guaranteed benefits *per se*. However, there were other ways in which the worth of pension schemes was reduced. The list of companies closing their final salary pension schemes to existing employees and replacing them a mixture of defined benefit and contribution schemes included Aegon, Aviva, Barclays, CBG, HSBC, IPSL, Legal and General, Nationwide, Northern Rock, United National Bank and Zurich Financial Services while AXA and RSA changed their defined benefit schemes to defined contribution schemes. Other companies like Aviva, CBG, NAG, RBS, HSBC, LBG and Zurich either raised employee contributions, ended non-contributory schemes and raised the retirement age, or ended future accruals to final salary pension schemes or put caps on pensionable pay rises, with companies like LBG and RBS implementing several of these changes. These latter reforming measures affected 163,000 staff, and quite often they were taken to alter existing final salary pensions prior to their complete closure.

This section examines some of these changes in more detail. In LBG, a cap of 2% on pay increases being pensionable for final salary pensions was imposed in 2011 followed by a 0% cap in 2014 (Accord press release, 10 November 2010, 12 August 2015). This affected around 35,000 staff and meant the final salary used to calculate the retirement income was to be based on earnings on 2 April 2014, regardless of how long staff continued to work or any subsequent pay rises or promotions. Also in 2011, LBG began using the lower CPI (Consumer Price Index)—and discontinued using the higher RPI (Retail Price Index)—for pension calculations (LTU *Newsletter*, 23 February 2011). In a joint membership survey between Accord and Unite in late 2013, '92% of respondents stated that if the proposals were implemented [on the 0% cap] they may or definitely would consider their commitment to remain with [LBG and o]ver 80% of respondents stated they would be substantially or devastatingly impacted by the proposed changes' (Unite *LBG Newsletter*, January 2014). Ahead of the 1 April 2014 implementation date, Unite reported that its members were 'furious' at LBG's imposition of a salary cap on contributions to its (defined benefits) final salary pension schemes with a number of comments being to the effect that this is '[y]et another reason to leave … or is this the point to get rid of long serving loyal and faithful staff', 'Another day, another kick in the teeth' and "The only reason I have stayed is because of the pension, this helps make my mind up for me for the future' (Unite *LBG Newsletter*, November 2013). As Accord was unable to mount industrial action against these impositions as a result of insufficient membership support (see earlier), it pursued an unsuccessful legal course. And although it delayed its introduction by 9 months, in 2016 RBS increased employee pension contributions by 2% over 2 years for 27,000 workers in a final salary pension scheme (Unite press release, 21 March 2016, Unite finance Newsletter, 15 August 2016). Unite sought to use the proposed settlement between FSU and Ulster Bank over the same issue, namely, a delay of a further delay implementation and only a 1% increase (Unite finance Newsletter, 15 August 2016).

Other Changes to Terms and Conditions

In addition to the aforementioned changes to pay and pensions, there were a number of other deleterious changes to the terms and conditions of employment of workers in the financial services sector. In 2010, HSBC reduced the sick pay entitlement of managers and extended the working week while in 2013 it then reduced holiday entitlement by 2 days per year and cut sick pay (Unite press release, 4 March 2013). Meantime, in 2012, Nationwide reduced overtime payments by increasing the span of the working day from 9 am–5 pm to 8 am–8 pm (NGSU *Rapport*, December 2012), AXA imposed a change of contract to extend working hours in one division and in 2016 both CBG and RSA imposed annualised hours and new shift patterns imposed in order to reduce overtime payments. In terms of redundancy payments, and notwithstanding the maintenance of JSAs/SEAs at previous levels of compensation (see Chap. 3), in 2013 Aviva reduced its redundancy payments by capping payments regardless of length of service and halving the amount for each year of service (*Guardian*, 19 April 2013) while in 2016 RSA lowered redundancy payouts drop from 4 weeks' pay per year of employment to 2 weeks (*Insurance Age*, 22 April 2016).

Rough Edges and Minor Victories

Given the challenges of collective mobilisation and the influence of partnership discussed in Chaps. 2 and 3, the various unions operating in the financial services sector have been unable to do little more than knock off the rough edges of employer policy and secure some minor victories on a range of issues. Put bluntly, redundancies have not been prevented but severance terms remained broadly satisfactory; performance management systems continued to operate but were tweaked at the margins, and; the sizes of pay pots were sometimes raised but distribution remained determined by individual assessment and market mapping. So there has been some amelioration of management actions and their effects. Given that unions sought to contest the processes by which pay, performance management and pensions were determined and administered, this section on knocking off the rough edges and gaining minor victories in terms of outcomes must be read alongside the discussion of those issues in Chap. 3. Before proceeding, it is also worth noting that there was a sense of 'swings and roundabouts' as union gains were sometimes offset by union losses. For example, in 2016, the by default pay rise for RBS retail staff after the removal of sales-based pay was countered by the increase in (employee) pension contributions these staff paid. Meantime, in 2014, LBG imposed its 0% cap on pensionable pay but agreed to a 3% increase in the pay pot for that year.

Some success has been recorded in increasing the size of the pay pots. The success of UFS in increasing the pay offer for 2016 to its members in Capita was unusual given that the pay pot rose from 0.8% of the pay bill to 1.0% and then 1.5% (UFS *Report*, Summer 2015). Almost all other concessions with regard to pay pots were much less than this. However, this has to be counter-balanced by the imposition of pay post increases like Norwich Union in 2008, RBS in 2012 and LBG in 2013 at less than the average settlement rate. At the behest of Unite in Barclays and HSBC, the salaries of the lowest paid have been raised by a combination of the effective suspension of PRP, *de facto* promotions by abolishing the lower grades and guaranteed rises especially from 2011 onwards. After a 3 year campaign by Unite, HSBC changed its policy so that those returning from maternity, paternity or adoption leave could do so in a part-time capacity (Unite press release, 4 January 2012). In 2014, Unite was able to negotiate an increase in paid maternity leave (from 12 to 26 weeks full pay) and paternity leave (from 1 to 2 weeks full pay) in HSBC as well.

In LBG, in 2014 LTU secured back pay rises for some 10,000 current and former employees who had refused to sign new contracts after taking three test cases to an Employment Tribunal. LBG responded by saying: 'While the tribunal decision applied only

to three colleagues, we have decided to review the pay of all current colleagues who did not originally sign our harmonised terms
and conditions in 2010. Where this shows an individual would have
been entitled to a pay increase in 2011 and 2012, we will make the
appropriate adjustment to pay and pensionable pay' (*Guardian*,
19 November 2014). On other issues, LTU was able to persuade LBG
to shelve pilots for opening on Boxing Day, end plans to scrap retired
staff liaison officers, stop the raising of the staff mortgage rate and
the introduction of car parking charges while more generally staff
bonuses were not deferred as long as employers wished (even though
they were reduced). In LBG, along with Accord, Unite achieved some
minor improvements on pay. For example, in 2014, in LBG a 'derisory offer of 1.75%' was increased to 'a less-derisory offer of 2%' with
a 'substantial increase in the number of colleagues receiving CPI or
above from about 13,200 to nearly 60,000' and a 'significant reduction of colleagues receiving a 0% pay award from 18,000 to 4530'
(Unite *LBG Newsletter*, February 2014). This was in response to
Unite's claim of RPI+2% on all salaries, grades and ranges, progress
pay to the minimum income standard of £16,850 within 2 years,
attainment of midpoint of market pay within 3 years, two 15 minute
breaks per day and an increase holiday entitlement by 1 day (Unite
LBG Newsletter, February 2014). While subsequent further negotiations resulted in some progress on faster pay progression (Unite
LBG Newsletter, March 2014), this was to be held in the context of
the imposition of the freezing future pay increases in terms of their
knock on effect on all final salary pension schemes (i.e., the amount
of pensionable pay).Finally, in early 2017, LBG budget limitations
on funding previously unpaid overtime of fifteen minutes or more
were loosened, and the process by which managers could set in train
remedial measures within LBG's performance management system
were revised to allow for the slowing down of entry into, and progress through, the informal and formal stages (Accord *Newsletters*,
29 March, 27 April 2017). Yet stringent customer targets remained
for LBG's Mortgage and Protection Advisers (LTU *Newsletters*,
21 October, 14 November 2016).

Gendered Pay

Although not necessarily a consequence of employer response to the financial crash, gendered pay remained a significant phenomenon. However, employers' willingness to address this was influenced by the financial crash. As with other issues, cost control and incentive systems like PRP militated against ending gender pay discrimination. As Chap. 2 highlighted, in 2009, women in the sector working full-time earned 55% less than their male colleagues (compared with the economy-wide gender pay gap of 28%). By 2016, the gender pay gap in financial services was 39.5%, compared with economy—wide average of 19.2% (*People Management*, 4 April 2016). The ability of employers in the sector to resist further erosion of the gender pay gap was because there was little legal compulsion upon them—and this situation arose in part from the lobbying of the employers in the sector and their actions in the voluntary arena to avert any legal compulsion. For example, one of the few mandatory changes was the gender pay gap reporting requirement under the *Equality Act 2010 (Gender Pay Gap Information) Regulations 2016* whereby from April 2017 for employers, with 250 or more employees, are required to collate and publish statistics on this matter. Prior to this, Barclays, HSBC, RBS, LBG and Virgin Money signed up to a voluntary charter on gender pay gap (but only for senior staff) (*People Management*, 4 April 2016) while 72 financial services companies including all the major and medium sized players pledged to set firm targets for helping women into senior positions (*People Management*, 12 July 2016). Another 22 had signed up by November 2016. Away from the arena of legal compulsion, for example, LBG resisted calls from Unite to undertake an equal pay audit. So while in mid-2013 Unite congratulated LBG's continuous commitment to increase female participation on its board, it had to recognise it was too weak to compel the bank to undertake an audit. Instead, LBG committed to working with Unite to identify and address equal opportunities for all despite, in 2011, Unite reaching an agreement on pay where LBG committed to undertaking a full equal pay review—which it then did not do.

Living Wage

By early 2017, the majority of the largest (independent) living wage employers were to be found in the financial services sector. Among them were Aviva, Barclays, CBG, HSBC, Legal and General, LBG, RBS, NAG, Nationwide, Prudential, Santander, Standard Life and TSB. Smaller employers in the sector also paying the (independent) living wage included Aberdeen Asset Management, ING and Leeds Building Society. This high propensity to pay the (independent) living wage indicated that some staffs in these companies were paid so little as to benefit from its introduction. For example, when Santander introduced the wage in 2013, it lifted up the bottom earners on salaries of between £12,000 and 13,000. By 2015, it lifted up bottom earners on less than £14,300. The introduction of the living wage in CBG in 2015, for example, benefitted some 300 staff according to BSU while in 2012 in HSBC it benefitted some 230 (*IDS Pay Report* 1108, January 2013). However, this introduction of the (independent) living wage only applied to the directly employed workers of these companies so that the GMB union campaigned to pressurise employers like LBG, RBS and Nationwide to stipulate that the contractors (Carillion, G4S, ISS, Mitie) they used for cleaning, catering, post, reception and security purposes also paid the (independent) living wage and provided sufficient hours of work for workers to be able to earn a decent wage.[10] By late 2016, only Nationwide and LBG had agreed instruct its contractors to pay the (independent) living wage (in the latter's case by 2018) so the GMB's campaign at RBS remained ongoing. The campaigns mainly took the form of demonstrations, lobbies and media (mainstream, social) actions.

Workers' Accounts

The following letters and comments by workers in the financial services sector put some flesh on the bones of the preceding analysis of the outcomes of the processes of employers recalibrating the wage-effort bargain in their favour. Thus, this section allows for workers as union members to speak directly and for themselves. Those from members of Accord took the form of letters to the union's members' magazine while those from members of LTU took the form of comments as responses to surveys of members on a number of issues. The particular salience of using this material from Accord and LTU is that, whilst it largely concerns the experience of employment in LBG and its predecessors (like HBoS, Halifax and Bank of Scotland), members of these two unions may be seen in some ways as being more moderate and less oppositional than those of Unite. Unfortunately, the publications of unions like Advance and NGSU did not provide such letters and comments so that those from Accord and LTU could be balanced out with members' views in companies in which there appeared to be less manifest conflict of interest.

The first set of letters in Inset 4.1 comprises letters from Accord members in chronological order which often record the reasons for flight from LBG. To summarise these, the experience of the job, work and employment had deteriorated to a point that the individual workers decided 'enough was enough', whereby the balance of the wage-effort bargain has tipped to far in favour of the employer and its agenda. Insets 4.2 and 4.3, drawing upon comments from LTU members, indicate, on the one hand, the extent to which pensions were viewed as deferred wages which workers had earned and, on the other hand, indignation and anger at the outcomes of the process of performance management systems.

Inset 4.1: Letters of Discontent, Despair, Dismay and Dissatisfaction

Having worked for the Halifax and then HBoS for the last 23 years the imposition of changes to our pay and pensions is the final straw! Thinking back to when I first started with the company, our position has deteriorated beyond belief. I am at the top of my pay scale, so will no longer receive any pay rises and will have my company car taken away at next renewal. The main things I had left to look forward to were my holidays and pension—both of which are going to be reduced. The goodwill that many staff had for the company was in large part due to the relations which they had with Accord, and the way a negotiated settlement was always reached. LBG is working fast to destroy any remaining goodwill.

I just wanted you to know that I fully support whatever steps the Union proposes, including not working overtime or industrial action if this was necessary.
Source: My Accord, Summer 2010.

I've been employed by Bank of Scotland and HBoS for more than 30 years and am now leaving through voluntary redundancy. What has happened to what was once a great bank which I was proud to be associated with?
Source: My Accord, Summer 2010.

I'd like to take this opportunity to thank [Accord reps] for all the help and assistance they gave me during my time with HBoS. Special thanks to [one] for his incredible support during 2005, when I often felt like walking out. He always advised me to behave with dignity, and not to get provoked in situations where I was made to feel extremely edgy, nervous and tearful. Again during 2009, he always responded promptly, helped me make the right decisions, was encouraging, saw my viewpoint and advised me of my rights and entitlements. I had worked for the company for almost 18 years. Eventually I was put in a situation where I did not have much choice but to take early retirement.
Source: My Accord, Summer 2010.

It was not my wish to leave the company yet; I am only 53 and had assumed I would continue until I was about 60. However, my role as a banking adviser had become unbearable over recent years with the pressure to sell more and more to customers who didn't really want what I was trying to sell them.
Source: My Accord, Spring 2011

I have finally decided to leave the company. Over the past weeks and months I have been feeling less motivated, more stressed, more of a number than a person. This week convinced me that I'd made the right choice when I 'celebrated' my 25 years service and did not receive a single message, gift or recognition of this event. It told me everything I needed to know about the new regime. Keep fighting for what you believe in. There are thousands of hard-working and dedicated colleagues who have simply had enough, but can't do anything about it. Yes, of course, I will miss the people—but not LBG
Source: My Accord, Spring 2012

I've just left the group after handing in my notice. I couldn't continue working under such tremendous pressure and stress levels prior to and since the migration with Lloyds systems. I used to enjoy working a 25-h week in branch, but the bullying emails and constant pressure we got from our manager was making all of us ill, on top of the increased workload and pressure from the system changes. I had a large cash error on the first day I started using the new card chip and pin system. I was summoned to my manager and told my errors were not acceptable and I'd have to go through an investigation to decide whether it was a 'will or skill' issue. Or

whilst I had my two days off, I could think and maybe consider a different career.
Source: My Accord, Spring 2012

I resigned in December after 27 years—just knew there must be more to life than working for an atrocious company like Lloyds. My own branch manager was lovely but she's the exception to the rule. My area manager didn't even email me or pop into thank me and wish me all the best. Frankly that says it all.
Source: My Accord, Summer 2012

I recently left the business after 19 loyal years. I have so many happy memories from over the years, but the past three have not been so pleasant. I persevered and tried really hard to adapt and move with the changes. But as time went on the 'people agenda' gradually disappeared and was replaced by more and more pressure! Finally, after four restructures in 4 years and a year of really bad health I came to realise that I no longer had that pride I once had and I was, like so many colleagues, very unhappy at work. Working in an environment with no respect or recognition for such hard work was demoralising, stressful and very, very upsetting. I was left to feel I was a bad and incompetent manager and unfit to do the job. Since leaving the business, I have regained my self-respect and confidence. My manager did not even ring me on my last day! I cried a few sad tears as I left for the final time. To not even get a text or a phone call after 19 years' service I think is despicable. Those still in the business have said 'you lucky thing, wish it was me'. Where has the respect and dignity at work gone?
Source: My Accord, Autumn 2012

We have both just tendered our resignations from the Bank of Scotland—a bank we used to be proud to work for. We started in 1976 full-time, left to have our respective families and for the last 9 years we've job-shared and not once have we let the bank down. We've been conscientious and proved popular with customers. However, recently we became disillusioned by the culture and ethics within the bank. The policies of treating customers fairly and meeting customer needs have to be addressed. We've witnessed so many instances where the bank is happy to help a customer when there's a potential sale in it. However if the customer comes back with a query, for example, they don't want to know. We felt we could no longer provide the level of service our customers deserve. The bank recently reviewed its complaint handling. To our amazement at a morning huddle we were told it was looking for more complaints as the number recorded had fallen! This can't be right? Surely the bank just had to take a look at the number of staff who are absent with work-related stress or leaving to realise there's a problem. We were in the fortunate position we could resign. We feel by agreeing to have the article published it may help our ex-colleagues and indeed action may be taken.
Source: My Accord, Autumn 2012

Having worked at the bank for 24 years I have finally had enough and left the company. As the years have gone by I have felt less and less valued as an employee and have found it constantly more difficult to achieve a reasonable performance rating. I got so tired of the constantly moving goal posts. The takeover by Lloyds felt like the straw that broke the camel's back. From that time onwards, all of the staff in my branch realised that they were just numbers. I lost count of the number of people who were shunted from branch to branch with no notice and no regard to their personal circumstances. I miss the team and a lot of the customers, but I don't for one second regret my decision to leave. I am at an age where I probably won't find another job but I would rather tighten my belt until it pinches than work for the bank again.

Source: My Accord, Autumn 2012

I've recently left the business after 6 years in a job that I loved. I thought HBoS was a great place to work and the rate of pay and the benefits were fantastic. Staff were made to feel wanted and if morale was low things were done. When Lloyds took over I dreaded coming into work. Lloyds didn't seem to care as much about their staff and as long as we sold products it would be happy. It was increasingly stressful to go into work so I began to look for another job. Luckily I found one. When I handed in my notice my service manager did not seem that interested in my reasons and said it was a good thing I was going. I feel sad that I have had to leave but the staff morale was so low and will continue to be this way until Lloyds treat their staff better.

Source: My Accord, Autumn 2012

I've worked with the bank for over 15 years—all the time under the HBoS flag has been rewarding, tough at times, but a job I loved. I was prepared to give my all as I was treated well and mattered. However, since integration I've never felt so undervalued, under pressure and bullied. I've seen colleagues around me break down due to the pressure and the public humiliations our manager liked to dish out. If things don't get any better, I will take the difficult decision to leave. I won't be the first and I'm sure I won't be the last, until someone with influence actually listens and acts on the information given by Accord and the feedback from the staff.

Source: My Accord, Autumn 2012

I work in the branch network and have seen many changes over the years, but never have I seen so many unhappy staff. Day to day in the branch is nothing but constant pressure to sell to customers—now rephrased as meeting customers' needs. We work hard to cashier, meet Net Promoter Score scores, balance our tills to reduce cash error numbers, ensure risk is complied with and on top of that we have to meet our sales targets. Why do we have such pressure to refer a certain number of appointments to be seen to be doing a good job, or save customers at least £1000 to have recognition and to receive a certificate? Why is it not acceptable any more for a member of staff to achieve 100% of sales targets? Why are we measured against peers? Why are staff constantly worried about their performance, and about being managed out if they don't hit all areas of their scorecards? Why is it that we cannot take 'no' from a customer? Why do we have to pressure them to book an appointment or arrange a call back regarding products? Where has the so-called 'customer service' gone?

Source: My Accord, Autumn 2013

I have resigned from the Halifax and am finally free after being employed by the company for almost 2 decades. I have loved my job, the people I worked with, and the customers. I have been with the company through many changes and embraced them, but sadly since being part of LBG I've been dismayed and disappointed at the way change has been handled. Cost cuts have been made so drastically to staffing and training, leaving loyal staff members in a position where it is not possible to provide the excellent customer service that the customers deserve. I am no longer proud to be an employee of a bank.

Source: My Accord, Winter 2013

All reproduced with permission from, and thanks to, Accord.

Inset 4.2: Pleas of Pension Poverty

What an utterly depressing state of affairs for me and my family. Having dedicated XX years (my entire working life) to this once great company, I find myself being sold out by another bunch of here today gone tomorrow, money grabbing, insincere, two-faced b******s.

The next time I am asked to go the extra mile for work, for no extra reward, I will certainly think twice as I don't see why I should put myself out any longer for a company that doesn't care about its employees (and I use that word deliberately instead of colleagues). Best Bank for Colleagues? I don't think so!

My pension is and has been a significant part of my total reward package. I feel now that making my pensionable salary frozen at 2014, Lloyds are effectively rewarding me with a big pay decrease.

'Thank you very much for all your hard work—so now come to work for less money' Great motivator
Antonio.

Utterly appalled. Yet another valuable benefit (in fact THE most important benefit) smashed to smithereens. Cynically timed just after the closure of the Colleague Opinion Survey. I fear what 2014 will bring when they review the other benefits. Very demoralised and as usual hard working staff are being punished for the actions of others.

The introduction of the 2% cap has already resulted in a significant pension gap for me personally and this latest change is a further kick in the teeth. This series of changes affects a population that have a limited opportunity to be able to make up shortfalls due to the length of time before retirement unless you are in the fortunate position of being able to commit a large percentage of your salary and even then it will only make a small difference.

It is us (now the minority) who have seen this company through thick and thin, not the opportunistic here today gone tomorrow 'professional managers' who take what they can get and then moves to the next victim. It doesn't make me feel wanted, respected, valued, or proud. Frankly, I am disgusted and I wouldn't trust this bunch as far as I could throw them. They will all have left LBG long before I retire to feather their own nests elsewhere.

Fight hard LTU... this is one battle that must be won. The Bank is overdrawn in my book... the decisions by people in the boardroom who are so far removed from the rank and file have mercilessly eroded any remaining goodwill and this is the final straw.

Another cynical kick in the teeth for longstanding and loyal staff which is almost certainly driven by preserving executive bonus opportunities. I understand the CEO is on for £2.5 million if the share price stays above 75 p for 30 days! [This is eroding the] remaining goodwill and this is the final straw.

Absolutely astounded, demotivated. As long as Antonio's bonus is intact that's OK.

I don't fully understand the impact of what is happening to the pensions, but I do understand that inflation will have a massive impact on what is left of my pension and will make it worthless to me when I retire. I have children, one income and can't afford to start another pension to be in the position I would have been in with my final salary scheme. This announcement will have added a number of extra years of employment. Gutted!

The Bank's own examples indicate I will need to pay £165 a month into an AVC just to get a pension £7 k a year less than I was expecting. Not sure where they think I am going to get that sort of money from given that pay rises have not kept pace with recent increases in my rail fares and utility bills. I can only assume the Bank see its longer serving members of staff as a drain on resources and is hoping we leave.

Cynical, cost cutting, stab in the back for long standing loyal employees. The Bank is increasingly demonstrating that it can't be treated as a trustworthy employer.

This is travesty. The [senior executives of LBG] are like politicians running the government, take, take, take, whilst their fat cat bonuses and retirement provisions remain intact and considerably more than mine.

[LBG] said in the announcement that the money saved would go towards pay rises, what a load of rubbish. Most staff I know have been in the Bank for 10 years or more and have not received any pay rises in the last 5 years and I can't see that changing in the near future, whether they save this money or not.

LBG is still making significant profits even after some disastrous Senior Management decisions which have killed our share holdings. Now they want to 'steal' our pensions. We should consider industrial action to fight this. It is not acceptable, in any way shape or form.
Source: LTU *Newsletter*, 20 November 2013.
Reproduced with permission from, and thanks to, LTU.

Inset 4.3: Market Pay Misery

I truly hope this is a major overhaul of the current process, as year after year we read about the same pay review priorities that have been established e.g. 'encourage the movement of employees from the Market Primary zone to the Market zone within their pay range'. However in reality the movement to the Market zone does not happen in an acceptable timeframe. I've personally been in my grade for almost 5 years now, a good performer every year, yet my position is still in the primary zone at only 86%. In fact I'm not even in the Market Zone of the grade below me yet.

For every person who has commented I would guess that there is 10 who agree but don't. I was going to be one of the 10 for all the obvious reasons of it being held against me at a later stage.

And if we are now going down the line of 'treating all staff the same' then I must have missed the announcement that you will be removing the final salary pension rights given to Mr Horta-Osorio. Did I miss that? He signed a contract just like everyone else did. So why is his set in stone, whereas the normal staff's contracts seem to have been written in pencil, rubbed out, and re-written at the banks whim? But hey, he is obviously better than the rest of us, so that is fine.

The performance management system is completely discredited. There is a forced distribution curve and pretending there isn't is part of the problem. The current process also drives the wrong behaviours. I have been in a meeting where a very senior manager said to his direct reports 'If you don't have a Developing performer, you will be the Developing performer'. There is also a dis-incentive to develop those who are genuinely Developing as the reality is you will just have to find someone else to be Developing to fit the curve at the end of the year. The whole system needs to be scrapped.

I am a line manager and I have successfully challenged an attempt to downgrade one of my direct reports ratings from 'good' to an undeserved 'developing'. I like to go to sleep at night with a clear conscience and it would have been morally indefensible not to have made this challenge. The unpleasant truth is that our current approach comforts weak leadership. Those individuals who lack the strength of character to lead by example employ it as a low-level bullying technique. Do as I say, or suffer the consequences. How have we ended up like this?

As many others on this thread have commented, you are currently not paying colleagues their salary within the correct zone. I've been awarded the equivalent of 'strong' and 'good' ratings for 8 years and my salary falls within the Primary Zone. The Primary Zone is defined as 'This is the zone that we would expect new starters or colleagues recently promoted to fall into. Colleagues may also fall into this zone if the market rate has increased.' I obviously don't fit into the first sentence of this category and the last sentence of this category was added later. Why are you not willing to pay colleagues who have many years of service and are receiving consistently 'strong' and 'good' ratings?

The Executives of this organisation care about no-one other than themselves. They had a charade of a 'consultation' about the Defined Benefit Pension scheme and completely ignored the response.

They will do whatever they like whenever they like with total disregard for staff (other than their own peers). ... what about THE REST? What about Band D & E who also work hard, long/longer hours and have far more responsibility. Do they not deserve the movement to Market zone?

Or is it OK to be with the Bank for years and stay at the bottom all the time???

Source: LTU Newsletter, 16 February 2015.
Reproduced with permission from, and thanks to, LTU.

Finally, and in response to the ever growing clamour of 'banker bashing' over City bonuses in the run up to, during and after the financial crash—and which have the effect of also tainting financial services sector workers—Unite published a 'myths v reality' leaflet for general distribution amongst the members of the public in order to counter the popular misconceptions about employees in the financial services based on 'guilt by association' with City bankers. It is reproduced in full in as Inset 4.4.

Inset 4.4: Truth and Lies About Financial Services Sector Workers' Wages and Conditions

Pay—Finance sector employees.

Against popular perception employees in the financial service sector are often poorly paid and suffer from much job insecurity. There are a range of myths relating to the pay of workers in this sector. Unite the union is campaigning to dispel these views and outlines the realities of work in the finance sector. The union is launching a campaign to address these issues.

MYTH: Finance sector workers earn well above the average wage.

REALITY: In reality the average starting salary for finance workers is only slightly above the minimum wage at around £11,500 with a relatively slow progression through the grades. A finance sector worker who has worked for 5 years as a customer service advisor can expect to be on around £15,800 (although regional variations exist). The financial services sector also has a larger gender pay gap than any other industry at 43%.

MYTH: Finance sector workers can earn huge bonuses.

REALITY: The majority of workers in the finance sector do not receive the type of bonuses publicised in the media—a few finance professionals in the City of London make eye-watering bonuses which skews the average bonus for all. Bonuses are not guaranteed and are usually linked to a combination of company and personal performance and in many cases are non-pensionable.

MYTH: Workers in the finance sector have it easy compared with other office workers.

REALITY: Many finance sector workers are given non-negotiable and often unattainable targets to deliver products and services. This puts increased pressure and stress on workers who can be disciplined if they fail to reach the target set and are then deemed to be underperforming by management. On a personal level this can affect morale and on a financial level can impact on any bonus due. Bullying behaviours from management has also been reported by union members in the sector.

MYTH: Finance sector workers receive above inflationary rises due to large profits made by companies.

REALITY: While Directors often receive well above inflation rises, the majority of employees in the sector receive pay rises in line with inflation. However there is a significant number of employees in the sector who receive no pay rise at all. Unite's campaign 'Zero Tolerance to Zero Pay' is targeting those employers who continue to operate this practice.

MYTH: Workers in the finance sector have a job for life.

REALITY: Far from being a job for life—the finance sector has lost around thousands of jobs in the past 5 years, more than any other industrial sector and with tens of thousands of jobs being offshored to cheaper economies, workers in the sector are increasingly concerned about job security.

MYTH: Finance sector workers have huge pensions to look forward to when they retire.

REALITY: Many finance sector employers have taken pension 'holidays' for years when they made no contribution to the pension scheme on behalf of employees during that time. Employers have also closed more beneficial pension schemes like Final Salary in favour of less generous

> and more risky schemes like Money Purchase. Women are particularly adversely affected by pension schemes, with women's income in retirement only around half that of men's, leaving them poorer in old age.
> *Source:* Unite leaflet, ES/942/1–08 (2008).
> *Reproduced in full and with thanks to, and permission from Unite.*

Given the reproduction in full of the Unite leaflet, it is also worth reproducing the comments of three its active members in Edinburgh and Newcastle:

We were always told by management that HBoS was a good business. The Bank of Scotland used to be a good employer. You were proud to work for them. It's having that rug pulled from underneath you. You think now, 'What were we working for?' ... [Now] there have been several small redundancy announcements every other week. It's death by a thousand cuts. Nobody on the staff knows who's going next. When people at the bank sit around together, they talk themselves into depression. (*Guardian*, 3 October 2009)

The 'reward' culture has meant that those at the top were further rewarded with unjustifiable and obscene bonuses. The average starting salary in the sector is around £11,500 and after 5 years you can expect to earn about £16,000. No matter what way you calculate it, a 5% or even a 10% bonus paid on that salary will never make you rich. The bonuses paid to workers have unfortunately become an integral part of their remuneration. As wages have been held down and more money poured into bonus schemes staff have come to depend on their bonus. Staff throughout the sector use bonus money to pay for a holiday or Christmas, but increasingly staff use their bonus to pay bills, debt and their credit cards. (Somerville 2009: 14)

It's hard to describe, working like we have done for over the past year [at Northern Rock]. It drains away any trust that you had in the company. You become disillusioned, you also feel deceived—after being encouraged by your employer to take shares as part of your remuneration and share in the company's success and then be left with nothing. (Unite *United*, Winter 2008/2009)

Strikes and Industrial Action

The greatest concentration of industrial action in the financial ser-vices sector since the financial crash has taken place in the pensions and insurance sub-sector of it (judged by the number of instances rela-tive to the size of the workforce). This contrasts with the pre-financial crash period of bank workers and ICT staff in banking taking limited amounts of action (see Gall 2008: 80–89, 136–138). The post-crash industrial action has centred upon issues which have been germane to the whole sector, and carried out solely by Unite members. This section examines the processes and outcomes of these actions.

The first noticeable instance of organised collective discontent after the financial crash was the ballot for strike action and industrial action short of a strike amongst Unite workers working for Steria on a con-tract with Cooperative Financial Services (CFS) in late 2008. The dis-pute concerned compulsory redundancies as a result of offshoring. The ballot of 176 workers saw a 71% vote for striking and an 89% vote for industrial action short of a strike on a 53% turnout. However, no action was forthcoming. In the late summer of 2010, Unite members in five workplaces in Capita Life and Pensions balloted for strike action over the imposition of changes to their pension scheme which eroded its worth. The ballot result was used to gain less drastic changes and a two year-phasing in period. Earlier, in 2009 (when company-level bargain-ing did not yet exist), Unite members in one of Capita's Glasgow work-places took 3 days of strike action in pursuit of a higher pay offer (while other workplace accepted across the board pay increases which were not based on individual performance assessments) and in 2010 Unite mem-bers in five Capita sites balloted for strike action against the closure of their final salary pension scheme. This resulted in the maintenance of the scheme but with some changes made to the terms of the scheme.

In late 2012, Unite members in four Capita sites undertook a lim-ited period industrial action short of a strike (a ban on overtime and on-call working) which compelled their employer to reverse its decision to offshore work and implement compulsory redundancies after a 4:1

vote for strike action and a 9:1 vote for action short of a strike on a 65% turnout. In the summer of 2013, Unite Capita members in its life and pensions and ICT services divisions in eight workplaces took strike action over an average 1.1% pay offer following a 65% rejection of the offer. Members voted in the life and pensions division voted by 62% for strike action and by 78% for action short of a strike on a 45% turnout while members in ICT services division voted by 84% for strike action and by 94% for action short of a strike on a 65% turnout. The contracted clients included Deutsche Bank (Abbey Life), Prudential, Royal London, Met Life, Phoenix and Friends Life. A single one-day strike resulted in a change to the performance distribution curve so that 65% of staff received the 'middle rating' compared to the 50% before (Email correspondence, senior Unite Capita shop steward, 8 November 2016).

In the spring of 2016, some 900 Unite members at eight Capita workplaces and working on contracts for Abbey Life, Aviva, Guardian, Met Life, Prudential and Royal London insurance companies, rejected by 88% on 72% turnout a pay offer and balloted for strike action. The pay offer was a 1.5% 'pay pot' distributed via PRP. They then voted for industrial action short of a strike by 90% and for strike action by 75%. The first strike took place in the early summer, being preceded by an overtime and standby ban from late spring. A second, two-day, strike followed in mid-summer, with a planned four-day strike called off to allow for negotiations, which led to a further 0.2% being added to the 'pay pot' (which allowed most to receive a 1.3% level rise equivalent to the then RPI), an additional day of holiday entitlement, and a pay pot for 2017 based on the December 2016 RPI (capped at 2.5%) (Email correspondence, senior Unite Capita shop steward, 8 November 2016). Some 150 new members were recruited in this dispute and strike pay of £60 per day per member was paid out.

The proposed closure of a Legal and General workplace in Surrey with 1700 job cuts led to an industrial dispute in late 2015. Unite members demanded the company minimised job losses through natural attrition, voluntary redundancy and by ensuring that all staff are offered realistic offers of relocation. Members voted in a consultative ballot by 63% for industrial action including striking on a 68% turnout. This then led to a formal ballot for industrial action with a 67% vote for industrial action, leading to the company offered to delay closure by a year and provide relocation for some. Prior to this, in 2014, Unite stated that with job losses at Legal and General's Ipswich site, 'industrial action to save these jobs can't be ruled out at this stage' (Unite press release, 2 September 2014).

In the summer of 2016, Unite members at Prudential in Reading balloted for industrial and strike action over plans to outsource about 80 jobs to India after the company rejected a counter-proposal from Unite asking it engage constructively in achieving efficiencies while retaining the knowledge and experience of current staff. At the end of the summer, these Unite members began industrial action after a 97% vote for strike action and a 100% vote for industrial action short of a strike on a 75% turnout. The action involved not co-operating with or undertaking any work related to Project Jupiter (which was the name of the plan to offshore work from the Reading site). The action, representing the first in the company since 1991, proceeded after some small movement on the part of Prudential in providing around a quarter of the affected workers with alternative jobs. In the early autumn, two 24-hour strikes were suspended after Prudential gave guarantees that alternative jobs would be found for all those affected. The industrial action short of a strike was also stood down. Prior to the outsourcing announcement, union density was 39% but before the ballot took place it rose to 60%, rising to 66% thereafter (O'Donnell 2017; Anonymous 2016).

Turning to the banking section of the financial services sector, and recalling the discussion concerning the difficulties in generating collective mobilisation in the Chap. 3, there were no strike ballots on job losses. The most that Unite could say was that, in the case of 2000 jobs losses at HSBC First Direct in 2013 where displaced workers were unlikely to be successful in applying for the new 1000 roles being created because of inappropriate skill sets or being unable to geographically locate, it could 'not rule out balloting its members for industrial action over the company's behaviour' (Unite press release, 23 April 2013) and it was 'assessing the mood among HSBC members with the possibility of a ballot on industrial action' after 3167 job cuts announced' (*unite-WORKS*, May/June 2012). In the case of pensions, in response to AXA closing its defined benefit pension scheme in 2013 and transferring

2300 staff to an inferior defined contribution scheme, Unite said it had 'not ruled out an industrial action ballot to put pressure on the company to think again' (Unite press release, 29 April 2013). In a survey of 1000 AXA staff carried out by Unite, 94% did not agree with the closure and 'only 20% of respondents said they would not consider taking industrial action to protect their pension benefits' (*Unite in AXA*, 13 June 2013). An offer of 15% compensation was then made which was rejected by 65% on a 67% turnout with Unite stating: 'Whilst this is a clear 'no' vote against the company offer, the Unite in AXA National Company Committee is of the view that although the company action is obviously hugely unpopular, that given the number of ballot papers not returned (over 30%) and the size of the 'no' vote, it does not give a large enough mandate to enable us to consider any further action on this matter' (*Unite in AXA*, 21 October 2013). Previously, when RBS planned to cap pensionable in 2009, Unite stated it would only go as far as to 'support its members in any action they choose to take to defend their pensions' (*Guardian*, 26 August 2009) while when NAG imposed an increase in employee pensions contributions, equivalent to a 9% pay cut in 2011, Unite only pledged to 'agree … to hold a consultative ballot to see if members are prepared to be formally balloted to take part in some form of action' (Unite press release, 4 October 2011). This sense of industrial inaction over pensions was broadly consistent with the period before the crash when schemes were closed to new entrants or final salary schemes closed (see Gall 2008: 137). The instances of merely threatening to ballot for strike or industrial action as Unite members did in 2009 in Barclays over closure of the final salary pension scheme (after a 92% vote to hold a strike ballot and which helped solicit a deferral of the closure and a reduction in the level of increased contributions) and in 2013 at the State Bank of India in order to (successfully) gain the payment of promised bonuses were exceptional (Unite press release, 19 December 2013).

So too was a consultative ballot by Unite members at Scottish Widows in 2015 on whether to hold an industrial action ballot over the company's decision to make the traditional Scottish bank holiday of January 2 a normal working day. The 74% vote in favour of balloting on industrial action led to Scottish Widows offering a day in lieu and triple overtime for the day (Unite Now! Executive Council report, March 2016). Lastly, CWU members in IPSL in 2011 voted 75% for strike action in a ballot in a dispute over the ending of their final salary pension scheme. This resulted in a compromise with the company. But, as highlighted before, more common were the situations of large rejections of pay offers and then consequent registers of failure to agree but without any ensuing action (as in LBG in 2013). Even with large numbers of employees receiving no annual pay rise as was the case in RBS (see earlier), no action was forthcoming even though Unite had taken action on this very issue in HSBC in 2005 when 10% of staff received no pay rise alongside 40% receiving a below inflation rise (Gall 2008: 137) .The figures for RBS employees in 2011 (61%) and 2012 (83%) either receiving no pay rise or one less than inflation were in excess of the situation in HSBC in 2005. This was not altogether surprising on account of not just the impact of the changed economic situation before and after the financial crash but also because union campaigns of 'zero tolerance' of 'zero pay rises' did not materialise in the period before the crash either (see Gall 2008: 137).

This overview highlights that industrial action was particularly concentrated within just one company within the insurance sub-sector, that industrial action short of a strike—in the form of non-cooperation—is a more effective tool than strike action in tackling offshoring (although the development of this tactic was relatively late in the day (see Gall 2008: 156–158)), and that for the vast majority of financial services sector workers there did not appear to be an obviously effective way to take industrial action. For the larger sub-sector of banking, the observation of IDS (2010: 12) that though 'The trades unions LTU, Unite and Accord have all recently held ballots at which the changes to the pensions scheme were rejected … it is as yet unclear what if any action this may lead to' provides a sense of the inability to engage in collective mobilisation (see also Chap. 3). This was further highlighted by the rather cautious tone of the content of Accord's message to its membership when facing, arguably, the greatest attack on its members' interests:

> The PEC [Principal Executive Committee] will be meeting again in two weeks' time to consider the bank's response and decide on what further

steps may be necessary to persuade the bank to behave decently towards its hard working staff. This will include further consideration of ballots for industrial action both short of and including strike action if the bank presses ahead with the current proposals following the consultation period. (Accord press release, 13 November 2013)

A senior Unite activist working in LBG and then seconded to Unite's organising department explained her perception of the nature of the challenge facing collective mobilisation:

> People got angrier and angrier, but the opposite side of that is fear, and it's fear that stops people taking action. The anger hasn't developed into a mood that the union has been able to take forward. People feel kind of stuck [:] if this had happened in isolation I think we could have tapped into that anger more, but because it is part of a much wider economic downturn people are fearful of losing their jobs, more so than they would have been otherwise. They might otherwise have just been a bit more gung ho about it and thought 'Well, okay, I want to have my say about this.' But now there is a paralysis there. (in Ellis and Taylor 2010: 807)

It is also worth noting that Unite created a £25 million dispute fund in 2012 (which had risen to the value of £35 million in 2016). The fund was available to help finance industrial disputes, mostly obviously through providing strike pay, and resource leverage campaigns. The fund was used on a small number of occasions in the financial services sector. However, it appears to have made little obvious difference to the willingness of Unite members (or workers) to take strike action (in terms of receiving strike pay) and the growth of the strike fund testifies, at least in the financial services sector, more to its lack of use rather than its ability to act as a deterrent to employers (thus, not requiring its expenditure). Practically, the dispute fund—especially with regard to industrial action—could neither resolve the issues concerning Unite members not having higher levels of union density that are required to provide the foundation for effective industrial action nor the challenge of identifying the most appropriate points of leverage.

Although this study does not seek to engage in comparative analysis with other Western European countries, it is worth noting in connection with the historically low incidence of industrial action in Britain overall and the financial services sector, in particular, that some countries have seen far more resistance to the ways in which capital has sought to resolve the financial crisis in its favour vis-à-vis labour. Taking Greece as an example would be an unwise comparator given the much greater depth of the crisis there (in addition to the historical weakness of its economy and its relatively small size). Therefore taking Italy as a better comparator, for example, highlights that in addition to a number of anti-austerity general strikes which finance sector workers took part in and while, inter alia, there were four strikes between 2011 and 2012 against redundancies and outsourcing, the major the major acts of resistance amongst finance workers were two sector wide strikes in 2013 and 2015 by some 300,000 workers to protest against the ending of the sector wide bargaining agreement and previously agreed wage rises. This illustrates that the structure of collective bargaining has an important bearing upon the process by which grievances are generated and expressed. By contrast, it would difficult to envisage such a sector-wide strike in Britain because of the decentralised nature of bargaining whereby different units of capital act at slightly different times and in slightly different ways. That said, Italy may well represent a country, along with Spain, which is at the upper end of the propensity to undertake industrial action in the financial services sector given that Tarren (2013: 36) reported that less than 25% of finance union respondents throughout the European Union had taken industrial action since 2007.

Reactive Radicalism

Surprisingly, while calls for genuine nationalisation (or public ownership) of the banks and the other financial institutions within the sector in the wake of the financial crash secured a wide public airing and much support amongst the public, there was little support for such measures amongst the employees, and especially, the union members in the sector. Some of this was at least attributable to the extensive holding of shares by financial services sector staff (see Unite *United*, Winter 2008/9; Somerville 2009: 14–15). An unusual instance was the debating of a motion at Accord's 2014 conference (but which was not passed) on nationalising LBG without compensation for shareholders.[11] The full response of LTU to this was laid out in Inset 3.3 in Chap. 3 but it is worth noting that in this LTU accused Accord of being both feckless and utopian (LTU *Newsletter*, 31 March 2014).

But the sense of a palpable unwillingness to change longstanding policy on such matters in times of an unprecedented crisis also reflected the ideological hegemony of neo-liberal capitalism amongst the workforce and their unions. Self-evidently, the continued embrace of partnership with management and employers meant that nationalisation would have constituted a massive rupture to their relationships, arguably being greater than the impact of the financial crash for post-crash period. In the case of managers, nationalisation may have ended their existence. In the case of employers, it would have ended their existence. What did happen was that Unite adopted a policy of a national maximum wage from 2009 onwards (Unite 2011), and made a submission to the High Pay Commission in 2011 which pointed out that in 2009 amongst six of the biggest financial services companies (Aviva, Barclays, HSBC, LBG, RSA, RBS), the salaries (excluding bonuses) of their chief executives were between 80 and 108 times the salary of the lowest starting salary in those companies (Unite 2011: 5). However, no manifest progress was made on progressing the policy of a maximum wage even though European Banking Authority (EBA) figures showed the number of high earners in British banks rose by 11% in 2012, with more than 2700 people earning above €1 million (then £833,000) (Unite press release, 29 November 2013) and in 2016 data showed that, on average, the difference in annual earnings between the highest 10% and lowest 10% paid workers in the finance and insurance industry (at £93,351) was the largest for any sector of the economy (*Guardian*, 11 January 2017).

Challenger and Mutual Status

In Chap. 2, the claim that challenger banks and mutual societies operated in employment terms in a less brutal and oppressive manner than their conventional counterparts was set out. In the former case, this was reasoned to be because of deploying a different approach to capital accumulation, essentially being to gain market share by generating customer loyalty (which required spurning a hardnosed, cost cutting approach). In the case of the latter, the same approach could be taken because they were no external shareholders to the account of policy holders (customers). This section examines the evidence to support this claim.

In the case of Santander, both the Advance and CWU unions regarded Santander as paying higher pay pot increases than most other banks even though the distribution of the pot was dependent upon the conventional pay matrix (individual performance mapped onto market rates). Thus, average pay rises have been in the upper quartile of those in the financial services sector since 2008 (and especially since 2013). Santander was also agreeable to the suggestion from Advance to pilot a team-based pay element to pay in late 2011, and from 2016, particularly as a result of CWU campaigning against the company's performance management system, in a 3 year pay settlement all elements of PRP were removed except for staff graded as 'unsatisfactory', only bonuses would be based on individual performance, and automatic annual pay progression was extended to previously excluded staff. In this regard, Nigel Cotgrove, CWU assistant secretary, in the case of ISBAN said: 'We've long championed reform of the process which members have long viewed as arbitrary, unfair and demotivating—largely due to the previous use of forced distribution of appraisal markings to achieve a pre-determined outcome and the use of peer group rankings' (CWU *Telecoms and Financial Services Voice*, November/December 2013). Whilst job cuts were made, none were compulsory, many operations that other employers either outsourced or offshored were kept 'in house' and the final salary pension scheme was not abolished. Notwithstanding the significance of the challenger status, CWU assistant secretary with responsibility for financial services, John East, said collective bargaining still 'therefore comes down to the usual balance of what is the price to be paid for the desired changes' (Email correspondence, 3 September 2016). In this, the CWU has, however, been able to use the opportunity of harmonisation to try to level up some of the terms and conditions its members are employed upon to those of the terms and conditions of members of Advance. Negotiations to guide the harmonisation of terms and conditions of employment (covering redeployment, redundancy and maintaining final salary pension schemes) produced outcomes which were endorsed by the CWU—through its Santander National Committee—and then its members in a ballots (by big majorities on high turnouts).Yet towards the end of the period of this study, Santander was reported to be using highly insecure 'on call' contracts (*Financial Times* 27 March 2017) as an alternative to zero hour contracts and the annual CWU conference in 2017 heard that staff attrition rates at the company were at 43% as a result of uncompetitive starting pay, slow pay progression and inflexible rostering (whilst other banks experienced 15 to 25% attrition rates). This began to call into question the extent of the worth of the 'challenger' bank status.

Turning to TSB, under Sabadell's ownership from mid-2015 onwards there was evidence of the positive influence of the challenger approach upon employment relations. As noted in Chap. 2, there was no attempt to erode terms and conditions upon transfer, pay rises were more generous than in other companies (although the terms of its SEA were not) and sales targets were not used. For example, in 2016 the pay post rise in TSB was 2.5% compared to HSBC (2.2%), RBS (2%) and LBG (2%). In TSB staff also received a 12.5% bonus, worth around six weeks' wages. The move away from using sales incentives and towards the same percentage rise for all staff subject to meeting customer satisfaction targets and the company being in profit took place prior to Sabadell's ownership (*My AccordTSB*, May 2015). This move was also part of the change to replicate a John Lewis-style partnership for the 8600 staff, whereby they are classified as 'partners' but without the very limited institutional rights that John Lewis grants its staff. Despite the changes, a joint Accord-Unite survey in late 2015 recorded '87% of [respondents] have considered moving to a competitor, while 65% report symptoms of work-related stress … 58% [thought] … the bank's annual [performance pay] review system is neither fair nor consistent, while 64% say the results are as good as rigged [with] … 92% report[ing] working unpaid hours … because of rising workloads' (Unite press release, 12 May 2016).

Virgin Money bought over Northern Rock in late 2011, with the sale taking effect on 1 January 2012. Under state ownership, the number of employees was reduced from 6500 to 2500 at the point of its sale.

When Virgin Money first announced its intention to but Northern Rock in 2008, it said it could not guarantee not to make redundancies. This was condemned by Unite (*Guardian*, 6 February 2008) but upon the sale to Virgin in 2011, Unite said it was 'cautiously optimistic' about the future of the existing jobs there (*BBC News*, 17 November 2011). This was because of the scale of the job losses already but, in the event, further redundancies were made albeit there was consultation with Unite over these. Virgin announced plans to reduce the number of jobs by a further 680 by the end of 2011 with 'compulsory redundancies [to] be avoided where possible' (*Virgin Money* press release, n.d. 2011). Virgin Money then gave a pledge of no compulsory redundancies for 3 years (*Manchester Evening News*, 17 November 2011). Virgin Money continued its recognition of Unite and like most other employers negotiated on the size of the pay pot which was then distributed as a result of performance management (individual assessment mapped on to market salary range). In 2015, this meant 'meeting some expectations' resulted in pay increases of between 0 and 2%; 'meets all expectations' between 0 and 4%; 'exceeding expectations' between 1 and 5%; and 'significantly exceeding expectations' between 2 and 6%.

According to Unite, the expectation was that CBG should act in a more ethical manner than its competitors given its heritage and history (Unite press release, 21 October 2013, 4 November 2013, 14 March 2014). In this regard, and despite its near collapse in 2013, conducting their research between 2012 and 2014, Chew et al. (2016) gave the bank a clean bill of health in regard of its ethical banking practices and socio-environmental development. But their study did not examine employment practices and behaviour in employment matters and, with regard to redundancies, pay, pensions and working hours (see this chapter and Chap. 3), there is no evidence that the expectation was delivered upon. Turning to Nationwide and mutuals, the NGSU's view was that the Nationwide's organisational culture was influenced by its mutual status, although not necessarily in a straightforward way:

> The business is keen to differentiate itself from the competition by trading on its values and working on behalf of members rather than shareholders. We're able to translate that back into the working environment and hold

the business to account, i.e., what's good for Society members is good for employees and it should practice what it preaches. But it's not always been the case though and prior to the financial crisis, Nationwide was as ruthless as the banks in its drive for sales and many of our members suffered bullying and stress as a result. External regulation has been a huge help here with more scrutiny on behaviours that can lead to poor customer outcomes, such as removing sales incentives and a crackdown on performance management practices that create undue pressure to sell. Management by humiliation ([through] sales league tables) is thankfully a thing of the past. Nationwide has been very responsive to this external pressures and it's a much happier place to work these days. I like to think we've [the NGSU] played out part in this and we've been very strong in calling out poor practice and exposing wrong behaviours. (Email correspondence, Tim Rose, NGSU Assistant General Secretary (Services), 27 July 2016).

Nationwide used a performance management system to determine pay rises where sales were prominent and mapped onto a pay matrix from the early 2000s, where NGSU was placed in a position of only being able to influence interpreting the application of the system rather than establishing its parameters and methodologies or the size of pay pot. Since the crash, NGSU has been able to influence Nationwide to accede to higher awards for the lower paid and pay rises for those at the top of their scales (in terms of the market salary range) but with less success recorded on accelerated progression through pay scales. This was a long battle 'in a climate where increasingly the choice is between controlling costs or cutting jobs' (NGSU *Rapport*, 30 October 2008) and despite NGSU calling for 'a credible performance management system' and making 'its acceptance and continued support of Future Pay conditional on performance management delivering a fair distribution of ratings for all employees' (NGSU *Rapport*, 30 October 2008). By 2016 and despite the aforementioned changes implemented as a result of external regulation, NGSU was 'increasingly concerned that performance management has simply become a process to deliver a set of ratings to distribute pay and that meaningful discussion about individual performance is stifled by calibration' (NGSU *Union Mail*, June 2016). Indeed, Tim Rose, NGSU Assistant General Secretary (Services), commented that: 'Calibration and performance ratings are a bone of contention and we were pretty close to refusing to agree this year's annual pay review on the basis of performance ratings but, ultimately, did so having secured a commitment to review and fundamentally overhaul the existing arrangements' (Email correspondence, 27 July 2016). He added that the dispute was 'very much behind closed doors and we're generally pretty good at agreeing a set of words that satisfy us that the issue is being taken seriously without being too confrontational. We sometimes get criticism from members who would like us to be seen to be more robust but we think we get better outcomes for members this way' (Email correspondence, 27 July 2016). Along with ending the final salary pension and replacing it with a defined benefit system and extending the scope of working hours (see earlier), the NGSU reported that in 2011 and 2012 especially significant amounts of unpaid overtime were being worked. In the case of NFU Mutual with 3500 staff and union recognition with Unite, PRP was used but without producing the same discontent found elsewhere on account of average pay rises being in the upper quartile. The LBSSA reported in 2016 that staff surveys at the Leeds Building Society recorded 'high levels of staff satisfaction' (Alliance for Finance minutes, 12 April 2016) with the employer increasing staff numbers and annualised hours operating flexibly along with PRP paying average rises in the upper quartile.

While Santander, TSB, Virgin Money and Nationwide are not inconsiderably sized players, challenger banks and mutuals still comprise a relatively small component of the overall financial services sector. Even if their approaches to employment relations were uniformly positively associated with their status in the marketplace—which the evidence above shows they are not—their very approach cannot be generalised throughout the sector precisely because the profitability of the main players is based upon a divergent approach.

Counter-Evidence

A CIPD (2013) survey of just over 1000 employees working in banking, brokerage and investment and insurance in April 2013 indicated that levels of pride and trust in employers were higher than the evidence presented here suggests. This was a similar disparity with regard to the perception of fair treatment at the hands of employers. However, on pay and incentives, there was strong evidence of dissatisfaction with performance management systems where 65% of employees agreed that there was a lack of transparency around how people are rewarded and what they are rewarded for (CIPD 2013: 23). Without a breakdown of the number of respondents in each of the four parts, namely, banking, brokerage and investment and insurance and the weightings as a result of this, it cannot be known whether the composition of respondents had a role to play—and how much of a role to play—in accounting for these results. For example, proportionately more respondents in brokerage and investment than in banking and insurance vis-à-vis the actual balance in the sector may have resulted in less critical responses. That said, as a one off snapshot, it is also worth bearing in mind that the survey took place after much of the worst of financial crisis had already taken place and a number of companies began to return to pre-crash levels of profitability. This brief consideration suggests that it would be wrong to assume, as alluded to in the appraisal of the research methods employed in chapter one, that the evidence presented in this study is complete or wholly impartial. However, the weight of evidence presented in this chapter does suggest that significant numbers of workers in the financial services sector were affected in gravely deleterious terms.

Eire

Despite a common project of neo-liberalism across the European Union, and the post-crash period resulting in widespread redundancies in these countries (see, for example, Soriano 2011), significant national differences remain between the countries, particularly with regard to collective bargaining structures, multiplicity of unions, legal regulation of employment and union traditions (see, for example, Eurofound 2011; Glassner 2009; Soriano 2011; Tarren 2013; Kornelakis 2014). Therefore, and in the limited space available in this study, comparative analysis of worker experiences and responses in the financial services sectors of these other countries has not been attempted other than in the case of Eire. This is because the Republic of Ireland, or Eire, provides scope for some productive comparison with Britain because of a number of companies and unions operating in both jurisdictions (such as Aviva, Bank of Ireland, Allied Irish Bank, Bank of Scotland (Ireland) and FSU and Unite),[12] bargaining takes place at the company level, union density in the private services sector overall is equally low and falling (see Walsh 2015), regulation of union recognition remains largely in the voluntary sphere and industrial action is regulated in a similar way to that in Britain. Moreover, the Irish state's response to an equally grave financial crisis was broadly similar to that of the British state, namely, 'nationalisation' and recapitalisation of its major banks. In the Irish case, this involved the Allied Irish Bank and Bank of Ireland. That said, there is greater state involvement in industrial relations in Ireland (through the Labour Court and Labour Relations Commission) although social partnership, regulating wage rises in particular, ended in 2009 (with only the public sector continuing to engage in it) and some have argued that the 'banking crisis was more severe in Ireland than elsewhere, due to the bursting of a national property 'bubble'' (Farrelly 2011: 1). The ending of social partnership in the private sector at the national level did allow employers to respond to the financial crash in a less restricted way.

In proportionate terms, jobs losses were equally widespread in Eire as in Britain. IBOA counted 6200 job losses by autumn 2010 with its prediction of 10,000 being met by 2014. By 2016, some 12,000 jobs had been shed. And, although redundancies and severance terms were negotiated, the IBOA reported that the extent of collective bargaining on issues of redundancy and restructuring was curtailed.[13] Indeed, this was particularly true with regard to pay for there were pay freezes in the years immediately after 2008. More recently, in 2017, Ulster Bank (in the Republic) unilaterally imposed new salary ranges. Subsequent to this, negotiations ameliorated some of the contentious issues. As found elsewhere in Britain, the FSU expressed concern at high and continuing levels of job losses (even though the losses were often voluntary and the severance terms jointly negotiated). In the case of AIB, it stated: 'While the redundancies are being carried out under agreed terms, the FSU is concerned about the future structure of AIB and the impact on staffing levels across the network. We have sought assurances from the Bank that the current round of redundancies will not add to the already increased workload and stress on members in AIB … In addition, FSU has raised issues about AIB's focus on offering redundancy to long-serving staff which is leading to a steady decline in the availability of experienced bankers. The Union has also expressed a concern that promotional opportunities for remaining staff will be limited or non-existent' (FSU press release, 7 October 2016). FSU agreed to make concessions over pension entitlement in 2011 with the Bank of Ireland while Unite could only gain one agreement, with Permanent TSB in 2008, to allow for career breaks with job security protected upon return.

In an IBOA survey of some 600 of its union activists working in Eire (and Northern Ireland and Great Britain), 83% of respondents considered their employers' response to workplace stress was unsatisfactory in the context of almost 96% reporting that the levels of stress had become more intense since the banking crisis began (IBOA *Spectrum*, June 2013). The key factors leading to rising stress levels were heavier workloads (with 71% saying staffing levels were insufficient) and continuing pressure to meet sales targets (IBOA *Spectrum*, June 2013). Dealing with customer distress resulted in abuse of bank workers by customers reported by 78% of respondents (IBOA *Spectrum*, June 2013). Meanwhile, Unite carried out a survey of its 5000 members in late 2011 working in Irish Life and Permanent TSB, Educational Building Society, and Bank of Ireland. The results showed 'only 13% had confidence in the management of their company—but 60% did not; only 29% enjoyed their current working environment—but 58% did not; over three quarters of respondents in a customer facing role, felt uncomfortable taking actions management asked them to do over the last year; around 64% were not confident in their job's security …; 83% were concerned about their pensions; and well over half would support industrial action in defence of jobs and conditions' (*uniteWORKSforIreland*, January/February 2012).

In a strong parallel with the situation in Britain, instances of strikes and industrial action have been rare in Eire. However, they have not been as rare and in proportionate or relative terms slightly more noticeable with more contestation of job losses. IBOA members working at

Hewlett Packard on the Bank of Ireland contract took strike action in 2010 over job losses, with this group of workers having previously taken industrial action twice before in 2000s, and industrial action short of strike was taken by IBOA members at the Nationwide building society over the consequences of asset transfer in 2011. Unite members at Aviva balloted for industrial action over 950 job losses and the outsourcing of 350 jobs in 2011 leading to a delay in their introduction (*uniteWORKSforIreland*, November/December 2011, January/February 2012). Fellow Unite members at Bank of Scotland (Ireland) threatened to strike against the closure of the company while members at the Bank of Ireland made several similar threats over job losses and took strike action (on three occasions) as did members at the Central Bank and Financial Regulator in 2009. A ballot to strike against job losses at Hibernian insurance in 2008 saw Unite members win some concessions as did one by Educational Building Society members in 2012. Finally, although 1000 Unite members rejected strike action at Irish Life in 2011 by a 60:40 margin to protect terms and conditions after a demerger, in 2014 they voted by 94% for industrial action after the company froze pay and increments, leading to the company making an acceptable offer of pay increases, and they took a series of short strikes in late 2015 and threatened longer strikes in 2016 to prevent the company imposing changes to pay structures without agreement. The threat of more extensive action led the company to stand down its imposed changes.

The similarities of the experience of financial services sector workers and their unions in Eire to those of financial services sector workers and their unions in Britain is all the more striking given that the institutional framework in Eire in some respects is quite different compared to that of Britain. But that national social partnership broke down in 2009 with company-level bargaining on pay superseding it added further weight to the ability of employers in the financial services sector to introduce systems of performance management which focus upon sales (and not customer service), thus, forming the basis of individual pay rises. The consequence has been, in line with the situation in Britain, that '[p]erformance management has become an increasingly important part of working life: so much so that IBOA receives more queries on performance management than on any other workplace issue' (IBOA *Spectrum*, June 2015). Added to all this, the full or part 'nationalisation' of some banks did not lead to any state oversight or intervention in regard of employment relations. Like in Britain, the senior management were left to their own devices to manage as they saw fit.

Northern Ireland

Owing to some differences in employment law and the institutions of industrial relations, consideration of financial services sector in Northern Ireland merits separate consideration. Here, RBS had two subsidiaries, namely, Ulster Bank (which it acquired in 1917) and First Active Building Society (which it acquired in 2003).[14] The latter was merged into the former with the shedding of just under 1000 jobs in 2009 and setting in train a series of restructurings involving branch closures and the transfer of work to RBS facilities in Britain. A further 1000 job were 'lost' in 2011. In Northern Ireland, the IBOA had some 4000 members in Ulster bank in 2009, and it threatened to ballot its members for industrial action on unilateral changes to contracts in 2010 but used legal action in the end instead to resist these. Between 2011 and 2014, its members experienced a pay freeze and have experienced the introduction of performance management. The FSU and Ulster Bank agreed to extend their procedural agreement and current redundancy terms for a further 2 years until the end of 2018 in the autumn of 2016. The procedural agreement comprised negotiation and dispute resolution procedures with the use of third party mediation where deemed necessary by either side while current redundancy terms of four weeks' pay per year of service (following a recommendation by the Labour Relations Commission to AIB) remained in place. Unlike in Britain, there is a more prevalent use of mediation in Northern Ireland and IBOA has used this to defend its members' interests in Ulster Bank. The only instance of intended industrial action in Northern Ireland took place when IBOA served notice of industrial action at the Clearco bank in Belfast in 2009. Negotiations expedited the matters in the dispute so that the action was not taken.

Conclusion

Along with the Chap. 3, this chapter provides the basis upon which to assess the impact of the financial crash, via the hand of capital, upon the employment experience of the employees in the financial services sector in Britain. For large swathes of the workforce in the sector, the terms and conditions of the wage-effort bargain have worsened since 2007–2008. In other words, levels of exploitation rose through the intensification (through performance management and reduced staffing levels) and extensification (through unpaid overtime) of work while the recompense in terms of wages (pay and pensions (as deferred wages)) has not kept up with the rise in the value of this effort. Neither the few rough edges that unions have knocked off the policies and practices of employers, nor the recognition that not all labour shedding was directly attributable to the crash because of changes in ICTs and customer behaviour, make a substantial difference to this conclusion. The traditional psychological contract of not great pay in exchange for job security, good pensions and other terms and conditions has been broken with a negative impact upon trust towards employers in the sector. Indeed, the selection of vignettes of workers' accounts of their post-crash experience of work and employment (especially when using the comparison to their pre-crash experience) supports this conclusion. Performance management systems were deployed not just to control staff attitudes and behaviours (in terms of punishing undesired attitudes and behaviours as well as eliciting and compelling desired ones) but also, some evidence suggested, to control wage costs. For example, in LBG, LTU (*Newsletter,* 2 November 2016) found a majority of members believed risk criteria were so difficult to satisfy that this was used as a deliberate ploy to reduce or deny staff bonuses. And while it was found that the challenger and mutual status of some employers did make some difference to the experience of employment in the post-crash period, it is doubtful whether this can be considered to be sufficient to mark out a viable alternative to that practiced by the large banking and insurance employers. For example, some changes to performance management systems were late in the day while redundancies were commonplace. The comparison with Ireland served to highlight that while some differences existed in the institutional framework of industrial relations, the outcomes were broadly similar to those experienced in Britain (with exception of more widespread pay freezes) and state 'nationalisation' and recapitalisation did not become tools by which unions could create leverage. The similarly limited collective mobilisation by workers and their unions also stands out.

Notes

1. Unite reports are used because Unite was the only union operating across the whole of the financial services sector and was one of the few organisation with the interest and resource ability to collate these figures.
2. Of the new jobs created with the traditional sub-sectors of banking and insurance, most have concerned compliance, enforcement and arrears. For example, in HSBC the number of staff working in compliance rose from 3200 to 7200 (*Guardian*, 9 June 2015).
3. It is unknown whether the relatively buoyant employment levels in the sector overall have had an influence on the ability of workers taking redundancy to gain employment elsewhere in the sector afterwards. Two factors are likely to have an important bearing here. The first is the applicability of the skill sets of redundees vis-à-vis the new jobs in the sector. The second is the demographic of the redundees, for many of the older redundees may in effect have taken earlier retirement (as some of the evidence in the workers' testimonies in this chapter suggests).
4. For example, 632 TSB branches were to have been sold off, as a result of European Union regulations on state aid, initially to the Coop. Eventually, TSB was floated as a separate company and then sold to Sabadell.
5. However, it should be noted that Amicus (2007) reporting that in Barclays, for example, unpaid overtime without time off in lieu was already a significant problem indicates there was a pre-history to this.
6. Only the Phoenix Group (with 600 staff represented by Unite), Provident Personal Credit (with 200 staff represented by USDAW) and West Bromwich Building Society (with 800 staff represented by SUWBBS) were found not to use PRP. Meantime, the Bank of England paid across the board rises to those staff passing the threshold

of satisfactory performance assessment while NAG was unusual in that it was only major company not to use a pay market matrix after employees had been assessed to be in different performance categories.

7. There were majorities to move to a statutory ballot for industrial action on pensions and terms and condition but not on pay in the consultative ballot.

8. The exceptions were those at the top and bottom of the pay scales who would receive no pay increase. Accord sought unsuccessfully at ACAS talks to gain a 'token' recognition payment of £250 for each affected member of staff.

9. Albeit, in none of the reporting of these membership surveys did Unite give the overall respondent rates of return.

10. For example, the GMB organised a consultative ballot in the spring of 2016 in which members voted for industrial action. This compelled Carillion not to cut the hours workers worked.

11. The 'resolves' section of the motion read: 'Conference resolves that in order to protect the pay, pensions and jobs of colleagues, and to ensure the stability of the bank as a public service, it is necessary to nationalise the bank entirely, and to run it under the democratic control of the workers employed by the bank, and in society at large'. Prior to that, it read: 'Conference recognises the interests of the large shareholders, and their profits, are not compatible with the interests of those workers employed by the bank and society as a whole. For profits to increase, colleague pay, pensions and working conditions must be decreased. For colleague conditions to be protected, and the services provided to society to be maintained, expanded and improved, it is necessary to take the bank into public ownership entirely, and operate it as a public service—that is to nationalise the bank, without compensation to the large shareholders who have enjoyed years of profits and more than received back their initial investment' (*Socialist Appeal*, 18 March 2014). The motion was not mentioned in Accord's reporting of the conference in the post-conference Spring 2014 edition of *My Accord*.

12. Mandate (some retail bank staff) and SIPTU (bank ancillary staff) had small numbers of members in the financial services sector.

13. Notwithstanding that some new union recognition agreements were gained with the likes of NIIB finance, EDS, Nationwide building society and an RBS subsidiary.

14. SIPTU had a small number of members in the First Active building society as well.

References

Affinity. (2012, August). *Banking standards written evidence from Affinity.* Bedford.

Amicus. (2007, February). *Amicus the union for you in Barclays' newsletter.* London.

Anonymous. (2016, September 8). How prudential staff built to a strike against offshoring. *Workplace Organising blog.*

Chew, B., Tan, L., & Hamid, S. (2016). Ethical banking in practice: A closer look at the Co-operative Bank UK PLC. *Qualitative Research in Financial Markets, 8*(1), 70–91.

CIPD. (2013). *Focus on rebuilding trust in the City. Employee outlook series.* London: Chartered Institute of Personnel and Development.

EHRC. (2009). *Financial services inquiry: Sex discrimination and gender pay gap report of the Equality and Human Rights Commission.* Manchester: EHRC.

Ellis, V., & Taylor, M. (2010). Banks, bailouts and bonuses: A personal account of working in Halifax Bank of Scotland during the financial crisis. *Work, Employment & Society, 24*(4), 803–812.

Eurofound. (2011). *Representativeness of the European social partner organisations: The banking sector.* Dublin: European Foundation for the Improvement of Living and Working Conditions.

Farrelly, R. (2011). *Ireland: The representativeness of trade unions and employer associations in the banking sector.* Dublin: European Foundation for the Improvement of Living and Working Conditions.

Gall, G. (2008). *Labour unionism in the financial services sector: Fighting for rights and representation.* Aldershot: Ashgate.

Glassner, V. (2009). Government and trade union responses to the economic crisis in the financial sector. Working Paper No. 09, European Trade Union Institute, Brussels.

IDS. (2010, August). *Pay in the financial services sector.* IDS Pay Report 1055, 6–12.

Jameson, H. (2010). *Partnership at HBoS.* London: IPA.

Kornelakis, A. (2014). Liberalization, flexibility and industrial relations institutions: Evidence from Italian and Greek banking. *Work, Employment & Society, 28*(1), 40–57.

Laaser, K. (2016). 'If you are having a go at me, I am going to have a go at you': The changing nature of social relationships of bank work under performance management. *Work, Employment & Society, 30*(6), 1000–1016.

LRD. (2013, December). *'Time to ring down the curtain on this performance'* *Labour Research* (pp. 23–25). London: Labour Research Department.

Martin, G., & Gollan, P. (2012). Corporate governance and strategic human resources management in the UK financial services sector: The case of the RBS. *International Journal of Human Resource Management, 23*(16), 3295–3314.

O'Donnell, S. (2017). Victory at Prudential. In Unite (Ed.), *Brexit: Unite demands protections for you* (p. 7). London: Unite.

Somerville, L. (2009). Economic crisis hits financial workers. *Frontline, 2*(10), 13–15.

Soriano, C. (2011). *Recession and social dialogue in the banking sector: A global perspective.* Dublin: Eurofound.

Tarren, D. (2013). *Building trade union capacity for social dialogue through the provision and analysis of change within the European finance sector.* London: Syndex/Unite/UNI Global Union (Europa finance).

Taylor, P. (2013). *Performance management and the New Workplace Tyranny—A report for the Scottish Trades Union Congress.* Glasgow: University of Strathclyde.

Traxler, F., Arrowsmith, J., Nergaard, K., & Molins Lopez Rodo, J. (2008). Variable pay and collective bargaining: A cross-national comparison of the banking sector. *Economic and Industrial Democracy, 29*(3), 406–431.

Unite. (2011, February). *Unite submission to the high pay commission.* London.

Unite. (2014, November). *Unite seeks urgent meeting with Barclays to discuss resourcing crisis in the branch network.* London.

Unite. (2015). *Unite members' survey—Finance sector.* London: Unite.

Van Wanrooy, B., Bewley, H., Bryson, A., Forth, J., Freeth, S., Stokes, L., & Wood, S. (2013a). *The 2011 workplace employment relations study—First findings,* London: ACAS/BIS/ESRC/NIESR.

Van Wanrooy, B., Bewley, H., Bryson, A., Forth, J., Freeth, S., Stokes, L., & Wood, S. (2013b). *Employment relations in the shadow of recession: Findings from the 2011 workplace employment relations study.* Basingstoke: Palgrave.

Walsh, F. (2015). Union membership in Ireland since 2003. *Journal of the Statistical and Social Inquiry Statistical Society of Ireland, 44,* 86–100.

5

Conclusion

Introduction

In the context of the sharp and stark contrast of the professed (mutual gains) philosophy of partnership to its actual practice, it may be said—using a pseudo-military analogy—that since the financial crash of 2007–2008, labour unionism in the financial services sector in Britain has failed the 'test of war', that war being the class war, for capital—as a class—has waged a war on labour—as a class—*and* won this war, amounting to a significant defeat for labour (although not of labour *per se*). The palpable sense of failure concerns labour unionism having not been able to rise to the challenge of repelling the offensive of capital against labour on the front of wage-effort bargain (and its associated components like redrawing the frontier of control). Put around another way, the crisis of, and for, capital in the sector has been resolved in favour of capital, and in not favour of labour. This most obviously refers to job shedding, pensions as deferred wages and the intensification and extensification of the wage-effort bargain for those remaining in employment in the sector under regimes of performance management. (Of course, the characterisation of failing this 'test of war' can also be levelled at labour unionism in the rest of the

© The Author(s) 2017
G. Gall, *Employment Relations in Financial Services*,
DOI 10.1057/978-1-137-39539-9_5

private sector as well as the public sector in Britain and with regard to the same issues.) As such, the presence of flight, fright and falling-in-line have far outweighed the limited evidence of fight, and successful fight at that (even where fight should not be made synonymous with its most obvious manifestation, namely, industrial action). Hence, the characterisation of being capable of doing not much more than 'knocking off the rough edges' was used.

Explaining the rather one-sided nature of this class war in the financial services sector requires an explanation that is specific and general—specific to the sector and the labour unions-cum-labour unionism found within it, and general to labour unionism overall within Britain. The former refers to the features like the prevalence of partnership, the modernisation of the legacy of 'internalism' into a form of company-orientated unionism, the impact of job security/security of employment agreements on propensity to mobilise, and low union densities. The latter refers to the overall state of health of the union movement and the dominant approaches which guide it in its relations with capital and the state. Employees and labour unionism in the financial services sector have found to their cost that the state has been captured by the forces of neo-liberalism and no longer can be characterised as a social democratic state. This was most graphically highlighted by the absence of social democratic 'nationalisation'. Whether the emergence of Corbynism—as a revitalisation of social democracy within the Labour Party—from late 2015 onwards will have a material bearing on this still remains to be seen. This study has worked its way through the former, namely, the specific components of emloyment relations and labour unionism within the financial services sector, by way of examining the players, processes and outcomes in the previous three chapters, and has done so upon the foundation of the introductory chapter. This final chapter presents an overall assessment of the preceding chapters, guided by posing a number of critical questions about partnership, labour unionism and relations with capital and the state.

Surveying the Wreckage

With the earlier caveats entered into regarding not all change in employment conditions being attributable to the financial crash and the implications of the nature of the research methods deployed leading to an orientation upon union organised companies, the exploration of the employee experience has shown that the human toll as a result of the impact of the financial crash upon the financial services sector has been deep, deleterious and extensive—deep in the sense that the changes wrought upon have been profound; deleterious in the sense of being negative to their material interests; and extensive in the sense that they have been widespread. Few workers have not been affected by labour shedding (directly as 'victims' and indirectly as those 'left behind'), pension impoverishment and ramped up versions of the diktats of performance management. Large swathes have also seen reductions in the (real) value of their wages as a result of performance management leading to pay freezes and below inflation rises. Meanwhile, remuneration for senior managers and executives has not been impacted in the same way. Indeed, under the professed need to 'pay the going rate' and 'attract the right talent', remuneration packages for such staff have continued to rise in real value. It is important to restate that at this point that the outcome of the human toll for workers has been the result of the responsive decisions of capital and its lieutenants (executives and senior managers) because of their ownership and control of the companies. They have acted to protect their material interests through the use of their ideological and power resources (notwithstanding the existence of state intervention). But what capital does to labour is only, as it were, one half of the equation. What labour does in response is the remaining half. Therefore, it is salient to also state again that overall the unions in the financial services sector have not been able to halt and turn back the attacks on their members' terms and conditions of employment, whether through responses more akin to militancy or those based upon partnership. What they have been able to do, on the one hand, is smooth off the rough edges of employer policies and actions and, on the other, achieve minor victories. In regard of the former, for example, the use of performance management systems was continued despite union opposition, with the result of union resistance being modification not abolition. Partnership did not prevent significant number of redundancies and job cuts in successive swathes. Examples of this were to be found at Aegon, Aviva, Barclays, CBG, HSBC, LBG, Legal and General, Northern Rock, RBS, RSA and Zurich. Moreover, there was no strong evidence that partnership was able to moderate or ameliorate the level of redundancies and job cuts. The bottom line for unions was the demand of 'no compulsory redundancies'. For reasons explained earlier, this was achieved in the main but the same cannot be said in regard of outsourcing and offshoring. While no demands emerged for short-time working and pay cuts in order to protect jobs (as did occur in manufacturing), no success was gained in introducing career breaks to ameliorate the pressure towards labour shedding.

The Fs and Ds of Financial Services Labour Relations and Labour Unionism

The supremacy of flight, fright and falling-in-line amongst the employees in the financial services sector resulted in fight barely registering, suggesting the relationship is a deeply symbiotic one. For the supremacy of flight, fright and falling-in-line to be ended would require that fight became a substantial component of the employment relations in the sector in terms of its processes and outcomes. In other words, extensive and successful fight would lessen the ability of employers to command flight, fright and falling-in-line while at the same time reduce workers willing to engage in flight, fright and falling-in-line. But as this was not the case, the relationship between flight, fright and falling-in-line becomes a more salient one. Those leaving should not be presumed to have been the more discontented given that the ability to leave was heavily influenced by individual financial considerations (where most redundancies were voluntary). By the same token, those staying should not be presumed to have been the more contented. Thus, those that engaged in flight comprised different complexions as did those that stayed through fright and, consequently, fell in line.

Partnership was an obstacle to fight. In spite of its mutual gains agenda, it has not served the cause or interests of workers well. It is an obstacle to constructing and mobilising fight because of the 'institutional enclosure' (Gall 2008: 146) that it represents. But partnership is not the only obstacle, or even the main obstacle for it is symptomatic of a wider malaise in terms of the continuation and acceleration of the processes and their outcomes of disorganisation, dissolution, dislocation and demoralisation of labour unionism in the sector. Part and parcel of disorganisation and has been atomisation, churn and fragmentation of membership and the organs of collective representation. But, of course, partnership has also helped, to some extent, to facilitate these developments. So, in the period under study, labour unionism in the sector has further experienced not only dissolution in terms of its membership and organisational presence but also greater demoralisation, comprising demotivation and disillusionment of active members and activists, as a result of the ascendancy of the power of capital, its material benefaction at the expense of workers in the sector and the prevalence of its ideology of partnership as a cloak for, and enabler of, this power. And, labour unionism has become disorganised as a result of the constant organisational churn of capital. While not quite a case of having to start from scratch after every external re-organisation much less every internal re-organisation, scarce resources have been compelled to be spent upon accommodating and adjusting to these environmental changes. Heavily related to this process of disorganisation is that of dislocation due to much employment in the sector moving out of the realms of that which labour unionism has traditionally organised within as a result of the application of ICTs.

Of course, these aforementioned processes and outcomes were not the preserve of the post-crash period alone. They were well in evidence before so, especially in regard of the period 2000–2007 (see Gall 2008: Chap. 5). In this respect, their constellation is the product of a much longer genesis involving weak tendencies towards unionateness and combativeness, the hold of internalism, and the underdevelopment of workplace unionism (Gall 2008). Partnership added to this and may be seen as the continuation of ideological internalism and company unionism (albeit modernised ones). The basis for their continuation despite the decline of institutionally-based unionism was found, in the cases of Unifi/Amicus/Unite (being the only major example of a multi-institutional based union), in their autonomy of its national company committees.

Servicing, Organising and Partnership

All unions in the sector can point to this or that membership recruitment and organising success (like Unite at LBG Speke or RBS Greenock or CWU at Santander Bootle) and this or that collective bargaining success (see Chap. 4) as result of organising. But instances of either cannot convincingly mask the wider picture that the scale and intensity of the organising practiced across the sector has not successfully overcome the significant challenges of either creating majoritarian unionism or colonising new workplaces and units of capital (see also Gall 2008: 7–8). For example, the arguments put forward by the proponents of merger in the cases of Unifi and Amicus concerning greater resources to facilitate growth, stronger voice and economies of scale were neither realistic nor realised. Indeed, Unite membership in the sector is at least a third less than when Unifi ceased to exist with 147,000 members (Gall 2008: 124) and Unifi itself lasted for only 5 years. Neither union organising nor servicing proved be no a panacea (see also Gall 2008: 130–131). The context of partnership clearly provided no basis for union revitalisation or renewal. But its existence does beg the question of how would labour unionism have acted without it? Would labour unionism have been freer to act more robustly than it did without being confined by institutional enclosure? Could 'free' traditional collective bargaining have delivered more negotiating gains than union involvement in partnership? And, did partnership provide the institutional support to help sustain labour unionism itself that it could not find the means to generate elsewhere and by other methods?

The survival of partnership suggest that for the largest units of capital in the sector it provided a key strategic means by which to institute a managed and controlled process of increasing the rate of labour exploitation while simultaneously engaging in widespread labour shedding (given the two are not necessarily synonymous). The senses of management and control are derived in large part from the consent afforded to the process by union involvement. Without partnership, the risk of confrontation could not be entirely ruled out. And, even where consent was not particularly forthcoming, the alternative avenues open to workers and union members to resist were greatly reduced by the involvement of labour unionism in the process. The price for capital of gaining a managed and controlled process was some limited union influence (aided and abetted by support for a certain form of unionism). In this process, and in line with the characterisation of Advance and Accord in Chap. 2, unions (including Unite) have been forced to engage in acts of helping to manage rationalisations. They have been cast almost as sub-contracted organisations to smooth off the rough edges in terms gaining (more) transparency and mitigation, ensuring employers abide by their own policy and rules.

The questions of whether unions chose partnership out of free choice in an ideological sense or chose it for instrumental reasons as a result of weakness; whether the lack of resistance and mobilisation was due to inherent weaknesses which were added to by partnership; and whether unions could have quickly thrown off the 'shackles' of moderation and partnership were all posed earlier. The degrees to which unions accepted partnership out of compulsion or their own volition varied given the combined effect of the variables of their own membership densities, available financial resources and ideological predispositions. There was more sense that Unite accepted partnership as a result of compulsion (as a result of low membership densities) such that partnership was more contested where it did organise than was the case with Advance or NGSU (which accepted it more as a result of ideology). Accord, CWU and LTU, amongst others, would fit in between the two ends of this spectrum. Historically, independent labour unionism in the financial services sector has been relatively weak (see Gall 2008) so that partnership, dating from the 1990s, cannot account for all of the weaknesses of contemporary labour unionism in the sector. Therefore, partnership can be said to have continued a pre-existing trajectory, even if it may have deepened it by seeking to colonise labour unionism by institutional and ideological means. The weak tendencies toward adversarialism and oppositionalism prior to the financial crash in the sector (see Gall 2008) made it highly unlikely that new and alternative *modus operandi* and union forms to partnership and extant forms of directed democracy would emerge easily and quickly.

Just Another Hard Luck Story?

An important point for discussion in contextualising the fate of workers in the financial service sector is to consider the experience of workers outside the financial services sector. Whether in the public services, manufacturing or private services, significant deleterious change has been experienced by workers too in terms of their pay, pensions and workloads. For example, 34% of the FTSE 100 companies had closed their final salary pensions by 2013 (compared with 4% in 2010) (*Guardian*, 28 May 2013) while pay freezes were common in manufacturing and the public sector (*IDS Pay Report* 1058, October 2010). It is beyond the scope of this book to provide an analysis of the situation in the rest of the economy and society in Britain in order to benchmark the experience of workers in the financial services sector against other workers. It can reasonably be ventured, however, that workers in the sector appear to have been subject to one of the most concerted and effective attempts to raise the level of labour exploitation of any sector in Britain as a result of the pincer of reduced headcounts and increased workloads.

Within the financial services sector, the challenges for workers (and their unions) in terms of organising, mobilising and then counter-posing their own power, material interests and ideology to those of their employers are not fundamentally different to the challenges faced by workers and their unions in other sections of the private sector of the economy in Britain or in Britain overall. This can be most keenly seen in the processes by which capital and the state in other sectors of the economy have instituted redundancies, pay freezes, new forms of performance management systems, poorer pension provision and so on as means of managing the economic fallout from the financial crash turning into a recession. In these other sectors (including the more heavily unionised public sector), the absence of widespread and effective collective resistance by organised labour has also been notable. Indeed, in some parts of manufacturing, concessionary bargaining took place by which pay cuts and pay freezes as well as short-time working were introduced in order to try to safeguard employment. The widespread absence of collective resistance elsewhere suggests that it would be short-sighted to easily and swiftly attribute the relative absence of resistance in the financial services sector solely to the specific historical weakness of labour unionism and prevalence of partnership there. These two factors have, as outlined earlier, played a significant role in shaping the way in which organised labour responded to the impact of the way in which capital responded financial crash. But underlying them have been more universal and comprehensive factors which can be best encapsulated in the notion of a generalised crisis for, and of, labour unionism in the neo-liberal epoch of capitalism. One of the foundations of this is the increasingly prevalent phenomenon of job and employment insecurity despite 'flexicurity'. In this context, it is worth recalling that in the financial services sector job cuts, offshoring and performance management were present before the crash (albeit not so pervasively or persuasively). Union opposition to them was not any more successful then despite the less grave situation.

Challenges Ahead

If labour unionism is arrest to the trajectories towards disorganisation, dissolution, dislocation and demoralisation, it faces many challenges in doing so. The major one is to identify and use innovative levers of strategic power in the reconfigured organisational processes of the financial services sector given the decline in branches, concentration of functions and capabilities into contact centres, outsourcing and offshoring. Without this unions will be compelled to continue to criticise management behaviour without the ability to effect change in management behaviour. The ability to identify and use new levers of power is a highly difficult and complex challenge for it is, in part, predicated upon and strongly related to increasing membership in absolute and relative terms. It is also related to membership cohesion, where one of the facets of disorganisation, in addition to atomisation, churn and fragmentation, has been the loss of many older and more unionate members. Younger workers, unable to take redundancy on account of their less conducive financial position, were often those remaining. As Chap. 2 suggested, while they may not be hostile to labour unionism, they are also often largely ignorant of it.

Final Remarks

At what point can employers' actions in the financial services sector with regard to the experience of employment no longer said to be directly related to their response to the financial crash of 2007–2008? And, at what point in time do their actions become normal and normalised in the post-crash era? As time progresses onwards from the financial crash, the legacy of the crash remains although its potency no doubt diminishes in some respects as the normal ways and contexts of capital accumulation and labour exploitation begin to re-assert and re-establish themselves. Assessing the human toll of the crash in the sector over a period of around 10 years seems a fair and appropriate canvas upon which to do so. Stopping at around 10 years also seems appropriate for, just as the point of departure of the earlier study (Gall 2008), the exit position here is also one of new and heightened uncertainty. This is because it remains unclear what the extent of the impact of Brexit will be upon employment levels within the financial services sector (even if the impact of the financial crash of 2007–2008 in all likelihood outweighs that of Brexit). Nonetheless, the potential exists for significant employment contraction amongst those employers which sell financial services within the European Union if they are barred from being able to trade in an unimpeded way with regard to tariffs. An immediate estimate after the referendum in June 2016 was that in excess of 100,000 staff were involved in such operations (*People Management*, 24 June 2016) while a report for the London Stock Exchange suggested that 'as far as the entire United Kingdom is concerned, 232,000 jobs would be at risk or likely to be lost' (*Scotsman*, 11 January 2017). By mid-January 2017, preparations for up to 5000 jobs (or staff) to be moved had been set in train (*Reuters*, 18 January 2017) following clarification by Prime Minister, Theresa May, that a 'hard' Brexit without access to the EU single market was being sought. If Brexit does lead to heightened costs for access to the market within the European Union, it can be expected that employers will transfer these operations to within the European Union (or other countries where the costs are lower than in Britain). Reports in the spring of 2017 suggested many large financial services sector employers were undertaking such measures (*Guardian* 31 March, 5 April, 26 April,

9 May 2017). Yet, much will depend upon whether financial services 'passporting' rules, which allow firms to sell financial services into EU member states, are resolved in favour of Britain, and this process will be of an indeterminate length of time given the complexity of negotiating new trade deals. However, there may also be a counter-boost to the financial services sector if Britain pursues the path of becoming a tax haven. Yet a salutary reminder was that regardless of the Brexit impact, extensive job losses, branch closures and offshoring continued strongly into early 2017 for reasons not related to Brexit as the actions of HSBC, NAG and the Yorkshire Building Society as well as the Cooperative, First Trust Bank, LBG, RBS, Standard Life and Aberdeen, and Swinton insurance showed. At this point in time, the European Banking Authority (press release, 2 February 2017) published its annual report on high earners—those earning more than one million euros per annum—in banks within the EU. Not only did it show an increase of a third in their numbers to 5,142 in 2015 but 4,133 of these were located in Britain, representing some 80%. The *Guardian* (21, 23, 25 February 2017) highlighted that the number of staff paid more than £1m per annum in Barclays, HSBC and LBG was 667.Contracting labour markets amongst both unionised and non-unionised employers in the financial services sector, whatever their cause, do not provide particularly auspicious circumstances for the regeneration and renewal of labour unionism in the sector, much less its transmogrification into a more robust form. This suggests that unions effectively tackling the growing sectoral wage inequality as well as increased levels of labour exploitation (through the intensification and extensification of work) remains at, best, a 'work-in-progress', and, at worst, something of a forlorn 'pipe dream'.

Reference

Gall, G. (2008). *Labour unionism in the financial services sector: Fighting for rights and representation*. Aldershot: Ashgate.

Index

A

Abbey National Group Union (ANGU) 44, 45, 155
Abbey National Staff Association (ANSA) 44, 45
Accord union 23, 27, 40, 41, 52, 60, 69, 85, 88, 101, 111, 112, 115, 116, 120, 122, 128–137, 139, 149, 153, 154, 159, 171, 187, 189, 199, 219, 224, 225, 245
AEGIS—The Aegon UK Staff Association 23, 47, 60, 83, 87, 88, 90, 103, 156, 159
Affinity union (also known as LTU) 26, 27, 29, 41, 42, 52, 53, 60, 86–88, 93, 94, 102, 111, 116–122, 125, 128–134, 136, 137, 140, 148–151, 153–155, 162, 163, 167, 171, 174, 185, 186, 189, 199, 202, 205, 210, 219, 222, 245
Alliance for Finance (AfF) 69, 227

Alliance and Leicester Group Union for Staff (ALGUS) 49, 90, 101
Amicus union 30, 68, 80, 88, 102, 155, 156, 234, 243, 244
Arrowsmith, Jim 28, 145
Austerity 1, 32, 221
Autonomy (of unions in companies) 58, 64, 80, 102, 103, 243
Aviva 59, 60, 82, 96, 141, 173, 181, 182, 185, 198, 200, 204, 216, 222, 229, 231, 241
AXA 33, 59, 66, 91, 92, 98, 99, 109, 111, 138, 139, 148, 156, 181, 191, 195, 198, 200, 217, 218

B

Bacon, Nick 111
Bain, George 6, 45, 143, 170, 171
Ballots 8, 45, 50, 62, 66, 79, 84, 102, 103, 126, 157, 165, 217, 219, 220, 224

© The Editor(s) (if applicable) and The Author(s) 2017
G. Gall, *Employment Relations in Financial Services*,
DOI 10.1057/978-1-137-39539-9

Bank of England 59, 174, 181, 195, 234

Banking 1, 2, 14, 19, 22, 33, 34, 43, 48, 51, 52, 59–61, 63, 75, 76, 86, 89, 92, 94, 102, 123, 124, 127, 128, 132, 136, 141, 146, 150, 153, 157, 166, 170, 171, 173, 174, 178, 179, 184–186, 198, 206, 215, 217, 219, 222, 225, 227–230, 233

Banking, Insurance and Finance Union (BIFU) 57, 84, 89, 102, 155, 159

Bank of Scotland 19, 60, 198, 205–207, 214, 229, 231

Barclays bank 59, 60, 62, 63, 66, 82, 92, 99, 102, 111, 139, 141, 142, 147, 151, 179, 181, 185, 191, 194, 197, 198, 201, 203, 204, 218, 222, 234, 241

Brexit 248, 249

Britannia Staff Union (BSU) 48, 49, 60, 90, 91, 100, 140, 159, 168, 191, 204

Brittannic Field Staff Association (BFSA) ix

Brown, Geoff 169

Cairns, Liz 23, 60, 194

Capita 33, 57, 67, 97, 141, 155, 166, 201, 215, 216

Capital 2–7, 10–13, 16, 18, 19, 21, 23, 24, 29, 46, 47, 54, 55, 76, 82, 83, 87, 95, 96, 99, 109–111, 124, 140, 142, 171, 173, 178, 187, 193, 221, 222, 233, 239–241, 243–248

Capitalism 1, 2, 4, 5, 12, 13, 20, 21, 124, 222, 247

Cheshire Building Society Staff Association (CBSSA) 55

Cheshire Group Staff Union (CGSU) 55

Collective action 5, 27, 30, 169

Collectivism 15, 16, 64, 144

Communication Workers' Unions (CWU) 23, 49, 50, 70, 81, 87, 90, 97, 100–103, 156, 158, 171, 219, 223, 244, 245

Co-operative Banking Group (CBG) 48, 49, 59, 60, 67, 140, 151, 168, 182, 198, 200, 204, 225, 241

Cooperative Financial Services (CFS) 48, 59, 143, 156, 215

Corbyn, Jeremy 158

Corbynism 240

Corbynistas 89

Credit crunch 1, 29, 32

D

Demobilisation 159

Demoralisation (of labour unionism) 9, 11, 243, 247

Derbyshire Group Staff Union (DGSU) 54, 90

Derecognition (of labour unionism) 52, 53, 116, 120, 121, 130, 140, 153, 155, 157

Deregulation 5, 12, 21

Dislocation (of labour unionism) 9–11, 76, 184, 243, 247

Disorganisation (of labour unionism) 9–11, 30, 76, 184, 243, 247

Dissolution (of labour unionism) 9–11, 17, 30, 56, 76, 243, 247

Dunfermline Building Society Staff Association (DBSSA) 55, 90

E

East, John 23, 50, 97, 223
Eire 172, 180, 229–231
Employed Union Officer (EUO) 45, 58, 64, 80, 86, 87, 90
Employee involvement 55
European Works Council (EWC) 39, 99, 111, 157, 159

F

Falling-in-line (of employee response) 2, 3, 8, 9, 25, 27, 30, 31, 171, 177, 178, 240, 242
Fight (of employee response) 2, 7–9, 25, 27, 30, 31, 58, 65, 80, 134, 136, 137, 179, 180, 206, 210, 211, 240, 242
Finance capitalism 12, 21, 124
Financial Conduct Authority (FCA) 21, 22, 52, 174, 184
Financial crash 1–3, 17, 18, 22–24, 28, 29, 32, 40, 52, 63, 69, 76, 78, 80, 82, 84, 85, 97, 98, 104, 112, 116, 131, 151, 153, 159, 164, 165, 169, 171–173, 177, 178, 180, 181, 183–185, 187, 193, 194, 198, 203, 212, 215, 219, 221, 222, 229, 233, 239–241, 245–248
Financial Services Authority (FSA) 94, 149, 151, 156, 174
Financial Services Union (FSU, formerly IBOA) 23, 50, 51, 60, 87, 90, 101, 199, 229–232

Flight (of employee response) 2, 7–9, 25, 27, 30–32, 65, 136, 171, 177, 178, 180, 181, 205, 240, 242
Friends provident 59, 109, 181
Fright (of employee response) 2, 3, 8, 25, 27, 30, 31, 171, 177, 178, 240, 242

G

Gall, Gregor 4, 6, 9, 16, 18, 24, 28, 32, 40, 43, 53, 60, 61, 64, 68, 70, 76, 78, 80, 83, 99, 102, 103, 111, 112, 114, 143–145, 152, 159, 164, 166, 170, 172, 174, 185, 195, 215, 218, 219, 242–245, 248
GMB general union 68–70, 129, 204, 235

H

Halifax Bank of Scotland (HBoS) 18, 19, 22, 41, 59, 60, 100, 101, 111–117, 120–125, 128–130, 132–137, 139, 160, 181, 182, 205, 206, 208, 214
Halifax Building Society Staff Association (HBSSA) 40
Hong Kong and Shanghai Banking Corporation (HSBC) 59, 60, 82, 97, 99, 104, 141, 143, 151, 155, 156, 181, 183, 191, 195, 197, 198, 200, 201, 203, 204, 217, 219, 222, 224, 234, 241, 249
Hook, Dominic 20, 23, 60, 62, 65, 142, 151, 166
Hoque, Kim 28, 29

I

Ideology 5, 6, 9, 11–13, 16, 21, 22,
    46, 47, 129, 138, 140, 162,
    243, 245, 246
Incomes Data Services (IDS) 23, 195,
    196, 204, 219, 246
Incorporation 45, 112, 116, 138,
    142, 162
Independent Union of Halifax Staff
    (IUHS) 40
Industrial action 5, 8, 27, 30, 43, 45,
    56, 62, 80, 81, 111, 119, 121,
    126, 127, 130, 137, 143, 157,
    159, 160, 162–166, 171, 174,
    196, 199, 206, 211, 215–217,
    235
Information and communication
    technology (ICT) 10, 182–184,
    215, 216, 233, 243
Institutional enclosure 242, 244
Insurance 1, 12, 14, 16, 33, 53, 57,
    59–61, 63, 66, 67, 69, 76, 78,
    86, 89, 91, 92, 98, 100, 102,
    109, 113, 135, 138, 139, 149,
    156, 157, 164–166, 170, 171,
    185, 186, 194, 215, 216, 219,
    222, 227, 228, 231, 233
Inter-union relations 40, 69, 116,
    132, 155
Irish Bank Officials' Association
    (IBOA) 23, 50, 51, 87, 90,
    101, 229–232

J

Job losses 43, 70, 93, 94, 98, 109,
    116, 117, 123, 124, 126, 139,
    160, 177, 181, 182, 190, 216,
    217, 225, 229–231, 249

Job Security Agreement (JSA) 123,
    125, 127, 160, 172, 181,
    190, 200
Johnstone, Stewart 28, 96, 138

L

Laaser, Knut 191
Labour Force Survey (LFS) 70, 75
Labour Party 20, 59, 158, 165, 240
Labour Research Department
    (LRD) 194
Labour unionism 3, 6, 9–11, 13, 14,
    21, 32, 40, 59, 69, 76, 78, 79,
    82–85, 88, 89, 99, 100, 144,
    170, 239, 240, 243–245, 247,
    249
Labour unions 2, 3, 6, 21, 24, 39, 69,
    95, 99, 110, 171, 240
Leeds Building Society Staff
    Association (LBSSA) 70, 90,
    103, 159, 227
Leek United Building Society Staff
    Association (LUBSSA) 90
Legal and General 59, 111, 155, 181,
    185, 198, 204, 216, 217, 241
Lloyds Banking Group (LBG) 8, 19,
    20, 23, 26, 27, 33, 40, 41, 52,
    59, 60, 62–64, 67–69, 82, 93,
    101, 102, 104, 111, 112, 116–
    130, 132, 136, 137, 139, 140,
    147–150, 153–156, 160–163,
    171, 172, 181–183, 185–188,
    190, 195–199, 201–206, 209,
    210, 219, 220, 222, 224, 241
Lloyds Trade Union (LTU, also
    known as Affinity) 23, 52
LloydsTSB 52, 60, 114, 116, 122,
    125, 129, 130, 148, 160

M

Macgregor, Rob 23, 65, 131, 142, 197
Manufacturing, Science and Finance
    union (MSF) 60, 84, 89, 155
Marginson, Paul 28, 145
Martinez Lucio, Miguel 28, 33
Material interests 1, 6, 7, 12, 13, 22,
    47, 100, 177, 241, 246
Mobilisation 8, 9, 15, 79, 80, 111,
    127, 140, 144, 145, 159–163,
    200, 217, 219, 220, 234, 245

N

National Australia Group (NAG) 59,
    181, 182, 198, 204, 218, 235,
    249
Nationalisation 18, 19, 33, 122, 136,
    158, 173, 221, 222, 229, 232,
    234, 240
Nationwide 51, 53–56, 81, 82, 95,
    98, 99, 140, 159, 198, 200,
    204, 225–227, 231, 235
Nationwide Group Staff Union
    (NGSU) 23, 29, 53–56, 81, 82,
    87, 88, 90, 140, 159, 168, 200,
    205, 225–227, 245
Neo-liberalism 4–6, 12, 13, 18,
    20–22, 228, 240
Nichols, Ged 23, 41, 42, 113, 115,
    130, 131
Northern Ireland 50, 51, 156, 180,
    230, 232
Northern Rock 18, 19, 96, 178, 181,
    198, 214, 224, 225, 241

O

Offshoring 8, 10, 21, 45, 96, 98,
    100, 109, 117, 132, 142, 166,
    181–183, 215, 219, 242, 247,
    249
One Union of Regional Staff (OURS)
    union 54, 55, 58, 83, 90
Outsourcing 8, 10, 47, 53, 57, 82,
    100, 109, 124, 126, 153, 181,
    217, 221, 231, 242, 247
Overtime 8, 119, 135, 154, 163, 179,
    186, 188–191, 200, 206, 215,
    216, 219, 227, 233, 234

P

Partnership, union-management 6,
    17, 30, 42, 84, 88, 92, 93, 95,
    113–116, 124, 140, 143, 200,
    240, 245
Pay 7, 9, 14, 15, 18, 21, 31, 33, 48,
    64, 66, 77, 79, 91, 101, 104,
    110, 111, 117–119, 125–127,
    130, 132, 133, 136, 137, 140,
    141, 144–148, 150, 152–154,
    157, 160, 161, 163, 174, 177,
    178, 180, 189–205, 209–213,
    215, 216, 218–220, 222–229,
    231–235, 241, 242, 246
Pension 1, 7, 16, 33, 52, 70, 76, 78,
    80–82, 91, 97, 100, 109, 121,
    122, 126, 127, 135, 136, 155,
    161, 163, 165, 166, 169, 172,
    174, 177, 178, 180, 186, 187,
    198–202, 205, 209–219, 223,
    225, 227, 230, 233, 235, 239,
    241, 246

Performance improvement plans (PIP) 67, 146, 186, 193

Performance management 1, 8, 9, 15, 31–33, 46, 64, 70, 77, 79, 80, 110, 111, 113, 127, 143, 146–149, 151–154, 158, 161, 167, 169, 170, 172, 177, 179–181, 191–198, 200, 205, 223, 226, 228, 232, 233, 239, 241, 247

Performance-related pay (PRP) 15, 80, 145, 147, 150, 152, 161, 191, 194–197, 201, 203, 216, 223, 227, 234

Portman Group Staff Association (PGSA) 54, 56, 111

Power 5–7, 11, 13, 18, 21, 22, 32, 46, 65, 129, 153, 157, 158, 161, 241, 243, 246, 247

Prudential 33, 52, 59, 63, 66, 95, 98, 148, 155, 156, 174, 204, 216, 217

R

Recognition (of unions) 33, 44, 45, 47, 53, 63, 67, 68, 92, 101, 111, 114, 120–122, 124, 128, 141, 148, 152–157, 159, 174, 194, 206, 208, 227, 233, 235

Redundancies 1, 8, 21, 29–31, 46, 47, 58, 64, 65, 68, 75, 79, 109, 111, 121, 123–125, 128, 141, 160, 169, 172, 173, 181–183, 193, 200, 215, 221, 225, 228–230, 233, 241, 242, 246

Redundancies (voluntary) 65, 80, 125, 128, 167, 172, 181, 182, 188, 206, 216, 242

Redundancy (compulsory) 8, 15, 30, 31, 34, 46, 54, 65, 78–80, 87, 117, 123–125, 128, 143, 161, 162, 167, 168, 181, 182, 194, 200, 206, 214–216, 223, 225, 229, 230, 232, 234, 242, 247

Rose, Tim 23, 53, 226

Royal Bank of Scotland (RBS) 19, 20, 22, 24, 27, 33, 34, 59, 60, 63, 64, 67, 82, 94, 95, 103, 141, 150, 151, 169, 179, 181–185, 196–199, 201, 203, 204, 218, 219, 222, 232, 235, 241

Royal Sun Alliance (RSA) 59, 95, 104, 111, 181, 185, 198, 200, 222, 241

S

Sabadell 98, 153, 224, 234

Santander 44, 45, 49, 50, 69, 96–100, 102, 140, 156, 204, 223, 224, 244

Security of Employment Agreement (SEA) 98, 123, 125, 172, 181, 200, 224, 240

Services, Industrial, Professional and Technical Union (SIPTU) 70, 235

Skipton Staff Association (SSA) 90, 101

Somerville, Linda 194, 214, 221

Staff Union West Bromwich Building Society (SUWBS) 83

State intervention 20, 21, 241

Strikes 2, 30, 110, 164–166, 175, 217, 221, 230, 231

Stuart, Mark 28, 56, 57, 114, 139

T

Taylor, Philip 35, 146, 170, 192–
194, 220
Trades Union Congress (TUC) 44,
47, 54–57, 83, 100–102,
128–130, 132, 173
Transfer of Undertakings (Protection
of Employment) regulations
(TUPE) 67, 156
Traxler, Frank 28, 53, 195

U

Undy, Roger 64, 84
Union for Bradford and Bingley Staff
and Associated Companies
(UBAC) 45, 89, 100
Union of Finance Staff (UFS) 23, 57–
60, 86, 87, 90, 91, 101, 103,
152, 159, 168, 173, 186, 201
Union of Shop, Distributive and
Allied Workers (USDAW) 23,
67, 68, 70, 158, 234
Union organising 88, 92, 112, 144,
166, 185, 244
Union servicing 16, 26, 57, 66, 67,
79, 86, 88, 244
Unite union (formed from Amicus
and TGWU merger 90, 120

V

Victimisation 80, 112, 143
Virgin Money 59, 96, 97, 203, 224,
225, 227

W

Waddington, Jeremy 28, 87
Wage effort bargain 13, 31, 46, 193,
204, 205, 233, 239
Wood, Alan 23, 58, 59
Woolwich Independent Staff
Association (WISA) 89

Y

Yorkshire Independent Staff
Association (YISA) 48, 90

Printed by Books on Demand, Germany